The Politics of Survivorship

The Politics of Survivorship

Incest, Women's Literature, and Feminist Theory

Rosaria Champagne

New York University Press
NEW YORK AND LONDON

NEW YORK UNIVERSITY PRESS
New York and London

Library of Congress Cataloging-in-Publication Data

Champagne, Rosaria, 1962–
The politics of survivorship: incest, women's literature, and
feminist theory / Rosaria Champagne.
p. cm.
Includes bibliographical references and index.
1. American literature—20th century—History and criticism.
2. Incest in literature. 3. Feminism and literature—Great Britain—
History—20th century. 4. Feminism and literature—United States—
History—20th century. 5. American literature—Women authors—
History and criticism. 6. English fiction—19th century—History
and criticism. 7. Adult child sexual abuse victims in literature.
8. Psychoanalysis and literature. 9. Patriarchy in literature.
10. Women and literature. I. Title.
PS169.I5C43 1996   CIP
813.009'353—dc20   96-10125

New York University Press books are printed on acid-free paper,
and their binding materials are chosen for strength and durability.

Manufactured in the United States of America

10 9 8 7 6 5 4 3 2 1

For Teri A. Vigars and Karen J. Hall

Contents

Acknowledgments

This book was written in two years, from August 1993 to July 1995. New to a tenure-track job, with no eligible leave time to save me, I wrote between chapters of my own life. A number of people helped me stay afloat during the writing of this book, and I owe them for their generosity.

I owe deep intellectual debts to teachers, mentors, and colleagues from both Ohio State University and Syracuse University. Linda Alcoff, Steven M. Cohan, Susan Edmunds, Laura J. George, Marlene Longenecker, Debra A. Moddelmog, P. Joy Rouse, Linda M. Shires, Clare A. Simmons, and Harvey Teres have read sections (or complete drafts) and have given me excellent—and sometimes painful—criticism and advice.

Richard Fallis, Bob Gates, Margaret Himley, Pat Moody, Duane Roen, and Chuck Watson have been extraordinary advocates and friends. Timothy Bartlett and Despina Papazoglou Gimbel, editors at New York University Press, have been encouraging and supportive of me and scrupulous with my book. Robert G. Jensen, Dean of the College of Arts and Sciences at Syracuse University, generously granted funds for professional indexing. Susan Ostrov Weisser, Jennifer Fleischner, and anonymous readers from New York University Press and from the editorial boards of *Discourse* and *Genders* have contributed greatly to this book's progress. Cheryl Dumesnil, Teresa Goddu, Anne Hall, Mary Ellen Kavenaugh, Linda Malik, Mick Markham, Margaret Mathews, Radell Roberts, Mark Schoenfield, Susan Pasco Teres, and Deborah Welsh have also contributed survivor backlash articles, skilled readings, research assistance, and kind words. My best friends and running partners, Barb Genton and Sally Gewinner, patiently listened to first-book traumas on our training runs; they kept me both sane and fit—no small feat. Karen J. Hall gave this book its title and believed in its importance when I forgot. My mother, Dolores Champagne Otis, sacrificed for my education and with my stepfather, Theo N. Otis, supports my political and intellectual endeavors. Teri A. Vigars, my lover, celebrated feminist theory and psychoanalysis for breakfast during this book's completion.

Finally, this book owes its existence to strong allegiances between the academic Left and community-based feminist movements.

Versions of chapters 2, 4, and 6 were published in *Genders* 21 (1995), *Feminist Nightmares: Women at Odds* (New York: New York University Press, 1994), and *Discourse: Journal for Theoretical Studies in Media and Culture* 17.2 (1994/95), respectively; I gratefully acknowledge permission to reprint.

The Need to Politicize Survivorship

> The traumatic event challenges an ordinary person to
> become a theologian, a philosopher, and a jurist. The
> survivor is called upon to articulate the values and beliefs
> that she once held and that the trauma destroyed. She
> stands mute before the emptiness of evil.
>
> —Judith Herman, *Trauma and Recovery*

This book explains why incest survivorship should be understood as an urgent feminist political issue, and why community
and academic feminists alike should embrace survivorship as a
potential site of feminist political intervention in heteropatriarchy. Denial of the prevalence of incest and its damaging effects
on people and communities, a position advocated by the seemingly rational and scientific discourse of the False Memory Syndrome Foundation and its disciples, is a vestige of antifeminism
and needs to be publicly critiqued and excoriated for small-
minded sexism. This book is about a war against feminism that
is being waged under medicalized notions of psychological
repression. Let me define my terms.

A survivor of incest is someone who has been molested or raped by a family member, who lives through and remembers the experience, and who comes to understand—through therapy or feminism or some combination of the two—how the experience of childhood sexual violence is "political."

To say that something is political is to understand both its impetus and its consequences as being lodged in the social and public structure of society. Because there is no such thing as "generic feminism," I will explain the three characteristics of the feminism I espouse: it (1) challenges sexist, racist, homophobic, and classist stereotypes, in order to (2) render unthinkable and impotent those ideological systems that hold oppression in place, and therefore (3) transform oppressive institutions from tools of intolerance into peaceful, compassionate, and educational practices.

The difference between a survivor of violence and a victim of violence is the political meaning made of the traumatic experience and its resulting and residual aftereffects of abuse. Under the law of heteropatriarchy,[1] women who are molested when children start out as victims. Victims become complicit with abuse and honor injunctions posed by perpetrators to dismiss the abuse's import or impact. Survivors, in contrast, move to a place where they reject the demand to remain politely silent. They remember, speak up, and take every opportunity to "make political" incest experiences. Politicizing abuse is a lifelong effort aimed at "denaturalizing" abuse (thereby making it socially untenable) and disabling its aftereffects (thereby transforming memory from the register of current phobias to the record of past events). Polite silence condones the social order of the law of heteropatriarchy, a system of domination that reduces women to objects for exchange and men to tools carrying out this exchange. The law of heteropatriarchy damages women by systematically denying their potential to shape and inform their own lives; it damages men by forcing on them the social role of either oppressor or savior. Feminism seeks to right the heteropatriarchal wrongs waged against both men and women. In contrast to silence, politicizing a lived moment connects that experience to the social orders of language, history, and critical theory, frames which make that experience material and recast men and women as political agents, not labels, tools, or victims. This does not mean that experiences only really happen if we have the language to name them but rather that experiences have psychoanalytic and feminist meaning only when we can name them openly and "exchange" these meanings in an interpretive community. Politicizing incest makes personal healing contingent on progressive feminist change.

Why Literature?

We begin to politicize survivorship by developing methods to read aftereffects of abuse that make survivor literature visible, because reading is the first step to political activism.

My privileging of novels as opposed to, say, survivor testimonials may seem to some an inappropriate entry to survivorship. After all, by privileging such a genre, aren't I implying that survivor stories are untrue and made up? And if survivor narratives *are* fictions, then aren't I aligning myself with antifeminists—from "Freud"[2] to the False Memory Syndrome Foundation—who denounce survivor recollections as fantasies and survivors as hysterics?

But "fictions" are not lies. Rather, they are narrative recastings of events unrecognized by history. The notion that novels represent untruths is historically a recent phenomenon. Prior to the nineteenth century, the novel represented a different—not lesser—epistemological entrance to culture. Its purpose was explicitly ideological and political; it laid the groundwork for a woman's participation in gender-specific tasks by providing the woman reader with a representation of her role in the social order. While novels historically engage the task of self-construction (as the novel of manners suggests), they also initiate the project of making and writing history. Their representations construct the subject (by allowing her to "imagine herself *into*" socially proscribed contexts) and mediate between the subject and the historical narrative that is supposed to resonate with that subject's life experiences (by providing a material site of either contestation, should the historical record not reflect the subject's life experiences, or connection, should the historical record adequately contain her life as she knows it). As Anita Levy suggests, the novel functions "as an agent that imaginatively produces cultural materials on the family, the self, and sexual desire," and thereby serves "as an agent of history, rewriting and redefining history itself."[3] If novels can thus be understood as a site of historical agency, then we can see how they serve to bridge the binaries that divide our social order: inside/outside, public/private, false/true. That is, novels are always already on both sides of the binary pair; they impact on the seemingly "private" ways we both define ourselves and name our identities, as well as determine the "public" frame for which that self-definition takes shape. As Mikhail Bakhtin suggests, "In a novel the individual acquires the ideological and linguistic initiative necessary to change the nature of [his or her] own image."[4] And the novel's reader carries this "ideological and linguistic initiative" from the novel's world into the social world.

Furthermore, this bridge between narrative representation and everyday life that literature constructs is of importance to the emerging definition of history. As Hayden White has suggested in his provocative essay "The Historical Text as Literary Artifact," and as New Historicists have declared, monological history is dead. White writes that "the older distinction between fiction and history, in which fiction is conceived as the representation of the imaginable and history as the representation of the actual, must give place to the recognition that we can only know the *actual* by contrasting it with or likening it to the *imaginable.*"[5] If the novel, then, is never exclusively separate from everyday life and the construction of history, the novel's reader is herself an agent of these vestiges of culture and cultural change by embodying the image and bestowing it with meaning. For the text of history does not carry intrinsic or inherent meaning, nor do the texts of literature or life. Rather, it is the readers who supply such meaning.

Reading makes memory. As Freud suggested in the late nineteenth century, memory is always an act of (re)invention and reevaluation. It is in the process of rereading self-invention that "experience" and "truth" are born. For this reason, I position reading as the first step necessary to initiate political intervention. It is reading that interrupts ideas at the level of ideology and thus before they become institutionalized, naturalized, and internalized as cultural norms.

I value lived experiences and believe that progressive political activists should practice and teach methods of making political sense out of local, everyday experiences. Indeed, political criticism that does not engage the experiences of the scholar-activist and then connect them to the social text that names and thus *invents as meaningful* those experiences is politically cowardly and intellectually bankrupt. My position differs from the "untheorized experience" typified by 1970s feminism in that I privilege not the *fact* of the experience but the *meaning* made of it. Thus, having lived through the experience of abuse is not necessary to politicize survivorship—in fact, all forms of liberation depend on the active participation of allies. Conquering abuse under the law of heteropatriarchy involves risk; if we are "improved" only to reconnect with heteropatriarchy and ascribe to apolitical silence and middle-class virtues, we are still victims.

Methods and Models

The project of politicizing incest shares its closest kinship to that of queer[6] liberation, because of the social stigma patriarchy has attached to those outside its law (of "normality") and also because both queer culture and survivor culture have strategically and historically constituted themselves in the closet and signified themselves through codes (nondiscursive symbols of inclusion or exclusion). In both constituencies, the closet has functioned historically as a site of subjectivity, and coming out of the closet has served as a political performance.[7] Eve Sedgwick, in *The Epistemology of the Closet*, states that "'closetness' itself is a performance initiated as such by the speech act of a silence" that "accrues particularity" to the subject.[8] The particularity accrued to the incest survivor is most often shame and self-hatred. Reading aftereffects as texts, which is the model that, I argue, initiates the project of politicizing survivorship, offers the necessary contradiction to this particularity.

Both the survivor and the queer subject share a complex and complicated sense of self and subjectivity, the effect of moving specific elements of our lives in and out of the closet with a strategic eye to audience and impact.[9] The solution to oppression posed recently in both movements has been "coming out," a gesture that configures the closet as the problem, thus occluding the heterosexism, homophobia, and victim-blaming maintained in our patriarchal society that make necessary private hiding places.[10] Philip Brockman writes, "That closet door—never very secure as protection—is even more dangerous now. You must come out, for your own sake and for the sake of all of us."[11] And Oprah Winfrey's TV documentary "Scared Silent" has the subtitle "Expose and End Child Abuse," thus declaring—in spite of overwhelming evidence to the contrary—that child abuse will simply stop once revealed. Coming out has, for both movements, been embraced as the political end rather than the political beginning.

But no matter how profound our need to feel in control of our social oppression, coming out does not put an end to the closet's function. Just as the popular feminist phrase "the personal is the political" (a concept that sought to connect private experiences to their political origins) fell short of waging the political impact it desired because it understood experience as presocial, so, too, "opening" the closet door in the hope of finding the solution on the other side fails to recognize how experience and the feelings that emerge from that experience find their meaning in the social, historical, and cultural text. Following Michel Foucault, I argue that the body cannot be wrenched from the social text; following Jacques Lacan and Sigmund Freud, I argue that what make human sexuality and sexual identifications (and their resulting identities) *human* are their excess of and resistance to procreativity as erotic foundation. And for these reasons, coming out does not end the oppression that constructs the closet as a significant and signifying symbol. One of the functions of this book is to provide a model for political change that connects personal experiences to the social text which makes those experiences meaningful. This model relocates the closet as a historical place-keeper—nothing more, nothing less.

Coming out also often fails as a singular political strategy when the person to whom one comes out feels implicated in and therefore threatened by this disclosure. "Erotic identity," writes Sedgwick, "is never to be circumscribed simply as itself" because it is never "relational" and "never to be perceived or known by anyone outside of the structure of transference and countertransference."[12] Transference refers to the client's unconscious projection of wishes and ideas onto the therapist (or in this case, the survivor's projection onto the outsider); countertransference refers to the therapist's unconscious projection of wishes and ideas onto the client. A political movement that seeks social change without the aid of allies is destined to reify the consequences of transference and countertransference and cement as social roles "insiders" (those authorized to know) and "outsiders" (those predetermined not to understand). But a model of social change that embraces and, indeed, depends on the work of allies recasts "implication" from the register of the disclosure received by one who is unprepared to the bridge that connects subjects through not (only) life experiences but shared political commitments.

Queer theory and activism and political incest survivorship meet with social disapproval on the level of either lived experience or representation. For lived experience we can use as an example those conservatives who see queer subjects as "responsible" for society's opprobrium by sinning against heteropatriarchy; in like terms, some conservatives read incest survivors as deserving social ostracization on the grounds that they asked for it, are lying about it, or are foolish dupes snookered by corrupt feminist therapists. And as an example of representation, consider the generally embraced liberal position that tolerates "sexual aberrations" but sees no reason to name them, to make a scene, to make others uncomfortable by representing marginal lived experiences.

Finally, just as queer theory and activism borrow eclectically from many disciplines and schools of thought, so the project of politicizing incest requires eclectic theorizing. But there are important differences as well. As a lesbian[13] woman, I feel pride in my love of and for women. I participate in Queer Pride marches and, in honor, share my love for women with (sometimes unsuspecting) colleagues and dog walkers. But the "pride" of survivorship is not born out of the experience that marks and names the subject as survivor.[14]

Chapter Breakdown

I write this book at a moment of critical importance to incest survivors, when backlash against survivors is powerful and organized by a group called the False Memory Syndrome Foundation, a "family-values" organization that, under the aegis of scientific interest and political neutrality, invests in publicly discrediting survivor memories and discourse and forcefully denying survivors the legitimacy to bear witness to their own lives and histories. (See chapter 6 for my analysis of this organization and its political agenda and effects.) The time to politicize survivorship has come. But survivorship is unlike other political markers. Unlike issues of gender oppression, incest survivorship is not located in one gender only and has no canonized literary history or political scholarship that provides models for political practice.[15] Unlike issues of racial oppression, incest survivorship (usually) leaves no socially obvious marker for social connection and recognition. Unlike issues of class oppression, incest survivorship emerges in secrecy, isolation, and privacy, not in the structure of economic organization. Rherefore, instead of employing an already-existing model of social change or genuflecting to first principles of academic thinking currently in vogue (e.g., "always historicize"), this book reconfigures psychoanalytic feminism, especially its understanding of the unconscious, desire, law, sexuality, language, fantasy, and the interiorization of oppression, as the model for social change. I believe that oppression depends on either occluding privilege or elevating it to an "inalienable" right.

Chapter 1, "Surviving Psychoanalysis," offers a method of reading incest as a form of cultural containment and shows how the privatization of incest survivorship results from the social and systematic exclusion of reading incest as a *necessary result* of the law of heteropatriarchy—not as an accident. The model developed here, "reading aftereffects as texts," reconciles as coterminous the concepts of heteropatriarchy and the superego (the internalization of parental censorship and desire).[16] This method of reading can be understood as psychoanalytically grounded cultural studies. "Cultural studies" refers to the social, political, and textual construction of subjectivity; it uses the critical theories loosely enveloped by poststructuralism: Derridean deconstructivism, Lacanian and Freudian psychoanalysis, Foucauldian historiography, and poststructurally informed feminisms and Marxisms. The subsequent chapters read the aftereffects of incest as texts in themselves within the following women's novels: Mary Shelley's *Mathilda* and *Frankenstein*; Flora Rheta Schreiber's *Sybil*; Joan Francis Casey's *The Flock: An Autobiography of a Multiple Personality*; Katherine Dunn's *Geek Love*; and Carolivia Herron's *Thereafter Johnnie*. All but one of these texts—the infamous *Frankenstein*—are noncanonical and remain outside the ordinary interest of academics, even though the issues raised in them are of critical importance to feminist readers who concern themselves with the institutionalization of violence against women. These chapters explore the incest taboo and its cultural injunction against reading; mothers as perpetrators; the daughter's desire and the problem of an agency created under the rules of incest; sibling incest and the blurred the boundaries of peers and consent; and the "Name of the Law of the Father" (Lacan's term) and its narrative and political role.

The last chapter reads Oprah Winfrey's television documentary "Scared Silent" and examines the connections between "spectatorship" and "survivorship." In addition, this final chapter critiques the False Memory Syndrome Foundation and shows how the backlash created by this institution can be countered by remapping the "spectacle" of the incest survivor and thereby inverting these socially inscribed roles, so that incest survivors become activists and spectators of this political moment and incest perpetrators and their implicit allies in the False Memory Syndrome Foundation become the spectacles— the objects—of this psychoanlaytic-feminist reading practice. "Personal healing" without social change is simply not enough, and social change without critical self-reflection lacks the ethics of compassion that initiates moral political impulses in the first place.

In *The Politics of Survivorship*, I do not offer a "tour guide" to women's incest narratives and therefore do not chronicle every moment of incest or suspected incest in all women's literature of the nineteenth and twentieth centuries. The project of canonizing the literary history of survivorship is both important and vexed, but it is not my project here. I emphasize throughout that we politicize incest survivorship by developing scrupulous, rigorous, vigilant methods of reading aftereffects of incest. We stop incest by politicizing its impact on our lives and families, and it is strategies of reading that negotiate the transition from victim to survivor. Incest will not stop merely because we expose its presence in our society or our families; nor will it stop by ostensibly punishing perpetrators with legal sanctions while simultaneously valorizing violence by calling war "patriotic," heterosexism and homophobia "God's law," racism "deserved," and sexism "natural." Systems of political change fearful of engaging psychoanalytic theory and opposed to developing methods of reading the interiorization of oppression are condemned to benign inefficacy or cruel totalitarianism.[17] The politics of survivorship is located not in being the body invaded but in reading the meaning of sexual invasion and then using these readings to reconfigure definitions of love, respect, duty, family, and universe.

CHAPTER ONE

Surviving Psychoanalysis

The literature [on incest] suggests quite clearly that as a rule
intellectuals have either ignored or unintentionally denied
the existence of incest in propounding their theories about
the universality of the prohibition.

—W. Arens, *The Original Sin*

Pathological lying. Post-traumatic stress disorder. Self-starvation. Nightmares. Panic attacks. Body tremors. Waking dreams. Chronic insomnia. Self-hatred. Self-mutilation. Repetition compulsions. Amnesia. Body memories.

These represent common aftereffects of incest. Sometimes a woman molested as a child connects her aftereffects to early-childhood sexual abuse; sometimes she receives counseling; sometimes she politicizes her experience and, in community with survivor-activists, works to fight social injustices. But usually the victim/survivor does not connect the aftereffects that punctuate her day to violation, especially violation that happened long ago. In these latter cases, the aftereffects take on a life of their own. Chronic symptoms proliferate, with no known origin and no known finish. Because of the role that repression plays in memory, currently a hotly debated subject, many survivors learn to "remember" the abuse through reading aftereffects as texts. This process of reading backwards, reading the body morphologically through the effects it has on the mind, opens avenues for memory, avenues necessary to politicizing incest narratives and the experience of survivorship.[1]

I focus on aftereffects of incest, calling these the "texts" of my reader's gaze. I do not privilege the incest event itself or the supposed "universal" prohibition against incest—the incest taboo—because as a crime that takes place in privacy, secrecy, and isolation, often the only material evidence of incest a survivor carries into adulthood is represented by aftereffects. First identified by Sigmund Freud in 1896 and then revised in 1905, redefined as "symptom" and made textual by Jacques Lacan, made public and popular in the twentieth century by feminist self-help activist texts such as Ellen Bass and Laura Davis's *The Courage to Heal,* and dismissed as unreadable and unimportant by the False Memory Syndrome Foundation, the aftereffects of incest are now the subject of debate about their validity, reality, and "readability" that rages on throughout modern U.S. culture.

Incest is the oldest taboo. It also is a very ordinary part of many children's lives: one of out of three girls; one out of seven boys.[2] In the United States, incest became a legal crime in the late 1860s.[3] In England it became illegal in 1908.[4] In both cultures, the social construction of sexual abuse ensured that victims would go it alone. Shame, secrecy, and victim-blaming would contain the problem and remove it from social discourse. Unnamed and untexted, aftereffects of incest would remain the unpoliticized demon of the individual victim; and with the incest experience thus contained by individual bodies and psyches, society could remain untouched by the needs of victims and oblivious to its role in creating a world where incest is, quite simply, ordinary. To "honor thy mother and father" meant (and means) don't remember—and if you do, then don't talk. In England and the United States in the nineteenth and twentieth centuries, only feminism successfully marshaled concern for children's welfare and women's safety to the forefront. The recognition of incest as a crime—instead of as a parent's privilege—"usually grew when feminism was strong and ebbed when feminism was weak."[5]

One chapter of Linda Gordon's *Heroes of Their Own Lives: The Politics and History of Family Violence* focuses on father–daughter incest as reported to the Massachusetts Society for the Prevention of Cruelty to Children (MSPCC) from 1880 to 1960. By defining the changing categories into which patriarchal culture lodged victims, her research provides a useful map of the social construction of incest. According to Gordon, in 1880 the MSPCC noted that incest ran rampant: "One of the most striking things about incest, that most ordinary and heinous of transgressions, is its capacity to be ordinary."[6] But because parents—especially fathers—hold political power and children do not, patriarchal institutions such as laws and rules needed to recast, in name or definition, sexual transgressions against children. Thus, by 1910 "the incest problem was virtually redefined as a problem of sex delinquency."[7]

As Gordon points out, most incest victims could only "confess" the crime if it was put in the past tense—even when they were still being abused. Psychologically, this reconstruction of time created a false safety net that allowed the survivor to speak. Because they were often "trapped" in the lie of time, they were said to be "feebleminded" liars, a term that implied moral retardation: "Feeblemindedness thereby justified the incarceration of victims, for these girls could not be expected to look out for their own virtue. At the same time, the girls' alleged mental inadequacy made them bad witnesses and interfered with the prosecution of sex assailants." With the interpretive and textual power of incest victims diminished with victim-blaming and public excoriation, the category of incestuous parents or caretakers virtually disappeared: "While incest victims were changed into delinquents, incest perpetrators became strangers."[8] This intentional misreading—for then as now, child abusers were most likely social intimates, not strangers—succeeded in making incest a crime in theory only.

Finally, "by 1960 [in the United States] incest was conceived by experts and described in textbooks on family problems as a rare sexual perversion, a one-in-a-million occurrence."[9] How do we know if incest occurs in one out of three cases or one in a million? One answer asks us to examine the ideology that declares the keepers of culture incapable of punishable transgression. The move from "one out of three to one in a million" demands that culture redefine transgression to a cultural norm, sacrificing the safety and sanity of the child for the entitlement of the father. For this reason, political survivorship *reads back*—and thus takes back—the right to define life experiences and their impact on relationships and social and legal practices.

Gordon concludes by stating that life became harder for the girls in the MSPCC records who told. Their fathers were rarely, if ever, punished, and their abuse continued—now with the added shame of being named public liars.[10] Incest had become so normalized it hardly needed a name. Without a signifier to make the connection between the body and the culture, incest became semiotically forgotten and thus culturally ordinary— ordinary not because "victims or other family members believed these incestuous relations to be legitimate" but because they functioned to rearrange the division of labor within the family. Incest became assimilated, and the family dynamic operated around this transgression. While the sexually molested daughter became known as feebleminded and a liar, her perpetrator grew in patriarchal glory as his entitlement to his child's body was sanctioned: "The largest single factor in creating the aura of 'normality' in these families was the father's attitude of entitlement. Not a single incest assailant expressed contrition for what he had done or guilt for having hurt his daughter—only denial, self-justification, and/or shame and humiliation at being discovered."[11] Incest is a crime that originates in sexual invasion and textualizes itself in aftereffects. Aftereffects are the signifiers of despair.

Aftereffects of incest are overdetermined and somatized symptoms. According to Freud in 1896, aftereffects result from sexual, physical, and psychological assault; if left unhealed—which declaring victims "feebleminded" renders inevitable—they become lodged in the unconscious and remain both repressed and functionally insidious. It is Freud who allows us to connect aftereffects to incest, and Jacques Lacan—Freud's most famous disciple—who helps us textualize them. If the unconscious is structured like a language (probably Lacan's most quoted concept), then aftereffects, too (since they reside in the unconscious) can be read as texts. To quote Jean Laplanche and Jean-Bertrand Pontalis: "The symptom (in the broad sense) is 'structured like a language', and thus naturally constituted by elision and layering of meaning." Furthermore, this language carries with it the poststructural warning that signifiers stand for more than the concepts they represent: "just as a word cannot be reduced to a signal, a symptom cannot be the unambiguous sign of a single unconscious content."[12] Thus, reading aftereffects as texts is not the simplistic project of plugging incest into a "checklist" of symptoms but rather the complex and risky business of giving narrative shape to symptoms and their probable cause. The former gesture privileges the perpetrator; the latter emphasizes the steps that make possible the shift from victimhood to survivorship.

Aftereffects of incest represent a quintessential reader-response text, for what the assailant did is determined in this paradigm by the meaning the survivor made of the event. The shared turf between reader-response criticism and feminist self-help literature can be seen in this definition of incest.[13] In *The Courage to Heal*, Ellen Bass and Laura Davis define childhood sexual abuse as any event that involves a child who is:

1. fondled, kissed, or held for an adult's sexual gratification;
2. forced to perform oral sex on an adult or sibling;
3. raped or otherwise penetrated;
4. made to watch sexual acts;
5. forced to listen to excessive talk about sex;
6. fondled or hurt genitally while being bathed;
7. subjected to unnecessary medical treatments to satisfy an adult's sadistic or sexual needs;
8. shown sexual movies or other pornography;
9. made to pose for seductive or sexual photographs;
10. involved in child prostitution or pornography;
11. forced to take part in ritualized abuse in which [children] were physically, psychologically, or sexually tortured.[14]

Bass and Davis make feminist the heretofore accepted definition of incest by removing it from the realm of the biological: prior to the feminist recovery movement, incest encompassed only reproductive possibilities. If only potentially reproductive transgressions of vaginal intercourse (father–daughter, mother–son, and brother–sister) fall under the "universal" prohibition, then every other sexual transgression simply means "nothing happened." Indeed, there really is no taboo fetishizing the most common form of child molestation: forced oral sex. Probably Bass and Davis's most controversial point—and one that I will defend—is that incest survivorship is not determined by a checklist or by parental entitlement over the family narrative but rather by the perceptions of the survivor. Bass and Davis write, "Violation is determined by your experience as a child—your body, your feelings, your spirit. The precise physical acts are not always the most damaging aspects of abuse." Indeed, "many kinds of sexual abuse are not physically painful."[15] Just as reader-response theory declares the reader responsible for making meaning, so feminist self-help theory puts the survivor in charge of naming her or his experience.

And like the project of politicizing incest survivorship, feminist reader-response theory privileges the reader over the text to effect political progress. Patrocinio Schweickart, in her influential essay on feminist reader-response theory "Reading Ourselves: Toward a Feminist Theory of Reading," declares feminist reading practices a form of praxis: "The point here is not merely to interpret literature in various ways; the point is to *change the world.* We cannot afford to ignore the activity of reading, for it is here that literature is realized as *praxis.*"[16] By teaching incest survivors to read aftereffects as texts, we make legitimate their perceptions and contest the legacy of dismissal by a culture that wishes to see them as feebleminded liars. By teaching incest survivors to read bodies as texts, to break the silence and "act on the world" by declaring sexual transgressions as ordinary but not inevitable, incest survivors can become strong political agents for progressive feminist change. Indeed, a revolution in this direction has begun: *The Courage to Heal* has turned a whole generation of women into feminists. I would like to carry their project into the realm of academic reading, because reading aftereffects as texts offers a method that politicizes the effects of the contemporary feminist recovery movement, instead of snidely dismissing it.

It is in the hope of connecting the experiential and the political that I refer to *The Courage to Heal* as "activist." And activist self-help literature is threatening not because of its subject—the recovery from childhood sexual abuse—but because of the power it ascribes to women via its explicit feminism. For the first time in the history of women's relationship to psychoanalysis, survivors—not Freud, Josef Breuer, or parents—are invited to read the body and give its aftereffects names and meaning. For embodying (feeling) pain is not enough; one must also make political meaning out of pain. And then one must be the reader of one's own invention, because "reading removes the barrier between subject and object" and thus "the division takes place *within* the reader." This division, the product of reading the text of oneself, "induces a doubling of the reader's subjectivity."[17] Reading the text of incest simultaneously fragments as it invents closure. Reading the text of incest invents incest anew by naming this ordinary abuse of children as an unacceptable transgression—no matter how seemingly benign the representation may be. As I said in the Introduction, literature is an important site of political engagement; reading aftereffects as texts is crucial to effect interpretation (reading) as an agent of political change. We must take seriously this activist self-help literature, because it is here that a whole generation of incest survivors are learning to read experiences outside of the social possibilities handed to them by heteropatriarchal culture.

The Feminist Freud

In response to the rejection Freud received from the Society for Psychiatry and Neurology in Vienna regarding his "seduction theory"—the theory that "hysteria" resulted from unprovoked and psychically damaging assaults, rapes, or molestations perpetrated by trusted adults against children—he wrote:

A lecture on the aetiology of hysteria at the Psychiatric Society met with an icy reception from the asses, and from Krafft-Ebing the strange comment: It sounds like a scientific fairy tale. And this after one has demonstrated to them a solution to a more than thousand-year-old problem, a "source of the Nile!" ... They can all go to hell.[18]

Indeed, the rising medical profession in the late nineteenth century understood hysteria[19] as a disease produced by a wandering uterus. By suggesting that incestuous fathers (and sometimes mothers, brothers, and nurses), and not the natural inferiority of women's bodies, caused hysteria, Freud delivered a powerful blow to the incest taboo. By doing so, Freud was the first to imply that the incest taboo was really a taboo against interpretation.

Freud's two theories of sexuality, the seduction theory and the oedipal theory, offer two seemingly different accounts of hysteria. In the 1896 seduction theory,[20] Freud sees a presexual child who becomes sexualized through assault, rape, or molestation; by 1905, according to Jeffrey Masson, the scorn of his fellow professionals and anxiety over the revelations of his own self-analysis had provoked Freud to advance the oedipal theory, a biological account of infantile sexuality which declared that psychic trauma resided inside. With his formulation of the oedipal complex, hysteria returned to the "natural" dysfunction of women's bodies.[21]

Masson's implication is that had Freud not been swayed from his original position, psychoanalysis might have affected women's lives in politically useful ways. But Masson fails to register that no one can conquer social mores in isolation; such a movement requires collective social action, not individual moments of brilliance. "The Aetiology of Hysteria" put forward a *potentially* feminist position whose social progressivity went unrealized because Freud could not single-handedly politicize it. What is important is that in 1896, Freud believed the women who relived scenes of childhood sexual abuse; just as hysteria gave credence to psychoanalysis and feminized it (especially through the body of Anna O.—Bertha Pappenheim—who coined the term *the talking cure*, a concept that continues to frame feminist therapy today), Freud made the crimes of incest visible to late Victorian and modern culture.

According to Freud in "The Aetiology of Hysteria," aftereffects become the hysteric's psychic prostheses; with them, the crime is veiled but (potentially) visible: "The symptoms of hysteria ... are determined by certain experiences of the patient's which have operated in a traumatic fashion and which are being reproduced in his psychical life in the form of mnemic symbols."[22] By referring to these symptoms as "mnemic symbols," Freud suggests that memory is invented, pieced together, read, interpreted like a text. Not a neutral "truth" or "lie," memory is a complex dance, shifting and filtering information between the conscious and the unconscious through language, which always already changes the possibilities of meanings.

In opposition to Josef Breuer (Freud's collaborator in *Studies in Hysteria*), who believed that "even an innocuous experience can be heightened into a trauma and can develop determining force if it happens to the subject when he is in a special psychical condition ... a *hypnoid state*," Freud believed that aftereffects result from "traumatic force,"[23] force originally imposed *on* the body which becomes a force inherent *in* the body. Instead of privileging "hypnoid states" as causal, Freud offers a "new idea," one so efficacious that it is still in use in feminist therapy today: repressed memories are painful and debilitating because of the aftereffects that they produce. The analyst's job is not to find hypnoid states but instead to lead the patient back to the feelings that encase the scene of memory:

Hysterical symptoms can be resolved if, starting from them, we are able to find the path back to the memory of a traumatic experience. If the memory which we have uncovered does not answer our expectations, it may be that we ought to pursue the same path a little further; perhaps behind the first traumatic scene there may be concealed the memory of a second, which satisfies our requirements better and whose reproduction has a greater therapeutic effect; so that the scene that was first discovered only has the significance of a connecting link in a chain of associations. And perhaps this situation may repeat itself; inoperative scenes may be interpolated more than once, as necessary transitions in the process of reproduction, until we finally make our way from the hysterical symptom to the scene which is really operative traumatically.[24]

Freud here is hunting for something *outside* the psyche that imposes itself on the body and is then repressed and harmfully embodied. Unlike the contemporary antifeminist stereotype of incest survivors—that they *love* to talk about their horrible experiences and do so at any opportunity—Freud's patients were reticent:[25]

If the first-discovered scene is unsatisfactory, we tell our patient that this experience explains nothing, but that behind it there must be hidden a more significant, earlier, experience; and we direct his attention by the same technique to the associative thread which connects the two memories.... A continuation of the analysis then leads in every instance to the reproduction of new scenes of the character we expect.[26]

To Freud in 1896, the "character" who would lurk in the scene—who still has the power of the gaze—was the perpetrator.

Importantly, aftereffects of incest emerge from the "overdetermination" inherent in childhood sexual abuse: "No hysterical symptom can arise from a real experience alone, but ... in every case the memory of earlier experiences awakened in association to it plays a part in causing the symptom."[27] Overdetermination means more than repetition; it refers to the multiple determinations of meaning. According to Freud, puberty separates the (at least) two stages of trauma. In the first stage, the incest occurs when the child is presexual. During the incest event itself, the child remains passive. Laplanche and Pontalis show this passivity as twofold: the child both *behaves* passively (she does not disobey the adult) and *interprets* violation passively: she "undergoes it without its being able to evoke a response in [her], since no corresponding sexual ideas are available."[28] It is through the interpretation phase of passivity that the event is not yet repressed. The second stage occurs in puberty. An event—not necessarily a sexual one—offers an associative link, which allows the pubescent child to reread the first scene as sexual. Filled with shame and fear, the child now represses the first sexual scene. In this way, the incest event becomes overdetermined.

Laplanche and Pontalis define overdetermination as:

> The fact that formations of the unconscious (symptoms, dreams, etc.) can be attributed to a plurality of determining factors. This can be understood in two different ways:
>   a) The formation in question is the result of several causes, since one alone is not sufficient to account for it.
>   b) The formation is related to a multiplicity of unconscious elements which may be organized in different meaningful sequences, each having its own specific coherence at a particular level of interpretation.[29]

Thus, symptoms that occur from childhood sexual abuse are triggered originally from violation and abuse but ultimately, the pain resides in the unconscious; it is located in memory, especially repressed memories: "It seems to me really astonishing that hysterical symptoms can only arise with the co-operation of memories, especially when we reflect that, according to the unanimous accounts of the patients themselves, these memories did not come into their consciousness at the moment when the symptom first made its appearance."[30] What is important is that aftereffects take on a life of their own. The bearer of the mark does not connect these somatized memories as memories at all; without analysis, these memory traces cannot become memory proper.

The point, of course, is that the etiology of hysteria is incest. Anticipating that his audience would reject his supposition, Freud offered a nonpartisan motive: "The singling out of the sexual factor in the aetiology of hysteria springs at least from no preconceived opinion on my part." He then explained that his teachers did not even approve: "The two investigators as whose pupil I began my studies of hysteria, [Jean-Martin] Charcot and [Josef] Breuer, were far from having any such presupposition; in fact they had a personal disinclination to it which I originally shared." Finally, Freud distanced himself from his thesis, saying in effect that "objective" evidence made him change his mind and believe incest survivors: "Only the most laborious and detailed investigations have converted me, and that slowly enough, to the view I hold today."[31]

Decade-delayed memory is not rare but is consistent with the pattern that aftereffects of incest follow: "At the bottom of every case of hysteria there are *one or more occurrences of premature sexual experience,* occurrences which belong to the earliest years of childhood but which can be reproduced through the work of psychoanalysis in spite of the intervening decades." Opposing the position that incest survivors "fake" memories, Freud declares that memories are undergirded by emotion, and feelings that accompany heinous memories cannot be fabricated: "The behavior of patients while they are reproducing these infantile experiences is in every respect incompatible with the assumption that the scenes are anything else than a reality which is being felt with distress and reproduced with the greatest reluctance."[32] He refutes the position that incest survivors plan and perhaps rehearse this performance in the analyst's office: "Before they come for analysis the patients know nothing about these scenes [of sexual abuse]." Furthermore, "they are indignant as a rule if we warn them that such scenes are going to emerge." The process through which unconscious memories become conscious is painful, not pleasurable: "While they are recalling these infantile experiences to consciousness, they suffer under the most violent sensations, of which they are ashamed and which they try to conceal." And even after an incest survivor remembers the sexual abuse, she does not necessarily believe it to be true: "Even after they have gone through [the scene of sexual abuse] in a convincing manner, they still attempt to withhold belief ... by emphasizing the fact that, unlike what happens in the case of other forgotten material, they have no feeling of remembering the scenes." To Freud, it is this denial, first of the incest event and next of its import, that offers "conclusive proof." He points out, "Why should patients assure me so emphatically of their unbelief, if what they want to discredit is something which—from whatever motive—they themselves have invented?" And in response to the accusation that overzealous therapists "plant" memories in their patients that turn out to be "false memories," Freud relies again on the feelings the patient has when reliving a repressed childhood memory and declares, "I have never yet succeeded in forcing on a patient a scene I was expecting to find, in such a way that he seemed to be living through it with all the appropriate feelings."[33] Furthermore, once "discovered," proof of the incest can almost always be found: "Without wishing to pay special stress on the point, I will add that in a number of cases therapeutic evidence of the genuineness of the infantile scenes can also be brought forward."[34]

Freud was the first to show that psychic pain lives on in the form of aftereffects well after the abuse stops, and that if left unhealed, aftereffects run—and eventually ruin—lives. In the middle section of his lecture, he anticipates two different ways to reject his thesis that incest is pervasive and devastating: the first tries to invalidate his thesis on the grounds that incest occurs only rarely; the second declares that it occurs often—so often, in fact, that if Freud were right, almost all women would manifest symptoms of hysteria.

Regarding the first challenge, Freud identifies three different kinds of incest perpetrators. In the first group we have stranger rapists: "isolated incidences of abuse, mostly practiced on female children, by adults who were strangers, and who, incidentally, know how to avoid inflicting gross, mechanical injury." The second, from which most cases of childhood sexual abuse come, includes "a nursery maid or governess or tutor, or, unhappily all too often, a close relative [who] has initiated the child into sexual intercourse and has maintained a regular love relationship with it." In this group we have children molested by trusted adults whose love they cannot afford to lose—not yet. The third group consists of siblings engaged in incest: "sexual relations between two children of different sexes, mostly a brother and sister, which are often prolonged beyond puberty and which have the most far-reaching consequences for the pair."[35] Of course, victimization by a member of one category does not prohibit victimization by a member of another. Perhaps anticipating the contemporary statistic that childhood sexual abuse survivors are most susceptible to adult assaults, Freud states, "In most of my cases I found that two or more of these aetiologies were in operation together; in a few instances the accumulation of sexual experiences coming from different quarters was truly amazing." Eerily anticipating the feminist self-help position that sexual "acting out" in children speaks previous abuse, Freud says that "children cannot find their way to acts of sexual aggression unless they have been seduced previously."[36]

In response to the second challenge—that incest is frequent and pervasive but that not all survivors of incest manifest symptoms of hysteria—Freud defends himself by pointing to the role of repression. If the event need not be repressed—for whatever reason—then it need not be acted out through somatized aftereffects; instead, it can simply be spoken. "Hysteria may almost invariably be traced to a *psychical conflict* arising through an incompatible idea setting in action a *defence* on the part of the ego and calling up a demand for repression."[37] Freud cannot explain why some events can be stored in conscious memory and others must be repressed. But he does state emphatically that no one manifests hysterical symptoms from conscious memories of abuse. Unconscious, repressed memories of sexual abuse provide the necessary precondition for hysteria: "Hysterical symptoms are derivatives of memories which are operating unconsciously."[38]

Why does repression create such an effect? Freud suggests that the repressed memory is potentially (and in some cases, actually) more harmful than the abuse itself: "It is true that we cannot help asking ourselves how it comes about that this memory of an experience that was innocuous at the time it happened, should posthumously produce the abnormal effect," resulting in "a pathological result while it itself remains unconscious." The reason that the repressed memory triggers the aftereffect is because "hysterical symptoms are over-determined," not because the scene of incest was innocuous.[39] It is for this reason that aftereffects of abuse need to be read semiotically, not dismissed as hysterical overreaction or a lack of self-control. Freud emphatically declares that the hysteric is not overreacting: "The reaction of hysterics is only apparently exaggerated; it is bound to appear exaggerated to us because we only know a small part of the motives from which it arises."[40]

In 1896, Freud advocated for a constituency that had never had a supportive and sympathetic public voice. Jeffrey Masson, Alice Miller, Judith Herman, Lenore Terr, Ellen Bass, Laura Davis, and I, among others, support the major theme of Freud's 1896 theory: that incest is pervasive and debilitating. Masson calls "The Aetiology of Hysteria" Freud's "most brilliant" paper and the seduction theory "the very cornerstone of psychoanalysis."[41] Alice Miller adds nonsexual trauma (such as verbal and physical abuse) as an additional cause of neurosis, but she embraces the overall implication of Freud's theory, the "recognition of the significance of trauma and of its societal suppression as the source of neurosis."[42] Yet, with the exception of the efforts of a handful of supporters, Freud's theory of 1896 has all but disappeared from the history of psychoanalysis. Indeed, even Freud wished he had never published this paper, and by 1905 he had revised his seduction theory in favor of the oedipal complex. According to most psychoanalytic theorists, Freud *had* to revise the seduction theory so that bigger fish—namely, Oedipus himself—could be fried.

What's Oedipus Got to Do with It?

Antipsychoanalytic feminists traditionally read Freud's transition from seduction theory to the oedipal complex as a betrayal because Freud—it appears—stopped validating abuse experiences and replaced this position with a hostile, masculinist theoretical overlay; one that witnesses the "birth" of "real" psychoanalysis. Psychoanalytic feminists, by contrast, find the seduction theory itself problematic: Elizabeth Grosz defines the seduction theory as that which "posits the intrusion of an external, alien sexuality which initiates the child (usually 'prematurely') into adult forms of sexuality," and then explains that this theory is, on its own terms, "problematic."[43]

Perhaps it is problematic because, as Masson explains, "every first year resident in psychiatry knows" that Freud "had to abandon his erroneous beliefs about seduction before he could discover the more basic truth of the power of internal fantasy and of spontaneous childhood sexuality."[44] Laplanche and Pontalis call Freud's change of heart "a decisive step in the foundation of psycho-analytic theory," because, without Oedipus, how could Freud (or anyone) bring into light "such conceptions as unconsciousness, phantasy, psychical reality, spontaneous infantile sexuality and so on"?[45] They quote Freud on this decisive move in the history of psychoanalysis:

> If hysterical subjects trace back their symptoms to traumas that are fictions, then the new fact which emerges is precisely that they create such scenes in *phantasy*, and this psychical reality requires to be taken into account alongside practical reality. This reflection was soon followed by the discovery that these phantasies were intended to cover up the auto-erotic activity of the first years of childhood, to embellish it and raise it to a higher plane. And now, from behind the phantasies, the whole range of a child's sexual life came to light.[46]

But this historical rationale is based on faulty logic. How can the seduction theory cancel out the theory of the unconscious or of psychical reality, when Freud in 1896 states that hysteria is *located* in the unconscious, and that the "scene" of trauma—a fiction—is painful because of how we "read" it? Furthermore, his oedipal theory clearly loads the cards against the incest survivor, who now does exaggerate ("embellish") her pain as a "cover-up" for the sexual fantasy she has created by herself. While I find one element of the 1905 theory helpful—the notion that symptoms (aftereffects of abuse) deserve to be taken seriously *on their own terms*, regardless of whether we can trace them to real events—Freud's relegation of incest to a primal fantasy gives (more) cultural credence to the notion that women lie.[47] That this shift held (and holds) enormous social impact is made clear when we see that, by 1905, sexual fantasies do not merely share turf with personal experience, they overshadow it: "psychoanalysis reveals," say Laplanche and Pontalis, "typical phantasy structures" that assume responsibility for "the organization of phantasy life, *regardless of the personal experiences of different subjects.*"[48] But by implying that fantasy is at the root of hysteria, Freudian psychoanalysis is not actually declaring that all women who suffer from what may be read as aftereffects of childhood abuse are dishonest or insane (although this is how it is traditionally read); rather, it is the social implication of fantasy at the root of hysteria that functions to declare dishonest or insane the women who suffer from aftereffects of trauma.

Peter Gay canonizes this death knell of the seduction theory by including it in *The Freud Reader*, with this warning: "['The Aetiology of Hysteria'] is at once elegant and eloquent, but it advocates an untenable theory—that neuroses are almost invariably caused by sexual aggression of adults against children."[49] Why should the notion that sexual abuse causes lasting emotional pain be so hard to accept? Precisely because, as Alice Miller makes clear, there exists a cultural injunction against reading the crime of parents; thus, "thou shalt not be aware" of parents' transgressions. Perhaps for this reason Laplanche and Pontalis declare seduction-theory revivalists "dangerous": "There ... [is] a danger in ... a revival of the seduction theory— namely that of re-opening the door to the preanalytical view of the child as sexual innocent."[50] A "danger" to whom?

Freud advanced his canonized theory of sexuality in the *Three Essays on the Theory of Sexuality*. The editor, J. D. Sutherland, declares the *Three Essays*, along with the *Interpretation of Dreams*, Freud's "most momentous and original contributions to human sexuality."[51] He restates the accepted narrative that Freud had to revise his "fairy tale" of sexual abuse for his hard and scientific theory that "sexual impulses operated normally in the youngest children without any need for outside stimulation." The oedipal complex offers the final word: "With this realization Freud's sexual theory was in fact completed."[52]

But the seduction theory does not foreclose the progressive elements of oedipalization—fantasy and the unconscious. Understanding these elements as an extension of the seduction theory implies that children can be simultaneously psychosexually active and psychosexually innocent, and that parents can love their children, sexually abuse them, and lie about it. In spite of the official record reproduced in the editor's note to the *Three Essays*, Freud's understanding of hysteria and the seduction theory did not outlaw the possibility that "sexual impulses ... operated normally in the youngest children," especially if we understand Freud's use of the word *scene* to include these sexual impulses.

What would happen if we read the oedipal theory and the seduction theory as complementary? Both theories declare that childhood sexual abuse is not *necessarily* trauma-producing (although it certainly is reprehensible and painful). While the editor casts the sexually aware child as present only in the *Three Essays*, Freud does not prohibit the possibility of a sexually aware child in "The Aetiology of Hysteria"; instead, his focus in "Aetiology" is on how the unconscious makes sense of unwanted sexual assault: "Only *aftereffects* produced by [incest] ... are [psychically] important, owing to the development of the somatic and psychical sexual apparatus that has taken place in the meantime."[53] Not only did Freud not have to "abandon" the seduction theory to initiate his theory of the unconscious, he had already established a working understanding of the unconscious in the seduction theory proper. The "contents" of the unconscious are themselves representations. Thus, we might think more productively of the oedipal theory either as Freud's own neurosis (as Jacques Lacan read it)[54] or as unconsciously operative in the seduction theory.

"Infantile Sexuality," the second of Freud's *Three Essays*, begins with a fall: "I cannot admit that in my paper on 'The Aetiology of Hysteria' (1896) I exaggerated the frequency or importance of [childhood sexual abuse], though I did not then know that persons who remain normal may have had the same experiences in their childhood."[55] But Freud anticipated and responded to such a position by stating in 1896 that only repressed memories lead to hysteria. After the fall, Freud changes the subject: "I ... overrated the importance of seduction in comparison with the factors of sexual constitution and development," and "obviously seduction is not required in order to arouse a child's sexual life." Freud fails to respond to his original thesis that the aetiology of hysteria is assault, not seduction. Suddenly, seduction (assault) means *seduction*—the simple arousal of a child's sexual life.

After Freud changes the topic, he reascribes agency, this time making the child's "spontaneous sexuality"[56] the cause for her own pain: "One of the clearest indications that a child will later become neurotic is to be seen in an insatiable demand for his parents' affections."[57] Suddenly, rape no longer triggers hysteria, loving caresses do, for parents who "are inclined ... to display excessive affection are precisely those who are most likely by their caresses to arouse the child's disposition to neurotic illness."[58] Assault, rape, and molestation have become "caresses."

After changing the initial experience from rape to caresses, Freud changes the agent of transgression. In "Transformations of Puberty," the third of the *Three Essays*, Freud refers to the frequently occurring "*child's* sexual impulses towards his parent."[59] And hysteria, aftereffects, and symptoms of incest, once located in the body and repressed/represented in the unconscious now become "proof" of a girl's weakness and ring the death knell for her future marriage, since those "who never got over their parents' authority" are "mostly girls who ... have persisted in all their childish lives [for their parents] far beyond puberty." Note that the gender of the child has changed. Even though most (but not all) of Freud's hysterics were women, the patient in 1896 was always referred to as "he" or "him"; by 1905 we know who the real criminal is, and we know her name is woman: for "these girls [who act on sexual impulses toward their parents] ... in later marriage lack the capacity to give their husbands what is due them; they make cold wives and remain sexually anaesthetic."[60]

These differences in position have convinced many feminist scholars to understand Freud's change of heart as a betrayal. But both theories share an important—and deeply troubling— feature: both try to "fix" the victim, and the fix does not offer an easy entrance into the politics of healing. What needs fixing at this point is society, specifically its definition of the incest taboo—the supposedly natural prohibition of sexual abuse crimes against children.

In *The Elementary Structures of Kinship*, Claude Lévi-Strauss states that "the incest prohibition is at once on the threshold of culture, in culture, and in one sense ... culture itself."[61] Actually, it is the simultaneous transgression of the taboo and denial of the crime that forms the foundation of patriarchal culture. By declaring perpetrators of abuse the keepers of culture, their transgressions cannot be marked *as* transgression because those who symbolize law are not judged by their actions but rather are privileged for their role.

The power of the taboo actually to prohibit incest assumes that adults have a natural repugnance to the notion of sex with and the eroticization of children. This repugnance is really more accurately understood as a wish fulfillment, for patriarchal culture consistently eroticizes the child.[62] In response to the notion that the incest taboo results from the natural repugnance of sex with children, Lévi-Strauss writes, "There is nothing more dubious than this alleged instinctive repugnance [for incest], for although prohibited by law and morals, incest does exist and is no doubt even more frequent by far than a collective conspiracy of silence would lead us to believe."[63]

Indeed, the frequency of child molestation and the concomitant denial of the crime establish Lévi-Strauss's definition of "culture." Since "there is no point in forbidding what would not happen if it were not forbidden,"[64] the incest taboo preserves culture through its simultaneous presence (in words) and denial (in action). The incest taboo provides the crucial link between nature and culture.[65] If the prohibition that fails to prohibit provides the necessary basis for the creation of culture, then it is the transgression of the incest taboo and its resulting textual erasure upon which culture depends. Incest has to happen, but we cannot read its trace. The only presence we can acknowledge is the taboo.

The taboo against incest has become a social myth as well, one that strategically simplifies the impact—both social and personal—that childhood sexual abuse has on a community. Defined by the taboo, incest is a known fact by both the perpetrator and the victim; it involves vaginal rape; it is only harmful if the abuse meets standards of high frequency and duration; it happens only in bad homes. The taboo further suggests that the perpetrator is sick, deranged, alcohol- or drug-addicted. He (and the myth only recognizes male perpetrators) clearly does not love the child he molests; he knows consciously that his behavior would be categorized as incest; and he is a visibly uncivilized member of society.

The victim or survivor, too, is constructed under the aegis of the incest taboo. She supposedly has full, conscious memory of the incest experience, which she triumphantly discloses to an authority figure who believes her and solves "her" problem by stopping the abuse. Furthermore, under the taboo, she hates and despises her perpetrator and knows, as the rest of the society does just by looking at him, that he is an evil person. Above all, she feels no ambivalence about the experience or the perpetrator; at the very least, she certainly feels no love or compassion for him. Even if the experience happened when she was preverbal, she knows that what she experienced was incest. Finally, she is able to put the whole experience "behind" her because the past does not converge into the present in unexplainable or confusing ways—that is, in the acting out and embodying of aftereffects—unless, of course, she is crazy.

If the victim has any memory loss regarding the experience, society knows how to dispense with her: the taboo declares that she is lying, or that she liked it, or that she falsely believes the experience was incest because of suggestions made by a therapist or friend or the media, or that she just didn't fully understand the intent of the perpetrator because Daddy was just giving her a backrub or teaching her what men want or because Mommy was just giving her an enema or good, clean bath. Finally, if the victim or surivor has no witnesses—not even by association—then she or he is a bad daughter or son, niece or nephew, brother or sister, for bringing unnecessary and unfounded charges against a poor, defenseless man or woman, whose life and career are now ruined because of the accusation.[66]

The approach implied by the incest taboo overrides psychoanalytic analysis about memory and trauma. As a strategy of containment, the taboo has authority because of its pervasiveness, not its authenticity. As socially constructed as a previous culture's "truths" may seem—such as the eighteenth-century belief that formal education of women in "male" disciplines was bad for a woman's uterus—some fail to see their own, contemporary myths as social constructions that benefit and perpetuate social hierarchies. That is, some fail to see their own "truths" as *political.* When they find exceptions to the rule, they call these exceptions "aberrations" and thus protect the rule. Perhaps because knowledge and discourse are based on available categories, previous legal precedents, and the subject's ability to interrogate her interpellation[67] into a particular social and gender role (which is, at the very least, an educationally elitist and time-consuming process), the incest taboo still determines for most people and institutions (including the present Western legal system) what incest is. Because myths about sexuality and gender, about violence and power, have everything to do with the perpetuation of a culture's values and nothing to do with empowering people outside of the culture's power structure to speak and be heard, it is no wonder the feminist recovery movement has struck a nerve. Embedded in feminist self-help, activist texts aimed at "healing" the survivor is a feminist theory of reading, a theory that, once developed, allows for far more than just "fixing" the survivor. It politicizes her.

Crimes of Reading: Activist Self-Help Strategies

A revolution in reading practices has taken hold in this country, and its genesis can be found in the feminist self-help industry. Ellen Bass, Laura Davis, Judith Herman, and Alice Miller have initiated a method of self-reading that relies on feminist understandings of the relation between sexism and sexual abuse. For all four survivor-activists, healing becomes possible through both individual work and social change: as Herman puts it, "The systematic study of psychological trauma therefore depends on the support of a political movement.... Repression, dissociation, and denial are phenomena of the social as well as individual consciousness."[68]

Ellen Bass and Laura Davis are the authors of *The Courage to Heal*, a controversial self-help book described by the False Memory Syndrome Foundation as the Bible of the incest recovery industry. Bass and Davis are self-described "non-experts" and explain in their preface to the third edition of *Courage* that their "perspective as laypeople" allowed them to "take the suffering of survivors out of the realm of pathology—and instead to present them as strong, capable people who'd been hurt."[69] Their method of healing is explicitly grounded in reading and writing practices. *Courage* offers writing exercises for each stage in recovery and understands the role of reading these written testimonies as acts of psychological integration. Bass and Davis make clear that this is not a rigid checklist but a trajectory of self-growth. These stages don't happen in any special order, for "healing is not linear" but instead "is an integral part of life."[70] In fact, the emergency stage and the stages of remembering, confrontation, and forgiveness are inapplicable to some survivors. I list here the stages of recovery (with full commentary by Bass and Davis):

1.   *The Decision to Heal:* Once you recognize the effects of sexual abuse in your life, you need to make an active commitment to heal. Deep healing happens only when you choose it and are willing to change yourself.[71]

2.   *The Emergency Stage:* Beginning to deal with memories and suppressed feelings can throw your life into utter turmoil. Remember, this is only a stage. It won't last forever.

3.   *Remembering:* Many survivors suppress all memories of what happened to them as children. Those who do not forget the actual incidents often forget how it felt at the time. Remembering is the process of getting back both memory and feeling.

4. *Believing It Happened:* Survivors often doubt their own per-
    ceptions. Coming to believe that the abuse really hap-
    pened, and that it really hurt you, is a vital part of the
    healing process.

5. *Breaking the Silence:* Most adult survivors kept the abuse a
    secret in childhood. Telling another human being about
    what happened to you is a powerful healing force that can
    dispel the shame of being a victim.

6. *Understanding That It Wasn't Your Fault:* Children usually
    believe the abuse is their fault. Adult survivors must place
    the blame where it belongs—directly on the shoulders of
    the abusers.

7. *Making Contact with the Child Within:* Many survivors have
    lost touch with their own vulnerability. Getting in touch
    with the child within can help you feel compassion for
    yourself, more anger toward your abuser, and greater inti-
    macy with others.

8. *Trusting Yourself:* The best guide for healing is your own
    inner voice. Learning to trust your own perceptions, feel-
    ings, and intuitions forms a new basis for action in the world.

9. *Grieving and Mourning:* As children being abused, and
    later as adults struggling to survive, most survivors haven't
    felt their losses. Grieving is a way to honor your pain, let
    go, and move into the present.

10. *Anger—The Backbone of Healing:* Anger is a powerful and
    liberating force. Whether you need to get in touch with it
    or have always had plenty to spare, directing your rage
    squarely at your abuser, and those who didn't protect you,
    is pivotal to healing.

11. *Disclosures and Confrontations:* Directly confronting your
    abuser and/or your family is not for every survivor, but it
    can be a dramatic, cleansing tool.

12. *Forgiveness?* Forgiveness of the abuser is *not* an essential
    part of the healing process, although it tends to be the

one most recommended. The only essential forgiveness is for yourself.

13. *Spirituality:* Having a sense of a power greater than yourself can be a real asset in the healing process.[72] Spirituality is a unique personal experience. You might find it through traditional religion, meditation, nature, or your support group.

14. *Resolution and Moving On:* As you move through these stages again and again, you will reach a point of integration. Your feelings and perspectives will stabilize. You will come to terms with your abuser and other family members. While you won't erase your history, you will make deep and lasting changes in your life. Having gained awareness, compassion, and power through healing, you will have the opportunity to work toward a better world.[73]

The purpose of writing and reading one's way through stages of healing is to effect integration. Judith Herman, a psychiatrist who has redirected psychiatric work through a feminist lens, explains why integration—a "normal" part of most folks' psyches—is so vexing for survivors. In *Trauma and Recovery*, Herman describes memories of trauma as "frozen" and "wordless" interruptions to the unconscious that are "encoded [only] in the form of vivid sensations and images."[74] Because "traumatic memories ... are not encoded like the ordinary memories of adults in a verbal, linear narrative that is assimilated into an ongoing life story," they feel like unwelcome interruptions; at this stage, survivors wish for complete amnesia, not integration.[75] Psychological disintegration is the signal aftereffect of abuse, one that is hard to read because it masks itself as almost anything else. According to Herman,

> Traumatic events violate the autonomy of the person at the level of basic bodily integrity. The body is invaded, injured, defiled. Control over bodily functions is often lost; in the folklore of

combat and rape, this loss of control is often recounted as the most humiliating aspect of the trauma. Furthermore, at the moment of trauma, almost by definition, the individual's point of view counts for nothing. In rape, for example, the purpose of the attack is precisely to demonstrate contempt for the victim's autonomy and dignity. The traumatic event thus destroys the belief that one can *be oneself* in relation to others.[76]

Because trauma to the body disintegrates the fiction of self-containment and conscious self-control, the psyche repeats this lesson. Because this repetition (re)covers an event when the victim's "point of view counts for nothing," a time when the victim must survive without "autonomy and dignity," the victim is put into an impossible place: for one cannot be a powerless reader; this is a contradiction in terms. Therefore, the victim must replay a text she cannot read; she thus embodies it like a badly constructed addition.

One must transform these somatic distresses and frozen images into words in order to render impotent flashbacks of trauma and become a fully engaged agent in social betterment. Herman says, "The goal of recounting the trauma story is integration, not exorcism.... The fundamental premise of psychotherapeutic work is a belief in the restorative power of truth-telling. In the telling, the trauma story becomes a testimony."[77] Herman's use of the word *testimony* is not innocent, for politicizing survivorship is a way to reconnect with the world. By defining politicization as reconnection, I challenge the "family values" camp's position that reconnection means reconciling with the values of the nuclear family on its terms, the result of which is forgetting the meaning (the "truth," to Herman) of violation in the name of daughterly subservience. Instead, the politics of survivorship defines reconnection to the social world as an effort to change that world. The politics of survivorship may come with the price of local family ostracization—a price one pays in the hopes of larger community change and reconnection.

Alice Miller is a Swiss psychoanalyst whose devotion to Freud is most evident through her departure from psychoanalysis. In particularly Freudian form, Miller left her profession and resigned from the International Psychoanalytic Association on the grounds that the psychoanalytic devotion to the drive theory obscures the real origins and effects of child abuse. I say she is being particularly Freudian because by inventing her professional self as Freud's disobedient daughter, she cements her relationship to the father she ostensibly wishes to "abandon."

In *For Your Own Good: Hidden Cruelty in Child-Rearing and the Roots of Violence* (1980; translated 1983), *Thou Shalt Not Be Aware: Society's Betrayal of the Child* (translated 1984), *The Untouched Key: Tracing Childhood Trauma in Creativity and Destruction* (1988; translated 1990), as well as in the preface—"Vantage Point 1990"—to 1990 editions of all three books, Alice Miller outlines her theory of pervasive childhood sexual and emotional abuse and its concealment by trusted institutions. What I find invaluable in Miller's theory is its usefulness as a theory of reading. It gives us the tools to read aftereffects of abuse and trauma as a text and to identify a trauma-induced aftereffect when we encounter it, instead of dismissing it as inconsequential or neurotic simply because it does not come with a narrative that identifies it *as* a text. Furthermore, Miller's intervention offers a useful critique to the essentialism in Freud's drive theory by showing how the latter outlaws the concerns that constitute aftereffects as legitimate by contextualizing them within the law that declares parents as always just, rules as always fair, and punishment as always "for your own good." (I privilege Miller's point in this section, but not because I want to suggest that she is "right" and Freud "wrong"; my focus lies not with the purity, rightness, or righteousness of a particular theory but rather with the ways we use theory to make meaning of our experiences.) Miller's specific contribution, then, to the project of reading aftereffects as texts is to feminize Freud's seduction theory, and thus her methodology infuses a theory of pain with political optimism by recognizing the transformation of pain into literature as an act of personal strength.

In *For Your Own Good*, Miller calls the child-rearing principles most people were subjected to from the late eighteenth to the early twentieth century "poisonous pedagogy." The church, the state, the patriarchal family structure, and cultural prescriptions that contained men and women in separate spheres[78] and then raised that separation to a cult all fed into that child-rearing strategy. And just as the issues of abolition, legalized abortion, and queer liberation (to just name a few) have historically been understood, by both friends and foes, as larger than the specific causes named, practicing poisonous pedagogy has as much to do with nationalism as it does with toilet training. Furthermore, because most people have been raised within this ideology, it is impossible to "see," both because ideology is always invisible to those immersed in it and because poisonous pedagogy facilitates the abuse of others as a repetition compulsion—an unwitting act of repeating an event of unnamed trauma.

According to Miller, poisonous pedagogy declares that

1. a feeling of duty produces love
2. hatred can be done away with by forbidding it
3. parents deserve respect simply because they are parents
4. children are undeserving of respect simply because they are children
5. obedience makes a child strong
6. a high degree of self-esteem is harmful
7. a low degree of self-esteem makes a person altruistic

8. tenderness (doting) is harmful
9. responding to a child's needs is wrong
10. severity and coldness are a good preparation for life
11. a pretense of gratitude is better than honest ingratitude
12. the way you behave is more important than the way you really are
13. neither parents nor God would survive being offended
14. the body is something dirty and disgusting
15. strong feelings are harmful
16. parents are creatures free of drives and guilt
17. parents are always right[79]

Although children may never "believe" these tenets to be true, most children know that they will be measured against some or all of these. Because we have been immersed in (at least some of these) values, those who have discursive power see to it, often unwittingly, that they stay in place. Miller's theory very usefully shows that poisonous pedagogy becomes dangerous once we stop marking it as a cultural option and instead see it only as a cultural norm.

One could respond to the problems posed by poisonous pedagogy by stating that our culture has always relied on it, both as a system of child-rearing and as an informing system of reading that puts into play the construction of receivable readings, not contestatory ones. One might say that since "we" have all survived poisonous pedagogy—as intellectuals and as citizens—then clearly, there is nothing really the matter with it. This all-or-nothing response that sees cultural interpellation as either wholly harmful or apolitically benign represents intellectual surrender. Psychoanalytic feminism teaches that nothing is safely contained in binaries. Miller offers a global metaphor to respond to the supposed amelioration of pain through an extended and institutionalized practice of trauma:

"It would be just as false to deduce from this fact of survival that our upbringing caused us no harm as it would be to maintain that a limited nuclear war would be harmless because a part of humanity would still be alive when it was over."[80]

Incest narratives both contain examples of aftereffects (splitting, addictions, obsessive-compulsive behaviors, self-hatred, etc.) and are themselves often narrative aftereffects. We need to ask under what terms a survivor transforms past abuse into narrative instead of (or more realistically, alongside) destructive aftereffects. We should also ask how both somatic and literary aftereffects offer a simultaneous release from and connection to an unnarrativized trauma.

According to Miller, artistic expressions of pain are possible only if (1) the subject had a witness to her abuse; (2) the subject can perform some repetition compulsion (either abuse of children or one's own body) that she does not "read" as an indicator of some problem, because these acts of violence fall within the boundaries of acceptability; or (3) the subject can intellectualize the experience—through either education or denial. By intellectualizing pain, the writer can transmogrify it into another text (this one outside of her body) and thereby ward off the need to repeat it without rereading it. (Importantly, the repetition compulsion functions to prohibit self-reading. Being in constant motion allows the subject to reenact the event in a veiled way, so that the trauma is both close at hand but in an unrecognizable form.)

Since many writers intellectualize abuse, we can usefully consider the ability to transmogrify trauma into a literary text as an extension of the repetition compulsion. The practice of writing involves repetition, and the act of repetition implies the presence of hope made possible by the act of forgetting. The five psychological stages abused adults undergo are useful to understanding this connection I am making between hope and pain. Here is Miller's configuration of these stages:

1. to be hurt as a small child without anyone recognizing the situation as such;
2. to fail to react to the resulting suffering with anger;
3. to show gratitude for what are supposed to be good intentions;
4. to forget everything;
5. to discharge the stored-up anger onto others in adulthood or to direct it against oneself.[81]

To this final stage I add another "or": to transmogrify the pain into a literary text and call it "fiction." These stages, especially the fourth and my addition to the fifth, are useful in the following ways. First, we can use them to generate readings of literary texts that imply the presence of unnarrativized abuse. Second, we can identify how the acts of reading and writing perpetuate already-established cultural possibilities and can therefore resist this perpetuation, seeking instead to read and write our way into better worlds. Finally, by identifying how our own experiences with abuse affect our suspicions about writers who unwittingly reveal themselves to us, we can use our constructions of our experiences as resources rather than liabilities.

Hope and pain imply (and construct) each other, as is evident by the fact that we often have to "forget" pain to keep hope alive. Knowing that overlies pain, as readers we can use our experiences with pain to read literary texts in "unthinkable" ways—that is, we can maintain the tension between hope and pain, rather than collapse one into the other. Ultimately, reading is the first application for both self-awareness and social change. According to Miller, when we read under the rules of poisonous pedagogy, we reify the cultural hierarchies that preserve the religious silence expected of abused children. What to do, then, with the epistemological quandary posed by a definition of reading as something that saves as it enslaves? Miller's suggestion is that we address the role of repression.

In *Thou Shalt Not Be Aware*, Miller centers poisonous pedagogy in the roles of repression—both the patient's (or text's) and the analyst's (or reader's). While reader-response criticism has made use of the role of repression in reading practices, especially in the criticism of Norman Holland[82] and David Bleich,[83] what distinguishes Alice Miller's position is her emphasis on cultural dissociation—the process by which individual experiences transform into shared experiences. Thus, reading is never "just" a response but always a highly charged epistemological system. While other psychoanalytically informed reader-response critics would also grant this, Miller's theory makes the additional point that while we can produce our "own" readings—and even read as resisters—we cannot, alone, apprehend what we need to learn from them. To provide the perspective denied to the primary reader, a second reader (or analyst) is necessary. To Miller, the smokescreen that makes parental privilege invisible is aided and abetted by psychoanalysis: "In psychoanalytic literature ... parents' feelings toward their children have scarcely been examined and are hardly ever the subject of research."[84] Miller sees no innocence in this omission; instead, it explains to her why "the psychoanalytic theory of 'infantile sexuality' actually protects the parent and reinforces society's blindness."[85]

To what is society blind? According to Miller, it is blind to the variety of ways in which parents can and do abuse their children, through practices and procedures that fall within the boundaries of acceptable parenting. Cruelty can take many forms, and the intentions of those in power (or their de facto "good" reputations) do not sanction their behavior as harmless. Miller writes that

> adults are more likely to make sexual advances toward their younger children than toward their older ones ... . Adults can rely more on a young child's discretion than an older one's, and until recently people were convinced—indeed, some still are— that what happens to very little children has no consequence at all and will never be divulged to a third party.[86]

Furthermore, the abusive parent need not rely on the "discretion" of the child, because children need to idealize and honor the abusive parent. This need "forbids them to notice, become aware of, or articulate the wrong done to them." Finally, the adult victim "forgets" (represses) what the child cannot afford to remember. The role of repression has maintained the reputation of many a parent and frozen the potential of many a child: "While ... repression ensures parents that their secret will be safe, the child's lack of conscious knowledge blocks access to his or her feelings and vitality."[87]

Outside of the nuclear family, the cultural family is similarly bound by repression. Miller cites Freud's Oedipus complex— the linchpin of post-Freudian constructions of Western culture—as one example. The relevance of Oedipus for Miller is that "Oedipus was assigned all the blame."[88] But "forgetting" that repression is a function of the unconscious and not a punitive crime, Miller closes her case against Freud by declaring:

> [The Oedipus complex] freed Freud from the painful isolation in which he found himself as a result of the discoveries he made in 1896 concerning parents' sexual abuse of their children. Shocking as people of that day found the idea of a child with sexual desires, this was still far more acceptable to the contemporary power structure, whose motives were disguised and buttressed by established methods of child-rearing, than was the whole truth about what adults do with their children, also in the area of sex-

uality. The Oedipus theory made it possible to continue to treat the child, now seen as having sexual desires, as the object of adult didactic (or therapeutic) efforts.[89]

But Freud was as bound by culture as we all are. It is a limitation in Miller's theory—and this weakness can be found in all totalizing theories—that she cannot move eclectically within psychoanalysis and recognize that Freud is no better able to control his unconscious than are any of us. In fact, by reading this shift in Freud as a critical fault line, we can make readers—and analysts—accountable for their practices and stop attributing to Freud the agency of a century. Freud simply is not responsible for the practices taking place in his name after his death. "Just say no to Freud" is as silly for critical thinkers as Nancy Reagan's advice is for crack addicts. By demonizing Freud, Miller fails to see that her inscription of poisonous pedagogy conveniently empties itself of unconscious functions by literalizing the complete power of conscious desire and social conscience for the abusing parent. Under poisonous pedagogy, only abused children repress. But repression points to human helplessness over the unconscious, regardless of the role we assume (victim, perpetrator, etc.) in the social order. Indeed, our sense of hope predisposes repression. But what we *can* do is read ourselves, knowing that we can never have a determinate text of our past. Understanding this gives us the license to read aftereffects in the text's gaps. Because the "knowledge stored up in the unconscious" is "a perception of reality stemming from the period of early childhood, which had to be relegated to the unconscious, where it becomes an inexhaustible source of artistic creativity," hence "the truth about our childhood is stored up in our body, and although we can repress it, we can never alter it. Our intellect can be deceived, our feelings manipulated, our perceptions confused, and our body tricked with medication. But someday the body will present its bill."[90]

We might think of literary texts as the body's bill—not the essentialized body of the author but a semiotic body nevertheless. By understanding the literary text as a mental apparatus, we can read—that is, name—aftereffects of abuse as operative textual functions. This method of reading engages with the play and terror of the unconscious and repression, an engagement that offers hope, for "the consequences of a trauma are not eliminated by repressing it but are actually reinforced. The inability to remember the trauma, to articulate it (i.e., to be able to communicate these earlier feelings to a supportive person who *believes* you), creates the need to articulate it in *the repetition compulsion*."[91] Thus, because some creative texts and actions "tell the encoded story of childhood traumas no longer consciously remembered in adulthood,"[92] Alice Miller's trauma theory provides readers with models to read aftereffects as texts and texts as aftereffects.

My appropriation of counseling theories for reading practices may seem inappropriate, but both are practices of invention and discovery. Wars result from conflictual readings because the threat of being misread is lethal to our identity and situatedness—in spite of the fact that reading, an act of qualitative invention, not an exercise in quantitative accuracy, necessarily misses the mark. Reading is an act of translation, and as in all translations, the "original" text is changed through the process. Without reading the text of our own experience and thus producing a text for others to read, we cannot construct our subjectivity and—as feminism deems necessary for social change—politicize our bodies as texts. Reading aftereffects as texts contests the assumption that only patriarchally approved evidence validates aftereffects of abuse as important or "real."

Aftereffects are text enough. Life is not a court of law, and when we become evidentiary purists, we fall into the old narrative of protecting parental reputations instead of inventing new ways of listening to those unauthorized to speak.

I turn now to the first example of women's literature that features psychological aftereffects of incest as texts: Mary Shelley's *Mathilda* (1819).

CHAPTER TWO

The Law of the (Nameless) Father

Mary Shelley's Mathilda and the Incest Taboo

Society expressly forbids that which society brings about.

—Lévi-Strauss, *The Elementary Structures of Kinship*

British romanticism, a literary movement spanning the years from 1790 to 1830, is the only canon to remain almost wholly resistant to feminist challenges. Still represented by six male poets (William Blake, William Wordsworth, Samuel Taylor Coleridge, John Keats, Lord Byron, and Percy Bysshe Shelley), romanticism is really the last bastion of male canonicity. Both a celebration of individualism and a place-keeper in intellectual history, marking the historical moment when *subjectivity* and *perception* became privileged terms, romanticism contains within its definition a potentially feminist understanding of epistemology. But this potential has not yet been realized. Mary Shelley, the only canonized woman romanticist—marshaled into the canon derivatively, as the daughter of William Godwin and Mary Wollstonecraft and the wife of Percy Shelley—is considered only a "minor" romantic, in spite of the fact that *Frankenstein* (1818) is easily the most popular piece of literature to emerge from this period. And Mary Shelley's minor status invites critics to dismiss *Mathilda* (1819), her unpublished and suppressed novella about father—daughter incest, for a variety of reasons. The most pernicious is that the incest taboo outlaws certain (feminist) methods of reading. We see this revealed in the suppression of *Mathilda*, a text whose 140-year burial at the hands of hostile fathers (not only Godwin but also those literary critics who serve as canonical standard-bearers) reeks of the heteropatriarchal privilege to silence incest narratives.[1]

Mathilda radically decenters the power of paternity and the Law of the Father in at least four ways. First, using trauma theory,[2] we see that *Mathilda* reveals how the Law conceals the ineffectiveness of the incest taboo by preventing a woman from reading the text of her sexual abuse. Second, since silence is the daughter's duty to the father, Mary Shelley's autobiographical heroine kills her father twice: by forcing him to name his incestuous desires and by writing about her body as a text. Third, *Mathilda* presents contemporary readers with a physical document, suppressed by William Godwin until his death and then dismissed by conservative critical standards until its first publication in 1959; this 140-year suppression demonstrates the physical struggle between this father and daughter, a struggle of great cultural and historical merit that has heretofore been untold. And finally, because Mathilda "chooses"[3] neither of the two possible responses to a sexually abusive father—be raped by him or kill him—and because, in trying to publish her novel, Mary Shelley transgressed the Law until stopped by her father, *Mathilda* reveals that heteropatriarchy can be restructured, although the impact depends largely on a woman's ability to write and (be) read.

Critical Responses

Certainly, since 1959, the year Elizabeth Nitchie edited and published *Mathilda* for the first time, many critical and cultural schools have changed the ways in which we read and teach literature. And yet, with regard to *Mathilda*, nothing seems to have changed: critics agree that the incest in this text resides in the air, not the body, and that there is no incest "outside" of the text. Either the incest taboo fashions as unthinkable the possibility that Mary Shelley was molested and represented this in *Mathilda* or heteropatriarchal conventions catalog the act of reading incest from the text to the body as a retrograde accusation against William Godwin, famous liberal philosopher, devoted husband to Western culture's first feminist, and beloved editor of children's books. Using Godwin's reputation as whiteout fails on two counts. First, a person's public character and repute in no way prohibit private crimes, motivated by psychological conflict, not political incorrectness. Second, Godwin is not on trial here. Rather, my interest is to account for the aftereffects of incest that inform Mary Shelley's fiction. Shifting from Godwin's reputation to Mary Shelley's representation of aftereffects offers an important feminist gesture to the task of academic reading, one that breaks with the entitlement that heteropatriarchy wields over writing from the margins. And it is with this shift that I turn to *Mathilda*.

Mathilda is a novella about a twenty-one-year-old woman dying of consumption, whose "last task" involves breaking the silence of father—daughter incest by writing her history for Woodville, the Shelleyan poet who, had it not been for the sexual stigma of her body, should have been her suitor. After her mother has died giving birth to her, her father departs to wander the world while an elderly maiden aunt raises Mathilda in isolation in Scotland. After sixteen years, Mathilda's nameless father returns. Suddenly the aunt dies, and Mathilda moves with her father to London. The father sexualizes almost every moment between them, until a "young man of rank" visits their abode. This eligible suitor for Mathilda brings the father's sexual desire to a crisis. The father responds by turning the young man away, emotionally battering his daughter, and, finally, physically moving with his daughter back to the house that he shared with his late wife, Diana. Eerily, the house has been preserved as a shrine to Diana; everything is as it had been sixteen years earlier. Once there, the father explains that Mathilda is to act as Diana once had: that is, his daughter is now to live with him as his wife.

The night after he declares his incestuous plan and before he physically acts on this plan, the father again abandons Mathilda, this time leaving behind a suicide note in which he blames Mathilda for his sexual desire. Mathilda reads his note, then follows his track by carriage, only to reclaim his dead body from the sea. After his death, Mathilda runs away from her guardians and lives ascetically in an isolated part of the country. There she meets a poet, Woodville, and rejects him as a suitor because she feels tainted by her father. Wanting a spiritual tie instead, she tries to engage Woodville in a suicide pact (as Percy Shelley had suggested to Mary Godwin before their elopement). With his rejection comes the onset of Mathilda's consumption. Attempting to make sense of her life and explain her strange secrecy to Woodville, Mathilda writes her history of incest.

Mathilda is an incest narrative, one that relies on both the fact of incest and its aftereffects to make narrative sense of the plot, the characters, and the resolution. I am not just a little intrigued that other scholars—both feminist and politically undeclared ones—who have read *Mathilda* conclude everything except the most obvious observation: that in a suicidal summer, Mary Shelley used Mathilda to concretize the aftereffects of incest that she herself experienced. That *no* critic has suggested this is no mere oversight: from a radical psychoanalytic-feminist perspective, the incest taboo has enforced critical interpretations of *Mathilda* that maintain the Father's Law. Predictably, then, the incest taboo functions to dismiss any reading of this text that accepts sexual violations as experiential "truth" as being hopelessly retrograde or a fantasy projections of the reader's own pathology. Indeed, by denying even the possibility of incest in the Godwin household, critics have located the sexual abuse anywhere but in Mary Shelley's body.

Since 1959, readers of *Mathilda* have protected and maintained, both wittingly and unwittingly, the novel's obscurity by finding "real" incest in the Godwin household impossible. Sylvia Norman's contribution to volume 3 of *Shelley and His Circle*, entitled "Mary Wollstonecraft Shelley (Life and Works),"[4] is so unabashedly hostile to this idea, one wonders why Norman wrote her biographical essay at all. Norman introduces her section on *Mathilda* with an interesting observation to which she never returns: "There seems little doubt that Mary had a half-obsessive love for Godwin, whose own immediate feeling for [his daughter] bordered on panic."[5] Although never mentioning incest, Norman cites Mary as the one who transgresses proper boundaries of feeling. Norman states that "*Mathilda* reveals Mary's second-rate sensite mind," not only because of the composition of this text but also because "she even dared to show it around to friends."[6] Norman clearly believes there are some secrets that must be kept.

According to Norman, Mary Shelley, is a minor writer in part because her inability to keep certain things secret creates disunity in her works: "One important gulf between the major (Percy) and the minor (Mary) writer is the presence or absence of a unifying motive, whether moral, political or aesthetic."[7] But incest narratives—like incest itself—are disruptive, not unifying. Aftereffects of incest and the narratives they produce can

never meet the standards of unity that Norman (and other literary critics) demand. To unify an incest narrative is to deny
the presence of incest, in literature and in culture. Furthermore, Norman's penchant for unity occludes a penchant for
conservatism: indeed, in writing both *Mathilda* and *Frankenstein*,
Mary Shelley demonstrates "her leading handicap as a novelist"
(no doubt as a woman too), which is "her appalling want of
humor."[8] By dealing aggressively with issues of pain and passion, Mary challenges repression and denial, the cornerstones
of civilization. For her writerly transgressions Norman declares
her "unsafe": "Mary was safest as a writer when the theme constrained her." Not surprising, the safest of Mary's literary occupations was as her husband's editor: "Mary's finest literary
gesture must be seen as the editing of [Percy Shelley's] poetry
and prose."[9] Sylvia Norman's outrage at Mary Shelley's writerly
transgression is second only, perhaps, to Harold Bloom, who
introduces the Chelsea House publication *Mary Shelley* with this:
"Had she written nothing, Mary Shelley would be famous
today."[10]

Jay MacPherson's essay "*Mathilda* and *Frankenstein*" (reprinted
from *The Spirit of Solitude* and selected in Bloom's *Mary Shelley*)
denies Mary Shelley the right to transgress—or anticipate—
Freud. In writing about incest in a way that suggests "incest in
Mathilda is by no means a mere device of plot," Mary Shelley
contradicts Freud's subsuming of incest within narcissistic love:
"Incestuous, homosexual, impossible, and vampiric loves: all
are disguises of self-love and ... usually there is no cure for
them."[11]

MacPherson wastes little time dispensing with *Mathilda*, and
she uses a particularly Freudian gesture to do so. Weighing the
text against the context is a balancing act at which Freud failed
in 1933. In his lecture "Femininity," Freud had to choose
between believing the traumatic experiences with father—

daughter incest that his patients revealed to him to be contributing sources of their depressions—a position he himself had advanced in 1896—or using this information to confirm what he already knew about women: that they lie. Freud wrote:

> Almost all my women patients told me that they had been seduced by their father. I was driven to recognize in the end that these reports were untrue and so came to understand that hysterical symptoms are derived from fantasies and not from real occurrences. It was only later that I was able to recognize in this fantasy of being seduced by the father the expression of the typical Oedipus complex in women.[12]

Freud's position here is obviously sexist and appalling; and that MacPherson would tuck the incest in *Mathilda* into this paradigm is a dangerous move.

Elizabeth Nitchie, the first person to bring *Mathilda* into print, is neither hostile nor transparently loyal to a critical father. Rather, by declaring *Mathilda* biographically important (Nitchie says, "It would be harder to find a more self-revealing work") but never explaining where and how its import functions, her 1959 introduction denies the implications that her observations reveal. Compare Nitchie's observation that "the main narrative, that of the father's incestuous love for his daughter, is not in any real sense autobiographical"[13] with her position that "the relationship between father and daughter, before it was destroyed by the father's unnatural passion, is like that between Godwin and Mary. She herself called her love for him 'excessive and romantic.'"[14] That Mary Shelley could describe her relationship with Godwin as "excessive and romantic" should have made Nitchie less confident in her position that *Mathilda*'s autobiographical import literally stops at Mary Shelley's skin—especially when Nitchie states that Mary Shelley felt the characters were "sufficiently disguised" to publish the story.[15] Why would Mary Shelley have to disguise something that is so obviously (to

Nitchie and others) untrue? Or with a different twist: why would Nitchie use a phrase such as "sufficiently disguised" and not address why incest, even as "fiction," had to be disguised? After all, at the same moment in literary history Percy was writing a play about father—daughter incest, *The Cenci*; not surprising, no critic has suggested that its publication depended on the author's ability to empty his life experiences from his work.

Anne Mellor's *Mary Shelley: Her Life, Her Fiction, Her Monsters* and Emily Sunstein's *Mary Shelley: Romance and Reality* rely on contemporary feminist theories to make sense of Mary's relationships with her husband and father. But by painting Percy Shelley as the evil patriarch, these critics unwittingly defend Godwin's paternal innocence. U. C. Knoepflmacher, in "Thoughts on the Aggression of Daughters," is the only other critic to acknowledge that while Percy's behavior contributed to Mary's depression, Godwin's was significant—as Mary Shelley's obsession with him suggests. Knoepflmacher sees both men as condensed sites of unnamed aggression: "Mathilda's passive withdrawal clearly stems from parricidal wishes which the narrative conveys and yet never fully dares to acknowledge…. By dispensing with the protective masks of male protagonists, the story places Mary Shelley's marital difficulties at her father's doorstep."[16]

In contrast to Knoepflmacher's appreciation of power that inheres in indirect disclosures, Mellor misreads incest as sexual consent: "Mathilda … embodies Mary Shelley's most powerful and most powerfully repressed fantasy: the desire to both sexually possess and to punish her father."[17] Sunstein uses feminist social constructionist theories to arrive at almost the same unquestioned juncture:

> Thornton Hunt would later suggest that Mary's "force of natural affection … had somehow been stunted and suppressed in her youth." In fact, that force was intensified while she had to keep covert what she later knew to be "excessive and romantic" love

for her father, along with jealousy and anger, which were suppressed by her inhibitions as a female, an idealist and by her training.[18]

A daughter's "excessive and romantic" love for her father, suppressed anger and rage informed by that love, and "female inhibitions" are neither innocent facts of nature nor uninterpretable features of Mary Shelley's life. Indeed, it seems hardly an innocent omission that Sunstein and Mellor fail to read how Mary Shelley's heretofore unnarrativized identifications of incest inform her "excessive and romantic" love for Godwin.

Rather than accept this love as innocent, we should ask what it means. For example, trauma theory shows that loving Godwin with fierce devotion provides one way for Mary Shelley to "forget." As suggested in the previous chapter, incest is often a transgression of love, a love naturalized by normative heterosexuality. Additionally, desire can be a sexual transgression, one not physically forced but still psychologically brutal. Judith Herman raises this point in *Father—Daughter Incest*:

> Because a child is powerless in relation to an adult, she is not free to refuse a sexual advance. Therefore, any sexual relationship between the two must necessarily take on some of the coercive characteristics of a rape, even if, as is usually the case, the adult uses positive enticements rather than force to establish the relationship. This is particularly true of incest between parent and child: it is a rape in the sense that it is a coerced sexual relationship. The question of whether force is involved is largely irrelevant, since force is rarely necessary to obtain compliance. The parent's authority over the child is usually sufficient to compel obedience.[19]

That Mary Shelley could describe her love for Godwin as "excessive and romantic" yet that incest, whether psychological or physical, could not be considered an important paradigm through which to read her life and works seems unthinkable from a psychoanalytic-feminist perspective. Perhaps the only answer is that the Law of the Father ensures that the emperor always appears clothed. And even if we know the truth, there are dangers involved in exposing his nakedness—dangers to the daughter's sanity, not the society's status quo. As Jane Gallop puts it, "'It would be good' to lift 'the mantle of the law' so that the father's desire and his penis are exposed. But that does not mean the 'answer' is for the father to make love to his daughter."[20]

Godwin's Mathilda

Mary Shelley's normal knack for self-repression was slipping during the writing of *Mathilda* (between August 4 and September 12, 1819),[21] because she was suffering from an acute depression that was complicated by the actions of her husband and father.[22] The death of her three-and-a-half-year-old son William, on June 7, 1819, initiated her depression. "I shall never recover [from] that blow," Mary Shelley wrote to Amelia Curran two weeks after her son's death.[23] Percy wrote to Godwin, asking him to comfort his daughter. Godwin responded with a series of letters that served to retraumatize Mary.

In his letters Godwin castigated Mary for not rising above her sex, stating that "it is only persons of very ordinary sort, and of a pusillanimous disposition, that sink long under a calamity of this nature."[24] He then threatened to withhold love: "Remember too, though at first your nearest connections may pity you in this state, yet that when they see you fixed in selfishness and ill humour, ... they will finally cease to love you, and scarcely learn to endure you."[25] Finally, Godwin blamed Mary's problems on her unfortunate marriage to a "disgraceful and flagrant person" and at last demanded that she coerce her husband to send more money to Godwin if she wished to have further contact with her father.[26] Percy speculated in a letter to Leigh Hunt, written August 15, 1819, that Mary's obsession with winning Godwin's love was fueled by Godwin's cruelty to her. He tried to protect Mary from Godwin: "Poor Mary's spirits continue dreadfully depressed. And I cannot expose her to Godwin in this state."[27]

Percy's behavior toward Mary, although not acerbic in tone or selfish in intention, nonetheless lacked direct acknowledgment of her pain. His actions, as indicated through the above-quoted correspondence, involved concealing information from Mary. And as Paula Feldman and Diana Scott-Kilvert suggests, "This policy of concealing unpleasant facts from Mary, which Shelley was to pursue for the rest of his life, was undoubtedly prompted by the best of motives, but it must inevitably have weakened the relationship of trust between them."[28]

Apart from protecting Mary from herself, Percy was characteristically self-absorbed while Mary grieved. But in the summer of 1819, he was grieving too, and their coping mechanisms collided. When depressed, Percy wanted more sex, for "death increased his desire"; Mary, six months pregnant, rejected him, in part because "making love seemed a cruelly ironic, impossible affirmation."[29] Also, superstitious as they were, Mary and Percy felt that their children's deaths (Clara the year before William) were acts of symbolic retribution for Harriet Shelley's suffering and suicide,[30] a catastrophe that arose from Percy and Mary's relationship and subsequent marriage.

In her depression Mary turned to her writing. She began a new "journal book" with an entry that was uncharacteristically self-revealing. She also began a new novella, *The Fields of Fancy* (perhaps a play on Mary Wollstonecraft's unfinished tale "The Cave of Fancy"),[31] which she later retitled *Mathilda*.

Writing during August of 1819 was not an escape from life, it *was* her life. For the first time in four years, Mary Shelley was not a mother; for the first time in five years, she didn't want to have sex with Percy. In her first journal entry in this state of mind and body, she wrote:

> I begin my journal on Shelley's birthday—We have now lived five years together & if all the events of the five years were blotted out I might be happy—but to have won & then cruelly have lost all the associations of four years is not an accident to which the human mind can bend without much suffering.[32]

Mary Shelley's journal is not the least bit self-disclosing, and often it seems intentionally mysterious. In the place of feelings and emotions, readers will find in the journals from the early years (1817 to 1822) page after page of seemingly innocuous lists. Most entries consist of lists of domestic chores and physical wants, books read and translated, the health of the house's inhabitants, walks taken, food eaten, laxatives needed, Percy's mood and his relationships with others. In spite of these domestic lists and the normalcy they command, we know that during the summer of 1819, Mary Shelley's tight hold on herself was breaking down. Feldman and Scott-Kilvert address this:

> Mary does not dwell in the journal on the two major tragedies of the years 1816-22, the deaths of their daughter and son; Clara's death is briefly noted, but William's is marked only by the breaking off of entries at the end of the second notebook, leaving only the prescriptions for purges and diuretics among the endpapers of the volume as a reminder of their useless efforts to save the little boy's life.[33]

And yet Mary Shelley's entry on August 4, 1819, asking that the last five years be "blotted out," reveals that her pain was slipping through her tight hold. From August through September 1819, Mary Shelley's rules for writing and for life did not remain in the separate domains she wished them to occupy.

Mary Shelley's desire to publish *Mathilda* and William God-win's ability to suppress it are documented in the surviving letters and journals of Mary Shelley and Maria Gisborne, Mary's dear friend. Godwin's responses to the novel, the most notable of which is his refusal to return Mary's only copy after years of badgering and begging by Mary Shelley and Maria Gisborne, have survived only through the writings of other people. As William St. Clair notes, for a family who threw nothing away, it is significant that important documents of the correspondence between father and daughter have not survived. Although St. Clair makes no reference to *Mathilda* in his "biography of a family" (an important omission in its own right), in its chronological place he observes that Mary's "own letters to her father have, with unimportant exceptions, all been lost, perhaps deliberately destroyed later by members of the family embarrassed by the strength of love they revealed."[34]

However, since Godwin apparently wanted to deny and conceal everything that had to do with *Mathilda*, it seems more likely that Godwin himself destroyed this correspondence.[35] To explore my speculation that Godwin destroyed these letters in order to conceal and deny the father—daughter incest that threatened to occur (or occurred? perhaps Godwin was the one "embarrassed by the strength of love" these letters revealed), I will piece together the letters and journals of Mary Shelley and Maria Gisborne and re-create the series of events that resulted in the suppression of *Mathilda* from May 1819 until Elizabeth Nitchie edited it for the University of North Carolina Press in 1959.

Mary Shelley gave her only fair copy of *Mathilda* to Maria Gisborne on May 2, 1819, and asked Maria to deliver this text to Godwin.[36] This in itself needs to be examined. The Shelleys never sent their only copy of a newly written work to any publisher, least of all someone as notoriously unstable as Godwin.

Mary had available to her the means to have *Mathilda* recopied (or to recopy it herself). That she did not suggests to me that this text functions as a material site for Mary Shelley's self-articulation. Mary Shelley was not careless. That she sent Godwin her own copy—and did not even deliver the text in person— offers one of the many gaps in Mary Shelley's biography that needs to be examined.

Maria Gisborne was traveling to England, and Mary Shelley told Maria that Godwin would probably read, edit, and publish her novel.[37] On the voyage, Maria read *Mathilda* and was duly impressed. In her journal she wrote:

> I have read *Mathilda.* This most singularly interesting novel evinces the highest powers of mind in the author united to extreme delicacy of sentiment. It is written without artifice and perhaps without the technical excellence of a veteran writer— There are perhaps some little inaccuracies which, upon revision, might have been corrected: but these are trifling blemishes and I am well persuaded that the author will one day be the admiration of the world. I am confident that I should have formed this opinion had I not been acquainted with her and loved her.[38]

Maria delivered *Mathilda* to Godwin, and on August 8, 1820, she recorded his response in her journal:

> Mr. G. spoke of *Mathilda;* he thinks highly of some of the parts; he does not approve of the father's letter. ... The deception on the part of the father with regard to his real design is too complete; for himself he says he should most certainly not have ordered a carriage to be prepared for the pursuit, after receiving such a letter. ... The subject he says is disgusting and detestable; and there ought to be, at least if it is ever published, a preface to prepare the minds of the readers.[39]

It is most interesting that Godwin declares the subject "disgusting and detestable." Interesting also is the fact that Godwin calls for a preface—perhaps to deflect the autobiographical readings *Mathilda* was sure to generate. Godwin also fails to address (or Maria doesn't record) the transparent autobiographical connections: the fictional Mathilda is the author's age (twenty-one) in 1819; Mathilda's mother dies giving birth to her, just as Mary Wollstonecraft died giving birth to Mary Shelley; and Mathilda's father disowns her when a male suitor arrives on the scene, just as Godwin disowned Mary when she fell in love with Percy. Furthermore, Godwin relegates *Mathilda* to a category he does not reserve for other incest tales: certainly, he fails to interpret Matthew Lewis's *The Monk* (1796), Horace Walpole's *The Castle of Otranto* (1764), or Percy Shelley's "Laon and Cynthia" (1817) and *The Cenci* (1819) as "disgusting and detestable" on the grounds that they deal with incest. Importantly—and I deal with this issue more fully in this chapter when I "read" *Mathilda*—Mary Shelley's novel does not only *thematize* incest, as the other romantic texts that address this subject do. Her text *teases out the aftereffects* of incest—aftereffects that were not in cultural or intellectual currency at the time. By relying on aftereffects and not themes, Mary Shelley anticipates Freud (by about seventy years) and trauma theory's contribution to feminist therapy: the narrative invention of somatic and psychological aftereffects of abuse. One has to ask: How did Mary Shelley know?

After receiving Mary's only fair copy of *Mathilda*, Godwin turned a deaf ear to her request for the manuscript's return. According to Peter Marshall, Godwin "quietly put the manuscript in the drawer. Three years later Mary was still trying to get it back, and the work was not published in her lifetime."[40] U. C. Knoepflmacher puts it this way: "Godwin made sure that *Mathilda* would never be published."[41] Meanwhile, on February 9, 1822, while Mary Shelley was recovering from Percy's passionate love for Jane Williams (in January 1821) and Emilia Vivianti (in February 1821),[42] she wrote to Maria Gisborne, asking her to steal *Mathilda* from Godwin's desk drawer: "I should like as I said when you went away—a copy of *Mathilda*—it might come out with the desk."[43] One month later, on March 7, 1822, Mary wrote again: "Could you not in any way write [to Godwin] for *Mathilda?*—I want it very much."[44] Maria's response was not encouraging. Godwin, subject to frequent and wild mood swings, was not receiving the Gisbornes. Maria wrote to Mary, "With regard to *Mathilda* ... as your father has put a stop to all intercourse between us, I am at a loss what step to take."[45]

Three years later, Mary was still anxious for *Mathilda*'s return and apparently was concerned that Maria Gisborne was not transmitting her desires to Godwin. On April 10, 1822, she wrote an exhaustive letter to Maria that wavered between desperation to get *Mathilda* back and concern over Shelley's recent arrest. As in all previous correspondence with Maria, this letter constructs Godwin as audience:

> I wish, my dear Mrs. Gisborne, that you would send Godwin, at Nash's Esq. Dover Street—I wish him to have an account of the fray [Shelley's arrest for cursing at an Italian officer], and, you will thus save me the trouble of writing it over again, for what with writing and talking about it, I am quite tired—In a late letter of mine to my father, I requested him to send you *Mathilda*—I hope that he has complied with my desire, and, in that case, that you will get it copied, and send it to me by the first opportunity.[46]

Significantly, this letter demonstrates, among other things, how Mary weaves *Mathilda*'s absence into the daily fabric of domestic anxiety and life with Percy. In her correspondence she makes similar gestures to her dead children, alluding to them in a way that incorporates them into the present. *Mathilda* thus functions in Mary Shelley's letters and journals as a relic of herself, as a dead child (like William and Clara) who is allowed to haunt the present. It is only after Percy dies (July 8, 1822) that Mary Shelley begins to construct *Mathilda* as a story that foreshadowed her husband's death.

In the letter that tells Maria Gisborne that Percy Shelley and Edward Williams drowned at sea when the *Don Juan* capsized, Mary Shelley also reveals that she displaces her needs so that the comfort she asks for will not really soothe her pain. In this August 15, 1822, letter, Mary begins by restating a dream that Percy had before he took the fateful voyage:

> [Percy] dreamt that lying as he did in bed Edward & Jane came into him, they were in the most horrible condition, their bodies lacerated—their bones starting through their skin, the faces pale yet stained with blood, they could hardly walk, but Edward was the weakest & Jane was supporting him—Edward said—"Get up Shelley, the sea is flooding the house & it is all coming down." S. got up, he thought, & went to the window that looked on the terrace & the sea & thought he saw the sea rushing in. Suddenly his vision changed & *he saw the figure of himself strangling me.*[47]

When describing to Maria Gisborne how she and Jane reclaimed their husbands' drowned bodies, Mary relies on Mathilda's experience: "It must have been fearful to see us—two poor, wild, aghast creatures—driving like Mathilda towards the sea to learn if we were forever doomed to misery."[48] Wife murder is to the present as incest is to the past. Percy's dream and Mathilda's fate foretell the future: even though Mary does not die, her role as Percy's wife dies with Percy. Likewise, in *Mathilda*, the daughter replaces the mother as object of sexual desire. This displacement cancels out Mathilda's childhood and adulthood simultaneously: the father's transgressive sexuality kills the child, while psychologically, the exchange of the live woman for the dead makes Mathilda fear being alive. Mathilda follows her father to the sea, where he has drowned; likewise, Percy follows his July 7 dream to the sea, where he meets the same fate.

By displacing her past and condensing her future, *Mathilda* becomes the site of Mary Shelley's rereading of her past, especially her adolescence, in an effort to understand how her past has transformed into the present. Its import was not lost on the author herself. One year later, in 1823, she reflected on this: "But it seems to me in what I have hitherto written I have done nothing but prophecy [*sic*] what has arrived.... *Mathilda* foretells even many small circumstances most truly."⁴⁹ It must have seemed appropriate, given Mary Shelley's obsessions about privacy, concealment and deception, that her most self-revealing text was never published in her lifetime.

Mary's Mathilda

Mathilda's concession to write her history for Woodville initiates the plot of *Mathilda*. Because heteropatriarchy codifies denial by making certain questions and observations "unthinkable" (both consciously, through social pressure, and unconsciously, through denial), Mathilda breaks the silence only when she is free to do so: after her father is dead and she is dying. Momentarily resisting the imposed silence the Law demands, Mathilda can represent the unthinkable. She writes, "While life was strong within me I thought indeed that there was a sacred horror in my tale that rendered it unfit for utterance, and now, about to die, I pollute its mythic terrors."⁵⁰ It is important that her "freedom" comes with the price of death; although her father is dead, the Law still reigns. This is made clear by the father's namelessness: his name is "only" father; he therefore is ever present, not simply historically specific. He is the Law, the role, the cultural place-keeper.

The incest taboo, in cultural, psychoanalytic, and political permutations, shows that the father need not seduce his daughter; instead, he imputes his desire onto her. Good daughters obey their fathers; good daughters anticipate and fulfill their father's needs; good daughters seduce their fathers so that their fathers don't have to be the agents of transgression. In this way the Law restructures and reconstitutes the daughter and her desires.[51] After sixteen years of parental abandonment, with mother dead from bearing Mathilda and himself absent because Mathilda's presence commands his grief, the father returns. It is he who sexualizes the reunion: "I cannot tell you how ardently I desire to see my Mathilda," the father writes in a letter to the aunt (186). Mathilda tells us, "As he approached, his desire to see me became more and more ardent" (187). Here we see how Mathilda takes over her father's vocabulary, thereby textually enacting the imputation of desire. He will not (at this point) speak his desire, so she says it for him.

At her father's return, Mathilda is emotionally neglected and sexually naive. Her aunt (who acted as her legal guardian out of duty, not compassion) made herself available only during specific hours, and then only twice a day (182). Her traditional, conservative, and thoroughly "anti-Wollstonecraft" aunt forbids her to befriend girls her own age because she might "catch" their Scottish accent ("great pain was taken that my tongue should not disgrace my English origin" [183]). When her father arrives, the possibility that he may love her makes her feel like a new person: "I felt as if I were recreated and had about me all the freshness and life of a new being: I was, as it were, transported" (188–89). She is not "awakened" sexually, however, and when her desire to be parented comes with the price of unwanted sexuality, she does not know that her father's lust will appropriate her need for care and protection: "I had no idea that misery could arise from love, and this lesson that all at last must learn was taught me in a manner few are obliged to receive it" (198). Here we see that the father's misappropriation of Mathilda's love confuses her sense of boundaries and reality. By calling incest "love," he teaches her a lesson that *not* all must learn. E. Sue Blume explains this lesson in detail: "As a distortion of intimacy, incest teaches many contradictions: to be cared about is to be taken from, to need someone puts one at risk of being taken advantage of, and to be given to leads to expected payback. For the incested child, intimacy equals danger and damage."[52]

As Jane Gallop and Luce Irigaray note, within the rules of the Law, the father's sexual desire is projected onto the daughter, who does his bidding and takes his fall. As Gallop puts it, "The Oedipus Complex, the incest taboo, the law forbidding intercourse between father and daughter, covers over a seduction, masks it so it goes unrecognized."[53] And Irigaray writes, "The *seduction function of the law* [works when it] suspends the realization of a seduced desire. ... The law organizes and arranges the world of fantasy at least as much as it forbids, interprets and symbolizes it."[54] Mathilda's power is located in her ability to create her own subjectivity—in trauma theory, to differentiate enough from her abuser so that she knows that there exists a difference between wanting to be loved and wanting to be fucked: "I disobeyed no command, I ate no apple, and yet I was ruthlessly driven from [Paradise]. Alas! My companion did, and I was precipitated in his fall" (198).

Writing about the intrusion of her father's sexual desire makes incest real for Mathilda; her naming the event offers a counterdiscourse to the Law. Mathilda takes the risk of writing her own text while reading her father's Law; but because she knows she is dying, she also knows she can afford this risk.

However, if incest is the secret women keep, then Mary Shelley is playing a much pricier game than her heroine. If, as I suspect, Mary Shelley writes her way into understanding her "excessive and romantic" love for Godwin as incestuous, then her reconstructed memories of love/incest deepen any explanation for why the summer of 1819 was so traumatic, for memories of sexual transgression are often accompanied by feelings of the terror she was not allowed to "indulge" as a child.[55] Most of what is known about Mary Shelley's depression during this summer comes through reading the absence: no sex with Percy,[56] little correspondence,[57] a journal filled with obsessive-compulsive lists.[58] She made "confessions" only when she thought people were not listening. To Leigh Hunt she wrote, "I ought to have died on the 7th of June last."[59] Mary Shelley "lived" through her writing of *Mathilda*. In this textual embodiment of incest—for whatever reason—she kept herself sane. The irony, of course, is that those around her thought she was going mad. By writing *Mathilda*, Mary Shelley was momentarily freed from the seduction of the Law: "The seduction fantasy is really about seducing the daughter to not read her own text, but instead to obey the law of the father."[60]

The first time Mathilda falls for the seduction of the Law, she unwittingly echoes her father's words, spoken sixteen years before, regarding the intrusion of third parties. At this point in the text, the father has moved Mathilda from Scotland to London and, seemingly without conscious intent, is grooming Mathilda to become his wife replacement. Just as, sixteen years earlier, the father and Diana "seldom admitted a third to their society" (180), so, too, Mathilda now says, "It was a subject of regret to me whenever we were joined by a third party" (190). In his life with Diana, the father's spoken aversion to the presence of a third party calls forth Mathilda, whose presence kills his wife. And now, Mathilda's internalization of her father's aversion to outsiders seems to make material a "young man of rank," whose presence galvanizes the father's violent desire.

According to M. M. Bakhtin in "The Problem of the Text," the third party holds a special dialogic relation to the text: "Each dialogue takes place as if against the background of the responsive understanding of an invisibly present third party who stands above all participants in the dialogue."[61] But in an incestuous household, third parties are not welcome because they threaten to expose how the Law of the Father denies, trivializes, or distorts the daughter's experience; they also threaten to expose the father's desire itself.[62]

The father's behavior toward Mathilda changes in response to her sexual potential, not to her behavior: "I now remember that my father was restless and uneasy whenever this [third party] visited us, and when we talked together [father] watched us with the greatest apparent anxiety" (91). The father typifies the behavior of seductive fathers, who, as Herman suggests,

> reacted to their daughters' emerging sexuality either with an attempt to establish total control or with total rejection. The message they conveyed to their daughters was, in effect, "As long as you remain my little girl, everything will be fine; but if you try to grow up, there will be hell to pay."[63]

Mathilda is paralyzed by her father's change in attitude and behavior, especially since she cares very little for this "young man of rank." This third party becomes significant because of what he does—he brings the father's incestuous desire into crisis—not who he is. Like the father, the third party has an unstable relationship to heteropatriarchy, and his namelessness makes his power to permeate Mathilda's life even greater.

Mathilda blames her self-in-body (the incested daughter knows that her body always already puts her in jeopardy) and her self-in-narrative for her father's shift: "I seem perhaps to have dashed into the description.... In one sentence I have passed from the idea of unspeakable happiness to that of unspeakable grief, but they were this closely linked together" (193). We know her self-blame is repeated in the act of writing, of creating a narrative, because the geography of her terror is the sentence that moves too swiftly. The link that Mathilda knows but cannot define or see shows that the Law must never be made into narrative; in breaking this commandment, Mathilda has exposed an important connection among narrative, representation, and violence.

Mathilda reads the text of her father's behavior while she writes her own text for Woodville; furthermore, she constructs a reading of her father's text that he would not endorse. Her grief is so "unspeakable" because the Father's Law imposes silence. This textual moment exposes a gap, a stopping of patriarchal momentum: Mathilda has not yet realized that once the incest is spoken (that is, represented or made discursively "real"), her "desire" will be overlaid by her father's law. The guilt that she will use to describe herself and her wants is the by-product of desire cut off from its origin.[64]

Equally important, Mary Shelley is also burdened by this convolution of desire and displacement, which explains why the covert incest described in her own admission (her "excessive and romantic" love, which can also be understood as her inscription and imputation of Godwin's desire according to the Law) can find voice only through the fictional Mathilda's body. Denial is not the simple act of knowing the truth and consciously lying about it to the outside world. Rather, denial is a complicated coping mechanism that relies on and is shaped by the reading and writing of one's own body as text: if I don't name it, it didn't happen; if I don't write about it, I won't make it real; since its reality depends on my reading, I won't read the experiences of my body. Because the Law determines what a woman reads about her body's experiences, it also makes reading and writing unlawful acts for the survivor of sexual abuse: "Laws shape experiences we have before we have them."[65] In the summer of 1819 in the text of Mary Shelley's life, both the "fictional" Mathilda and the "real"[66] Mary Shelley are at the precipice of the Father's Law. Although silence no longer seems natural, silence now takes on a greater power. It is both life-saving—for the daughter who can never grow up—and life-threatening—for the woman who can create herself and her own subjectivity only if she reads the text her father forbids and then writes herself out of the role he has constructed for her.

The father responds to Mathilda's physical maturation by moving her geographically and symbolically backward:

> He intended to remove with me to his estate in Yorkshire.... This estate was that which he had inhabited in childhood and near which my mother resided while a girl; this was the scene of their youthful loves and where they had lived after their marriage; in happier days my father had often told me that however he might appear weaned from his widow sorrow, and free from bitter rec-ollections elsewhere, yet he would never dare visit the spot where he had enjoyed her society or trust himself to see the rooms that so many years ago they had inhabited together.... And now while he suffered intense misery he determined to plunge into still more intense, and strove for greater emotion than that which already tore him. (194)

This passage reveals the father advancing the paternal power to plot the sexual control of his daughter. First, by fitting his daughter for the role of his dead wife, he fails to differentiate between mother and daughter. Second, this passage exposes the beginnings of Mathilda's denial: in agreeing to read her father's text and embody her father's reading, Mathilda does not suspect her developing body also functions as a third party (along with Woodville) that galvanizes their household crisis.

While a psychoanalytic framework shows how the Law pro-jects the father's desire onto the daughter, who does his bidding and takes his fall, an anthropological-sociological paradigm fur-ther problematizes the possibility of a daughter knowing or act-ing on her desire by defining her body as a "gift." By moving Mathilda backward, instead of letting her grow up and out of his house, the father exchanges his daughter for his wife. As I noted in chapter 1, according to Claude Lévi-Strauss in *The Elementary Structures of Kinship*: "The prohibition of incest is less a rule prohibiting marriage with the mother, sister, or daughter, than a rule obliging the mother, sister, or daughter to be given to others. It is the supreme rule of the gift."[67] The father who refuses to give to other men the gift of his daughter and fails to exchange her as a commodity in the marketplace of heteropatriarchy commits the ultimate act of narcissism by cannibalizing the gift. Just as readers cannot help but appropriate texts that they read (this is the cruder rendition of "the reader constructs the text"), so Mathilda's father uses the act of reading as incest foreplay: "When I was last here, your mother read Dante to me; you shall go on where she left off" (195).

The Law of the Father makes possible the daughter's place as gift. But ironically, by fitting Mathilda for Diana's role, the father makes himself vulnerable to parricide. By moving history backward, he moves himself into the territory of the living dead: "Although more than sixteen years had passed since [Diana's] death, nothing had been changed; her work box, her writing desk were still there and in her room a book lay open on the table as she had left it" (194–95). This open book functions as a symbol of textual necrophilia: if reading is like incest, because both are acts of the cannibal, then the father is eating and reading and fucking the dead.[68]

Most important, the exchange of women, while central to the proliferation of culture, is so pervasive that both its agency and its effects go unnoticed. According to Gayle Rubin in "The Traffic in Women," since "women do not have the same rights [as men] either to themselves or to their male kin,"[69] women "are in no position to realize the benefits of their own circulation."[70] Of course Mathilda is burdened by a guilt that cannot be expressed; something as routine as the traffic in women becomes representable only when it exceeds the Law of the Father. Ironically, while incest is representable to the father, it is often unrepresentable to the daughter ("secrecy, a necessary component of control, is imposed on the victim of incest").[71] This business of who gets to represent the victimization of a woman's body is significant because one's subjectivity depends on the act of representation. Thus, Mary Shelley's disrespect for the Law takes shape in the writing of her fiction, where she commits the ultimate act of bad-daughter behavior: she reads and writes the text of her body, a text that Godwin has censored.

W. Arens has suggested that incest has been linked to cannibalism because historically, sexual and nutritional excess signified the savage.[72] If "you are what you eat," we can see that the father's law fashions Mathilda in another way: as murderer. Mathilda unwittingly "kills" her father, because the presence of her body makes his role as father untenable. Because "the body is a model which can stand for any bounded system,"[73] we see that the father has cannibalized his way beyond satiation. Laws function not merely to define lawful behavior but also to inscribe "how, when, [and] in what ways to be lawless."[74] Thus, the father who transgresses the incest taboo has committed a representable crime. Unlike the daughter's, his transgression is not unspeakable. Mathilda becomes introduced to the connection between reading and cannibalism when she muses, "I did not yet know of the crime there may be in involuntary feeling" (197). Mathilda does not yet know that all reading is an act of appropriation and ingestion, and that we are what we read and misread. Therefore, she misreads the limitations of her power to "correct" her father's feelings. Before she knows about her father's sexual desire for her, she thinks, "When I know his secret then will I pour a balm into his soul and again I shall enjoy the ravishing delight of beholding his smile" (197). But after she embodies the text of his sexual desire, she becomes irrevocably and indescribably changed; she feels soiled: "I gained his secret and we were both lost forever" (197). The nameless father rapes his daughter with desire, not touch; only through Mathilda's embodiment (in body and text) of his crime can we find his trace.

Although *Mathilda* is a story of incest that doesn't involve touch, Mathilda becomes touched by her father's sexual desire when she reads the text of that desire. Just as Mary Shelley lived through the act of writing during the summer of 1819, it is through the act of reading that Mathilda is raped. The horror of this father's crime is located in its intangibility; because her rape does not fit the socially inscribed "model" standard (vaginal penetration), only Mathilda's aftereffects are materially evident. Mathilda is raped by words, by gestures, by her father's gaze, and by the textual gaps in all of these. Her father says, "You are the sole, the agonizing cause of all I suffer, of all I must suffer until I die. Now, beware! Be silent! Do not urge me to your destruction.... My daughter, I love you!" (200-201). The trap here is not lost on Mathilda. She wants her father to love her, but not sexually. Although the Law protects the father by always trivializing incest, in this case it recognizes physical rape as more "legitimate" than the psychological rape Mathilda endures; the fact that someone else's victimization is more physical does not lessen Mathilda's suffering.[75] There are many ways of minimizing sexual abuse, and one is to change the subject, indicating in this case that the construction of Mathilda's subjectivity is "wrong" because she wasn't physically violated.

Mathilda was betrayed and then abandoned. The source of both violations was her father's desire to possess her sexually; although he did not use his penis to penetrate her, the combination of his power and desire (i.e., the phallus) penetrated her past and present. His power and desire prevented her entry into a future as an adult, since adulthood requires taking stock of one's past whereas being a good daughter involves keeping the (father's) secret of incest, even from oneself.

Mathilda dies a good daughter. And in an uncharacteristic gesture, I imagine that Mary Shelley acted like a bad daughter in the summer of 1819. Mary Shelley took stock of her life that summer: she had been a good girl, yet nevertheless her husband had cheated on her, her children had died, and, once again, Godwin had threatened to abandon her if she didn't "cheer up." Because the self-image of "mother" died with her children, Mary Shelley was free to explore previously hidden psychological terrain, possibly triggered by this loss. Importantly, she allowed herself this freedom only when she thought people wouldn't take her seriously—or literally. Thus, her identification with incest was filtered into the "lie" of her fiction.

This commingling of truth and lies can also be understood as a function of the Law. Luce Irigaray and Jane Gallop revise Lacan's configuration of the Freudian Father's Law, which simplifies the power of patriarchal authority by separating it from the penis with which it wields its power. According to Lacan, "The phallus is a signifier ... intended to designate as a whole the effects of the signified."[76] Although Gallop contends that "it is only the law and not the body—which constitutes [the father] as patriarch,"[77] she makes the connection between representation and social control that Lacan bypasses: "As long as the attribute of power is a phallus which refers to and can be confused ... with a penis, this confusion will support a structure in which it seems reasonable that men have power and women do not."[78] Mary Shelley adds another dimension to the Law by "lying" about her body, that is, telling the construction of the truth that the father won't hear unless it is contextualized in fiction.

Mathilda carefully weighs the differences between the construction or invention of one's history and the telling of lies. After her father's suicide, her identity as daughter is also killed; thus, Mathilda is not sure what to do with her past, but she knows she must do something with it. Should she consciously lie to herself, and "over the deep grave of my secret ... heap an impenetrable heap of false smiles and words" (219)? She says she "dare not," because to "do nothing" with her past (that is, not to put it in narrative and thus construct/record it) or to bury it with false narratives would allow it to become an unimaginable weight. She considers feigning her own death so that her heirs can claim the inheritance she feels has prostituted her, and she decides against this only because self-support would involve writing, which would necessitate (even veiled) disclosure of her own history. Mathilda feels stuck because all systems for making sense of her past seem a lie. Because her father's crime was a crime of desire, Mathilda must name (invent, construct, make up, represent, write) the crime in order to "escape" it (216).

But herein springs the trap of the phallus/penis symbol/body Law. To name the crime is to give it shape and power; not to name it is to be silenced by it, to be the object of the Law's desire and power once again. Unlike Mary Shelley, who risks the Law by writing *Mathilda*, Mathilda decides not to decide. And so Mathilda copes by never growing up; she says, "In solitude only shall I be myself" (216). She contrives her own death, which symbolizes her death as daughter; in doing so, she leaves herself no place to live within the symbolic or cultural order:

> I escaped. I left my guardian's house and I was never heard of again; it was believed from the letters that I left and other circumstances that I planned that I had destroyed myself. I was sought after therefore with less care than would otherwise have been the case; and soon all trace and memory of me was lost. (219)

To escape to a place where she can write her history, Mathilda must construct the presence of a third party who reads her traces, those implications she drops like bread crumbs and "forgets" so that she may eventually remember.

As the penis/phallus conveniently confuses the agency of patriarchal Law, *Mathilda* problematizes another element of the Law: the role of the absent mother. In his suicide/abandonment letter the father writes to Mathilda, "In my madness I dared say to myself—Diana died to give [Mathilda] birth; her mother's spirit was transferred into her frame, and she ought to be as Diana to me" (210). As I have argued above, the economy of exchange explains and legitimizes the father's brandishing of power so that the incest taboo organizes this exchange by mediating a relationship between the incestuous father and the mother's absence. Because Diana died in the process of giving birth to Mathilda, the father has the right (within the Law) to exchange/change daughter for wife. Mathilda "kills" her father by resisting the exchange.

However, Mathilda resists in a complicated fashion: she does not say or do anything, but rather, she disobeys by not taking on her role as seductress, by not anticipating what her father wants and thus saving him the trouble of transgression by embodying his sexual desire. Furthermore, when she orders a carriage and follows her father after his departure, she does so because she finds her identity in her role as daughter: if he dies, then she "dies." She wants to exonerate herself as her father's murderer; by resisting the Law she kills his role, and since "it is only the law—and not the body—which constitutes [the father] as patriarch,"[79] she has unwittingly found him out, undressed the father, exposed his phallus as penis. Of her tale Mathilda says, "Oedipus is about to die." (176). (And it is worth pointing out that Oedipus, at death, is reconciled to his daughter, but his death also forces her into the market of exchange.) It is important that Mathilda is too late to fulfill the script of the Law, and therefore Mary Shelley sees to it that Mathilda successfully resists the Law. Thus, in reclaiming her father's dead body, Mathilda functions as a Bakhtinian third party who serves as the most important reader on the scene.

In constructing herself and inventing her history, Mathilda manifests many symptoms that result from incest: dissociation,[80] inability to mourn or name her pain, embodying self-blame and guilt, perceiving herself as soiled, and sensing that she has committed some crime she cannot name. Simply put, Mathilda embodies incest:

> My father had for ever deserted me, leaving me only memories which set an eternal barrier between me and my fellow creatures. I was indeed fellow to none.... Unlawful and detestable passion had poured its poison into my ears and changed all my blood, so that it was no longer the kindly stream that supports life but a cold fountain of bitterness corrupted in its very source. (229)

First, patriarchal societies claim that incest is harmless because children forget or lie;[81] good for daughters because it makes them more sexually open or simply the victim's deserving fault.[82] Next, patriarchal culture makes laws ensuring that legal authorities read the text of a woman's body in these ways.[83] Eventually, women write the texts of their bodies in accordance with this prescription. Because we learn to read and write within culture and ideology, what is most devastating about the lessons patriarchal cultures teach about incest is that eventually the survivor herself doesn't know how her body could have "allowed" this to happen. And when one feels betrayed by one's body, one feels responsible for the crimes that have been committed. After the intrusion of incest, Mathilda feels that the blood which pulses inside her isn't really hers anymore. This creates two related incest aftereffects for Mathilda: self-blame and splitting.

The Law constructs the daughter as always already anticipating the father's transgression. Even though Mathilda does not allow the father to project the role of seductress onto her, nevertheless she feels responsible, if not for his sexual desire then for the fact that she did not sacrifice herself, use her body as a wedge to separate the father from his sexual desire by embodying it, by "wanting" it. She says, "I believed myself to be polluted by the unnatural love I had inspired, and that I was a creature cursed and set apart by nature" (238). Because "the remembrance haunts [Mathilda] like a crime" (218), she responds by splitting, by not matching her depression to its source. She has to force herself to feel: "I often said to myself, my father is dead. He loved me with a guilty passion, and stung by remorse and despair he killed himself. Why is it that I feel no horror?" (215). Instead of feeling pain and anguish, she bypasses her body and tells herself what and how to feel.

Mathilda experiences a time warp between feelings and reactions, because splitting reverses the process of reaction. Instead of feeling pain and then thinking about why she feels this pain, Mathilda inverts this: "I do not weep or sigh; but I must reason with myself, and force myself to feel sorrow and despair" (215). As she becomes more practiced at splitting, she reads history not to understand the feelings of others but to know how she should feel: "I began to study more … to lose my individuality among the crowd that had existed before me" (222). (It is important to note that Mathilda is not trying to write her experience into the master narrative of history—she says, "Perhaps a history such as mine had better die with me." Rather, she tries to efface her history by borrowing the feelings of others [175].) Mathilda becomes so practiced at splitting that she stops living in her body and instead merges with her father; she converts the memory of her father's love into "the life of my life" (223). Eventually, when splitting seems more natural than feeling,

Mathilda says, "Even my pleasures were endured, not enjoyed" (223). And finally, splitting from the memory of incest causes Mathilda to "forget," and therefore she starts to believe she has made it all up (another aftereffect of incest): "There were periods, dreadful ones, during which I despaired—and doubted the existence of all duty and the reality of [the] crime" (221).

Secrecy, an element always present in crimes of incest, either eliminates or displaces the third party who reads and confirms the violation. Woodville exemplifies this displaced third party, whom Mathilda allows to read her story only when she is dying. And because Woodville's power as a third party has been displaced, Mathilda asks, in spite of Woodville's place as reader, "Who can be more solitary even in a crowd than one whose history and the never ending feelings and remembrances arising from it is known to no living soul?" (216). Mathilda can never grow into the role of adult woman—"I must shrink before the eye of man lest he should read my father's guilt in my glazed eyes"—because, unlike Mary Shelley, Mathilda writes her way into death, not life.

My Mathilda

As my introduction to this chapter suggests, as a literary movement romanticism demanded (and its canonization still demands) the privileging of the father's word over the daughter's—and, in fact, predetermines her silence. But in the summer of 1819, Mary Shelley broke this silence and used writing to heal her pain, specifically by creating an autobiographical character whose pain served to bear witness to Mary's pain. And whatever the "real" source of Mary Shelley's pain, it is important that she chose the theme of incest to reflect it. If, as Lacanian psychoanalysis declares (and as I believe), writing actually "makes" events narratively real, and therefore representable, by depositing secrets, impressions, dreams, and other events that occupy unnarrativized psychic places into language, it is significant that Mary Shelley chose to write about incest to represent "romantic and excessive" love between a father and daughter. Along with writing, Mary Shelley healed through reading—the other side of the coin. Without reading, even physical trauma is not "real," because it can never be made real without a Bakhtinian third party who reads its place. (It is important to note that the reader can be an outside "third party," the writer herself, or both.) When the unnamed topic is incest, one important way to make real the unbelievability of sexual transgression is through writing and then reading. In fact, without the act of narrative, the body of an incest survivor is forever trapped; if the survivor does not construct sexual transgression outside her body, her body will remain only a signifier of despair.

A century after Mary Shelley wrote *Mathilda,* Sigmund Freud and Josef Breuer, in analysis with female hysterics, developed the "talking cure," a method through which subjects construct their demons through—and deposit them in—language. Today, self-help books predominate which recommend that the subject write her way back to psychological health. Ellen Bass and Laura Davis in *The Courage to Heal* position writing as necessary to healing:

> So often, survivors have had their experiences denied, trivialized or distorted. Writing is an important avenue for healing because it gives you the opportunity to define your own reality.... By going back and writing about what happened, you also reexperience feelings and are able to grieve. You excavate the sites in which you've buried memory and pain, dread and fury. You relive your history.[84]

Unlike Freud, whose hysterics produced "talk" that became the intellectual property of Freud himself, Bass and Davis suggest that feminist self-help theory restores agency to the writing subject.[85]

There are many ways to minimize or deny the possibility that *Mathilda* may function as the site of Mary Shelley's reconstruction of her "excessive and romantic love" (love to heteropatriarchy; incest to me) for Godwin. One way is to declare that if she were *really* molested by Godwin, she would have "said" it somewhere else, somewhere more legitimate than in her fiction. But even if society believed sexual abuse survivors, obligating Mary Shelley to "confess" would naively imply that traumatic memories reside in accessible psychic places. In truth, unless the subject reveals signs of psychosis, experiences with past trauma are "civilized" into silent aftereffects, so that the body "talks" in disguised ways. This results in behaviors, nightmares, addictions, and a multitude of fears, visions, panic attacks, all of which "serve" the trauma survivor by keeping her secret. These aftereffects are evidenced in the "gaps" of Mary Shelley's letters and journals.

Mary Shelley manages—and perhaps even conceals—her identification with incest by letting her fiction become the repository for this "excessive and romantic" father—daughter connection. Any reader of Mary Shelley's life—especially during the writing of *Mathilda*—who minimizes the place of telling truths (making self-disclosures) within the narrative of "lies" (fiction) reveals how the incest taboo is a taboo against writing and reading, not against the act of sexual abuse. Remember the epigraph to chapter 1 from W. Arens, who writes, "The literature [on incest] suggests quite clearly that as a rule intellectuals have either ignored or unintentionally denied the existence of incest in propounding their theories about the universality of the prohibition."[86] Arens asks academics to interrogate the intellectual coercion—the Law—that denies the fact of incest (and its privileged place in maintaining patriarchal culture) by accepting without question that the taboo successfully outlaws the crime.

Accepting the spirit of this challenge, Diane Price Herndl, in "The Writing Cure: Charlotte Perkins Gilman, Anna O., and 'Hysterical' Writing," focuses on the subject's power to write her way out of the Law:

> As the "writer," the woman becomes not just a subject, but a subject who produces that which is visible and which will be visible even in her absence. She produces a discourse which will take her place.... Writing can provide an other to "hear" her discourse, even if such another is not present; "she" can be "read." That is, she can be seen. Writing can become the Other, insofar as she inscribes herself, represents herself in her text. Writing separates her from the unbearable presence of experience by representing it as other, as that which is written, as the not-me.... But writing is a poison as well as a remedy, because to cure the woman, it must kill the hysteric. Writing takes the place of the hysteric.[87]

This change of focus offers feminist readers an important gesture, one that reclaims bodily experiences through the piecing together of aftereffects. Reading aftereffects as a text appropriates poststructural interrogations of the unified subject on feminist terms.

Mary Shelley's depression lifted temporarily after she finished writing *Mathilda*. She gave birth to her fifth child, she fought with Godwin over his suppression of *Mathilda*, and she returned to her correspondence and journal keeping. It was the "writing cure" that killed Mathilda and temporarily soothed Mary Shelley. A letter she wrote to Marianne Hunt, dated August 28, 1819, approximately two weeks after Mary Shelley completed *Mathilda*, suggests that this "fix" was temporary: "Shelley has written a good deal and I have done very little since I have been in Italy."[88] And so, while *Mathilda* paves the way for another displacement, for another series of repressions, it identifies the way Mary Shelley embodied herself in the grips of depression.

The coping strategy Mary Shelley advanced anticipates both Freud and the feminist recovery movement, not because Mary Shelley was ahistorically clairvoyant but because, in spite of the tiresome academic catechisms of historical materialism, incest and its aftereffects are not contained (or containable) by specific centuries, classes, households, or families.

CHAPTER THREE

Covert Incest

Frankenstein after Oedipus

The terror was greatly intensified, moreover, by the
realization that the help that [Sybil] had always thought
would come from God was now coming from Freud.

—Flora Rheta Schreiber, *Sybil*

The narrative consciousness at which Mathilda arrives on her
deathbed does not arise out of nowhere, although its traces cas-
ily go unnoticed.

Since pain is not context-free, I turn to *Frankenstein* as the literary site of Mary Shelley's unconscious incest narrative. Before
her nervous breakdown in the summer of 1819, Mary Shelley
showed in her early writing insights into the aftereffects of
trauma and abuse. In 1817, after a notoriously incestuous "waking dream," she transformed these psychological configurations into a novel, an abreaction[1] that displaced the potential
for memory into a fictional creation. Because Mary Shelley
could claim she *authored* the text of *Frankenstein*, she could

thereby demonstrate to herself and others that she did not *embody* the nameless monster.

I argue in this chapter that *Frankenstein* functions as Mary Shelley's screen memory for the covert incest in the Godwin household.

Waking Dreams and Dissociating Memories

The story of *Frankenstein*'s conception is as romantic as the canon in which this text has been placed. As told in countless introductions to the historical period that defines romanticism, to the rantings and roamings of the later romantics, and to the novel proper and its modern film transformations, the story goes as follows: In 1817, one infamous sex criminal of England, accompanied by his current male and female lovers, and one unknown poet and his mistress, a young woman of famous parentage, gathered at Villa Diodati, a Gothic mansion, and told and wrote ghost stories. That summer, in the Italian mansion procured by Lord Byron and inhabited by Claire Clairmont—pregnant with Byron's child—Byron's nurse and jealous male lover John Polidori, the little-known poet Percy Shelley, Mary Godwin, and the sometimes-visiting Monk Lewis, "rainy days and nights" were passed "in conversation about philosophy, science, religion and literature; they rowed, walked, told tales, and proposed a contest in which each would write his own ghost story."[2]

After nights of writer's block, Mary Shelley had a vision that initiated the composition of *Frankenstein*. This waking dream is riveting. In her 1831 introduction, Mary Shelley describes it:

> I saw—with shut eyes, but acute mental vision,—I saw the pale student of unhallowed arts kneeling beside the thing he had put together. I saw the hideous phantasm of a man stretched out, and then, on the working of some powerful engine, show signs of life, and stir with an uneasy, half vital motion. Frightful must it be; for

supremely frightful would be the effect of any human endeavor to mock the stupendous mechanism of the Creator of the world. His success would terrify the artist; he would rush away from his odious handiwork, horror-stricken. He would hope that, left to itself, the slight spark of life which he had communicated would fade; that this thing, which had received such imperfect animation, would subside into dead matter.... He sleeps; but he is awakened; he opens his eyes; behold the horrid thing stands at his bedside, opening his curtains, and looking on him with yellow, watery, but speculative eyes.[3]

Of the waking dream in which Mary Shelley asserts *Frankenstein* was conceived, Emily Sunstein identifies the ever-present shadow of incest: "*Frankenstein* is rooted in Mary's family drama.... In the apparently incestuous nightmare that engenders the book when she was eighteen, a 'natural philosopher' flees from the hideous 'child' he has created from dead bodies and vivified with a powerful 'engine' (slang for phallus)."[4]

While Sunstein's explanation of the family drama manifested in *Frankenstein* seems similar to my argument, it is really very different, for Sunstein's narrative of this "family drama" functions in the same way that romanticizing the renegade poets in a summer hideaway does: as a metaphor that holds in place patriarchal law.

Sunstein is reading in complicity with the incest taboo. This closes the story so that radical interpretations, such as reading incest as a material issue, not only a metaphorical one, remain narratively unlikely. And it performs this exchange of metaphor for material by naturalizing and euphemizing the notion of incest. (Almost as if by example, Sunstein misuses the term *phallus* for *penis*.)[5] When critics rely on such metaphors, just as when subjects dissociate from their bodies, a topic such as incest may reside in a body or mind or plot configuration as an informing and present issue, but as in "real life," the privileged site is inside a survivor's body. Situating the body as the container of the evil renders almost impossible a shift of focus to the outside: to the perpetrators that lurk in the text. And it is by concealing the perpetrators that dissociating metaphors appear to exist without agency and names.

There are other important examples of Sunstein's dissociating the metaphor of incest from its materiality and thus relegating incest to a disease-like entity contained by a woman's body instead of a crime of bodily appropriation perpetrated culturally and globally: "If they had transmigrated directly from Jacob's tents instead of leading the avant-garde of an enlightenment age, father, daughter and lover could not have played out a more elemental patriarchal drama, one that was to end only with Shelley's death";[6] "Going so early from Godwin to Shelley, Mary lacked the confidence and the power to act in genuine freedom.... It followed from Mary's first sixteen years that she sought the father-lover-tutor-colleague she found in Shelley."[7] The ease with which father-lover collapses into a single role (as in the common use of expressions such as "He's old enough to be your father") suggests that incest, once dissociated from the body through language, functions simultaneously as a prohibition and an expectation. According to Georges Bataille in *Erotism*, this "organized transgression," makes "social life what it is": "The frequency—and the regularity—of transgressions do not affect the intangible stability of the prohibition since they are its expected complement.... Transgression is complementary to the profane world, exceeding its limits but not destroying it."[8]

After incest becomes operative solely as metaphor in her text, Sunstein addresses a common assumption about Mary Shelley and other women writers whose history with depression or mental illness is still kept in the canonical closet. Sunstein relegates speculation about Mary's private life to the silences in the text:

Her inculcated ideal of Ciceronian stoicism, moreover, had the result that even she herself and Shelley were to understand her emotionally *only after tragedy broke her down.* Independently, Shelley and Leigh Hunt were later to compare her to an apparently cool volcano. Her reserve and ironic badinage prevented her associations from perceiving her diffidence or her passionate essence, and *none probed beyond the apparent persona.* In her journal and many of her letters, except to Shelley, one has to tease out not what she thinks but what she feels or prefers not to say; one begins to know her in her silences and in her works.[9]

Although I agree with Sunstein that textual gaps are pregnant with meaning, I find it impossible to approach these gaps from the seamless completion of a romantic story, a narrative of the kind on which Sunstein invariably relies to construct her biography of Mary Shelley. Furthermore, this activity of pointing out the gaps but not filling them up/out with interpretations seems a cop-out; it effectively takes the critic off the hook of taking a critical risk. At the risk of being dead wrong, I fill these gaps with covert incest.

In his 1986 study *Mary Shelley and Frankenstein: The Fate of Androgyny,* William Veeder shares with me an obsession for the particular, and in this case, the particular climate that both produced and constituted Mary Shelley in 1818. But like Sunstein, Veeder introduces the subject of incest but does not place it in a feminist or any other political frame.

Veeder, in keeping with other Mary Shelley critics, outlines Mary Shelley's odd behaviors, especially those displayed during the years 1812 to 1822. First, he catalogs her psychosomatic illnesses: one in 1812 when her arm suddenly became paralyzed, the feeling returning only when she left her "chill upbringing in William Godwin's library" for the "liberation of rural Scotland and the orthodoxy of Isabel Baxter's family";[10] the other in the summer of 1819, manifesting itself in her nervous breakdown. Second, Veeder turns to Mary Shelley's mood swings. Her moods shifted unexplainably from repression to expression, the former directed inward as self-hate, the latter directed outward in her fiction: "Her private prose, her later novels, her relations with men, and *Frankenstein* all display Mary's need to express and her tendency to repress."[11] Third, Veeder points to her inability to separate from Godwin and from her own self-image as Godwin's little girl, with no voice: "[Mary Shelley] remains as an adult what she was in Godwin's library, the onlooker, critic, judge."[12] Fourth, he addresses her obsession with Godwin, which according to Veeder, Percy "catches": "Father [Godwin] looms so large for both Mary and Percy Shelley that no one critical approach can account for him fully"; "Percy's intricate conflicts with father are illuminated by Mary's incestuous attractions to father;"[13] "Percy's rebelliousness predates his reading of *Political Justice* because his anger was father-directed before it was political. Godwin serves less to generate rebellion than to canonize it"; "Mary can see so accurately into Percy because she shares with him more than an obsession with father: Daughter and son here share the same object of desire, William Godwin."[14]

Veeder's focus on the marital tension in the Shelley household, figuring Mary and Percy as siblings and thus subsuming them within another kind of incest paradigm, bypasses a political reading of Mary Shelley's relationship with Godwin and therefore of the cultural construction of the incest paradigm shared by fathers and daughters, even famous ones.

Lynda Zwinger addresses the power implicit in heterosexual desire and the daughter's "choice" for seduction in her study of novel daughters, *Daughters, Fathers, and the Novel: The Sentimental Romance of Heterosexuality.* Zwinger's approach is to

reveal *as choices* fictional constructs that present themselves to nonfeminist criticism as inevitable and inevitably incidental to the more serious business of the plot.... It is my intention to point out the extent to which those fictional choices ... ground the system of cultural constructs and prescriptions that we have learned to think of as heterosexual desire.[15]

We can extend Zwinger's exposition of "choice" to feminist readers as well. It is precisely because readers such as Veeder and Sunstein know that "a daughter gone wrong is a daughter no longer"[16] that they are unable to recognize how their critical choices rely on the centrality and materiality of incest. And because Mary Shelley's position in the canon depends on her status as a daughter, the choice to which Zwinger refers remains psychologically unavailable to Mary Shelley's critics. If Harold Bloom can state without hesitation that "had she written nothing, Mary Shelley would be remembered today,"[17] those of us who include Shelley in our university courses must protect her status as dutiful daughter—right?

Wrong. The political reading I advocate recognizes representation as an act of social control. If representation involves assigning events to established categories, then political readings challenge those categories (such as "dutiful daughter") on which we rely, because for the disenfranchised, categories remain elusive, invisible, or socially outlawed. Mary Shelley can behave as though she is a dutiful daughter, but that behavior requires that she not integrate her feelings—represented in her journal as numbness whenever Godwin sent one of his caustic letters—with her actions; and this low-grade dissociation comes with a price. By relying on Mary Shelley's "odd" behaviors to read her into the canon without first reading the pattern that these behaviors reveal, Veeder ignores a subject I wish to address: how his list of behaviors offers a pattern associated today with aftereffects of incest.

Because I believe that past traumas take up psychological space which then colors fictional narratives, I am concerned that our sole reliance on material evidence (evidence as defined by positivism) allows access to past traumas only when they are accompanied by identifiable and recognizable "proof."[18] As some feminist scholars are beginning to address, a cultural signifier (such as the patriarchal function of incest in culture and in heterosexism) cannot be overturned simply by adding more proof of its prohibition; this approach only reifies the cultural necessity of the transgression and of poisonous pedagogy, and unwittingly creates a more solid boundary protecting it from critical and literal deconstruction. Rather than offer proof of the crime, I instead ask my readers to join me in shifting the focus from origin of the trauma to its aftereffects.

Covert Incest

"Covert incest" refers to a sexual transgression and crime that does not involve touch, committed by a parent or surrogate parent against the child for whom this adult assumes responsibility. Kenneth Adams, in his study *Silently Seduced*, describes the aftereffects of this trauma, which is sometimes referred to as "emotional incest." By definition, covert incest covers so much territory as to render most children vulnerable; the pervasiveness of incest in any of its forms reflects not so much the sweeping breadth of the definition as our culture's notorious refusal to take seriously children in pain. Adams states, "Covert incest occurs when [a parent crosses] ... the boundary between caring and incestuous love" and "when *the relationship with the child exists to meet the needs of the parent rather than those of the child.*"[19]

I suspect that many, probably most, parents fall at times within this paradigm. How often do parents create needs so that their children become dependent? Why is separation, especially for daughters, a cultural taboo? Both in spite of and because of its pervasiveness, covert incest is harmful. Adams says covert incest is as debilitating as physical, or overt, incest:

"The child feels ... the same feelings overt incest victims experience.... Over time, the child becomes preoccupied with the parent's needs and feels protective and concerned. A psychological marriage between parent and child results. The child becomes the parent's surrogate spouse."[20]

Adams points to one important distinction between covert and overt incest:

> While the overt victim feels abused, the covert victim feels idealized and privileged. Yet underneath the thin mask of feeling special and privileged rests the same trauma of the overt victim: rage, anger, shame and guilt. The sense of exploitation resulting from being a parent's surrogate partner or spouse is buried behind a wall of illusion and denial. The adult covert incest victim remains stuck in a pattern of living aimed at keeping the special relationship going with the opposite-sex parent.... Separation never occurs and feelings of being trapped in the psychological marriage deepen.[21]

Adams's definition of covert incest highlights key points in Mary Shelley's relationship with Godwin: Godwin made Mary Shelley his surrogate intellectual partner at a very young age when Jane Clairmont proved inadequate;[22] Godwin punished Mary Shelley in spousal rather than parental ways: "Godwin took care to condition Mary not to think too well of herself," "Godwin never laid a hand on Mary, but punished her nonetheless with cold silent disappropriation, one of the few things that could make her cry;"[23] and, when Mary Shelley eloped with another man, Godwin "cut off his child."[24] Unprepared for her father's spousal wrath, Mary Shelley "spent the next month rereading *Political Justice* and *Maria* in order to marshall from her parents' mouths a vindication of her right to live with Shelley." Growing up and away portends the father's abandonment of the daughter only in a covertly incestuous household; this message was further driven home by Godwin's aggressive abandonment of both Fanny and Claire. Learning this in 1816, Mary Shelley never separated from Godwin: "She loved him so strongly that she could only break away violently, and had not broken at all in the sense that Shelley was his disciple."[25]

The most common misreading of incest portrays the "seductive" daughter as the cause of the father's actual or fantasized behavior. I extend that discussion here to accommodate covert incest and its ramifications. As I stated earlier, Freud provides the paradigm for this reading in his abandonment of the seduction theory, a change of heart informed by the weight of a father's authority in culture.[26] Although most of the women diagnosed with hysteria reported being sexually molested by their fathers or uncles, Freud was "obliged to recognize that these scenes of seduction had never taken place, and that they were only phantasies which [his] patients had made up."[27] Similarly, Veeder is "obliged" to declare, "The obsession is Mary Godwin's. She insists, however, that incestuous feelings are reciprocal.... When Elizabeth exclaims, "God preserve you, my more-than-father" ... Mary Godwin is speaking.[28]

But this cultural obligation to protect a father's name misappropriates the term *incest*; for incest is never reciprocal. Parents have power and authority; children may acquiesce and even desire (see chapter 5), but they cannot choose freely. Free choice exists only in the company of people who share the same relationship to cultural and political power and material goods. This underscores Zwinger's declaration that "if the specter of father-daughter incest, as a literal rendering of desire, is the cornerstone of anything, it is not civilization so much as heterosexual desire."[29] But why separate "civilization" from "heterosexual desire"? Is it not the "gift" of woman in marriage that undergirds both?

The "loss" of the correspondence between William Godwin and Mary Shelley has been documented but not analyzed. It seems possible that this correspondence was not lost but destroyed: somebody wanted to destroy the evidence. But at least one document—a letter from father to daughter written on June 13, 1820, including a copy of another written previously that year, on April 25—has survived (and has been recently published in the Carl H. Pforzheimer Library collection *Shelley and His Circle*, vol. 8). I quote this letter in full in the Appendix because it represents the degree to which Godwin casts his daughter in the role of spouse.

The April 25, 1820, letter enacts many of the strategies and identifies the expectations of a father in a covertly incestuous relationship with his daughter. In the opening paragraph, Godwin expresses his desire to "make no observation" so that he does not "offend"; rather, he intends simply to "put down a few plain facts"—disarming. His intention not to offend—even if we take him at his word—serves as a kind of front man to his emotional brutality. It wants to say, "Since I don't intend to harm, then no harm can be done." This belief that behaviors don't count as much as intentions allows Godwin to attack his daughter emotionally. Let us move to the outside structure of the April 25 letter: it is couched in the June 13, 1820, one. It is important to note that Godwin does not perceive the transparent brutality of his correspondence. If he did, he no doubt would have prefaced it, too, with this desire not to "offend" but merely to "put down a few plain facts."

In the April 25 letter, Godwin inscribes Mary Shelley in a spousal arrangement, evident by his expectation that Percy will make good on his offer and that Mary can control this. When he writes (and underlines), *"Everything therefore seems to depend on the return I shall receive to this letter,"* he requires two separate actions: one involves Mary Shelley confirming his feelings—that is, acknowledging that she is a bad daughter who is intentionally trying to ruin her father (vis-à-vis her marriage to "another" man)—and the other involves the sum of five hundred pounds. We should not conflate the two; although by doing so, Godwin can elicit sympathy for losing his spouse-daughter to Percy Shelley, by dueling with this same man over another issue and thereby expending the same emotional anger but channeling it in a socially acceptable way.

Godwin manipulates Mary Shelley into taking responsibility for his position in the same fashion that jilted lovers remind, "But you promised!" This is evident when Godwin writes, "It is in vain by words to paint my astonishment at finding … when your letter was put into my hands, that it was single. Not a shilling accompanies it." This statement is hardly made in vain; Godwin knows that writing such lethal letters may not produce the needed money, but it does remind Mary of her obligations to her more-than-father. Godwin purposely ignores the fact that Mary does not control Percy's money; with power and venom, he writes as if Mary is the agent and source of his pain. In a covertly incestuous relationship, this inversion of victim and perpetrator is often enacted. How else is the daughter to feel special, idealized, privileged—and confined?

Godwin closes his letter in the fashion of all jilted lovers—with an ultimatum: "If Shelley will not immediately send me such bills as I propose … my next request is, that he will let me alone." Here the ultimatum is veiled: Godwin wants no contact with Percy, but perhaps if Mary leaves her husband, her father will not hold her responsible for Percy's behavior in the way Godwin does now. Only in a covertly incestuous relationship does a daughter have to choose between parent and spouse. Furthermore, Godwin (re)signs his April letter, "Ever most affectionately yours," which must leave Mary Shelley unclear about which text to read: her father's actions (as evidenced in the brutality of the letter), his intentions (which annul this brutality), or his "ever most affectionate" words.

Finally, Godwin's postscript in the form of the June 13 addendum reveals the extent to which he feels he has lost his lover-daughter: "I can conceive nothing more < >kening to the heart than this correspondence. My < >ers seem never to be received." As if to highlight the emotional impact, the materiality of Godwin's text escapes notation. Perhaps it is just too much to imagine, that Mary is no longer "awakened" and that his "letters" fail to manipulate in the way a more-than-father's letters should. (Or if the missing word is *sickened*, his rage is still logical—within the rules he has established for Mary Shelley's desire.)

Mary Shelley's journal records a three-word response to this letter: "Letter from Papa."[30] Her sparseness does not indicate that Godwin's behavior did not hurt her but rather that once this behavior had become routine (as these letters from Godwin were, indicated by Percy's letters to the Gisbornes), she failed to record it as abuse. Mary Shelley's three-word journal entry is followed by Paula Feldman and Diana Scott-Kilvert's footnote:

> Godwin's letter to Mary has never been traced, but it is clear from Shelley's letter to the Gisbornes of 30 June, and from the draft of a letter from Shelley to Godwin dated 7 August that it contained a demand for an immediate loan of £500 to settle some of the debts arising from the court action of 1819.... Another letter from Shelley written the same day instructed the Gisbornes not to pay any money directly to Godwin without papers of release from further obligation and a signed undertaking from Godwin to pay the money to the proper quarter. He also added that unless the Gisbornes saw any prospect that Godwin's situation would be immediately improved by the loan (and that he would therefore cease to harass Mary with his demands), they should not advance any money at all.... The Gisbornes did not advance the money, and Shelley's draft letter to Godwin of 7 August attempts to explain how his own financial embarrassments, with debts amounting to nearly £2,000, made it impossible to assist Godwin any further.[31]

The "untraced letter" to which Feldman and Scott-Kilvert refer is, to the best of my knowledge, the one I quote from in the Appendix of this book.

Victor Frankenstein's Stages of Emotional Breakdown

Untraced letters pose as much of a problem for Victor's Creature as they do for Shelley scholars. In this section I follow the threads of the untraced father—daughter correspondence, the things left unsaid, into the text of *Frankenstein*. My hunch is that Mary Shelley plays out the aftereffect of dissociative disorders in her characterization of Victor Frankenstein. This speculation takes my reading in a different direction from those followed in the three most popular paradigms associated with *Frankenstein* criticism—the feminist readings that focus on birth metaphors and Mary Shelley's own (understandable) reproductive anxieties; the psychoanalytic readings that regard this text as reinscribed oedipalization; and the genre criticism that uses this text as the origin for science fiction.[32]

Frankenstein is Mary Shelley's textualized rage at Godwin, a rage she couldn't or wouldn't give voice to in her day-to-day dealings with him. That Mary Shelley could receive letters like the one quoted in the Appendix and respond only with three words in her journal invites many questions: What did she do with her anger? how did writing *Frankenstein* and then dedicating it to Godwin entitle her to respond? *Frankenstein* deals less ostensibly with the theme of incest than does *Mathilda*, but in this novel Mary Shelley explores aftereffects of abuse, albeit less transparently identifiable ones. Using psychological theories about dissociative disorders, we can read Victor Frankenstein, the Creature, and Robert Walton as psychic projections of the same body—Victor's. Victor acts as Mary's memory trace; the Creature "acts out" Victor's anger against his father; and Walton, who writes the story down, serves as the mediating core memory for Victor.

Early childhood trauma, especially sexual abuse, physical abuse, and extreme psychological abuse, can cause dissociative disorders in adults. A psychophysiological process, dissociation "alters a person's thoughts, feelings, or actions, so that for a period of time certain information is not associated or integrated with other information as it normally or logically is."[33] Adults who suffer dissociative disorders—including the most severe on the spectrum, multiple personality disorder (MPD)—tend to have high IQs. The spectrum of dissociation ranges from loss of awareness to the presence of other identities, or "alters"; in addition, people who suffer from dissociative disorders experience some combination of "amnesia, loss of time, ownership of possessions that they do not remember acquiring, fugues, depersonalization." Repetitive trancelike behavior plagues the subject with dissociative disorders, who can be "triggered" into dissociation by "innocuous stimuli or triggers that are reminiscent of the traumatic experience."[34]

Ian Hacking, in an article in *Critical Inquiry* titled "Two Souls in One Body," notes the specific dangers applying to those with MPD: "Multiples usually come with one or more vicious alters. Suicide—understood as internal homicide, one alter murdering the body to kill another alter—is regarded as a real threat."[35] These alters that embody the core are not innate aspects of this core but are created during moments of abuse, trauma, and captivity, when the child cannot escape physically or protect herself. So alters represent the core's psychological potential, not her "intrinsic" self. They are functional, not internal: "For a multiple, the easiest way to abreact repressed trauma is through the procedure of alters, eliciting one alter per significant trauma.... Without [alters] it is unlikely that [the patient] will bring to consciousness things that are of deep importance to her."[36]

The two most dramatic transformations in *Frankenstein* are in gender and in Victor's role as sole author of his trauma. To approach the second concept, I suggest that Victor's amnesia is dissociative. According to Philip Coons, "An absolute essential criterion for the diagnosis of multiple personality is the presence of amnesia. Usually, the original personality is amnesic for the other secondary personalities."[37] At the onset of each of the Creature's murderous rages, Victor is somnambulant. Because the reader is closest to Victor's point of view, the transparency of his displacements is veiled by his projection of self-knowledge. Victor's Creature "acts out" the murderous rages that Victor cannot accept as his own, largely because these rages are directed at the destruction of Victor's father, Alphonse. Similarly—and important—by writing both *Frankenstein* and *Mathilda*, Mary Shelley could fail to read Godwin's behavior as covertly incestuous by making fictions out of feelings that she had no place for—and by making her characters do what she would have liked to do.

Flashbacks come to abuse survivors in the way that Victor gives shape to his monster. Flashbacks carry with them the bodily pain and psychological isolation that a terrorized child or adult captive knows; in a similar fashion, Victor is conscious of his monster's size: "I resolved ... to make the being of a gigantic stature, about eight feet in height, and proportionally large."[38] His use of the word *resolve* typifies trauma memory: most survivors "know" of the sexual violations without "believing" that they really happened. And Victor's resolve follows a trajectory resonant with trauma theory. As he remembers (constructs the monster), he embodies physical pain: "Every night I was oppressed by a slow fever, and I became nervous to a most painful degree" (42). Finally, a vision comes to him in the form of a dream in which he kisses his father's "more-than-daughter" Elizabeth, his childhood sister and playmate and future wife, and his kiss kills her, transforming her corpse into the corpse of his dead mother:

I was disturbed by the wildest dreams. I thought I saw Elizabeth, in the bloom of health, walking in the streets of Ingolstadt. Delighted and surprised, I embraced her; but as I imprinted the first kiss on her lips, they became livid with the hue of death; her features appeared to change, and I thought that I held the corpse of my dead mother in my arms ... saw the grave-worms crawling in the folds of the flannel. (43)

Victor has a multilayered incest dream. That his father has implicated Elizabeth in an incest arrangement, and that Victor is conscious of this, is made evident later in the novel. More transparently, Victor "imprints" mother—son incest in this scene. This dream affects Victor viscerally: once he remembers (constructs the monster), he can never forget again. His horror represents the horror of someone who has to reread and recategorize her relationships with her family as well as her relationship to her body. Having "allowed" his unconscious to construct this dream, Victor blames himself for bringing into focus "the miserable monster whom I had created" (43). Once Victor's memory-monster is fully-formed, he reacts in horror, typical of abuse survivors who move from knowing to believing: "I had gazed on him while unfinished [knowing without believing]; he was ugly then; but when those muscles and joints were rendered capable of motion [believing means never being able to 'forget' again], it became a thing such as even Dante could not have conceived" (43). Victor realizes every survivor's worst fear: the "child within" is really a monster.[39]

This memory is too big for Victor, and so the Creature "becomes" an entity all his own. Although the Creature is really Victor, "he" has different physical and intellectual capabilities and, unlike Victor, has no history. The Creature acts out Victor's deepest desires.

After the dream "creates" the Creature, Victor becomes secretive and hysterical. He tries to hide what he knows about himself from the person he loves most in the world—Henry Clerval. Henry visits shortly after the Creature's construction, and in his presence, Victor becomes hysterical:

> I felt my flesh tingle with excess of sensitiveness, and my pulse beat rapidly. I was unable to remain to a single instant in the same place; I jumped over the chairs, clapped my hands, and laughed aloud. Clerval at first attributed my unusual spirits to joy on his arrival; but when he observed me more attentively, he saw a wildness in my eyes for which he could not account; and my loud, unrestrained, heartless laughter, frightened and astonished him. (45)

On seeing Victor, Henry exclaims, "How ill you are! What is the cause of all this?" (45). And of course, Victor cannot explain. Victor cannot keep his past contexts separate from present texts, and in his anguish he starts to dissociate. Victor sees the Creature: "I saw the dreaded spectre glide into the room." And he feels the Creature take over the (his) body: "I imagined that the monster seized me; I struggled furiously, and fell down in a fit" (46).

This event triggers Victor's first amnesiac fever—at least, the first that the reader sees. Because we understand this amnesia from Victor's perspective, not Henry's, we do not see Victor embody the monster. Nor is it odd for Henry (or later, Elizabeth and Alphonse, who also "see" Victor dissociating) not to confront Victor (and thereby alert the reader to the presence of his alters). If confronted or frightened in any way, Victor may "turn" into the Creature and embark on a homicidal rage, and it makes sense that Henry placates this rage. (Henry may or may not be conscious of exactly *why* he is so nonconfrontational with Victor.) Although the Creature is Victor's memory trace, he does not share his memories with Victor's consciousness; rather, he acts out the rage these memories produce. Therefore, Victor (and Mary Shelley) remains consciously unaware of both his memories and his behaviors. This text is written from the prismatic perspective of the character who knows the least and feels the most, albeit without "awareness." All Victor knows is that he loses consciousness, and when he returns to consciousness, his monster has killed someone—someone named William, it's worth noting—and someone whom he loves.

Victor has a breakdown and Henry nurses him. While semiconscious, Victor tells Henry what he feels and remembers, but his memories don't make logical sense. In similar fashion, incest narratives often reject narrative order. (This explains the prevailing notion that incest is a theme, not a story.) But as Roseanne Barry's case suggests (to offer one example of what is currently being called "celebrity incest"), the burden of proof still functions as secondary victimization. This prohibition we call "logical thinking" leaves little room for inchoate memories:

> Doubtless my words surprised Henry: he at first believed them to be the wanderings of my disturbed imagination; but the pertinacity with which I continually recurred to the same subject persuaded him that my disorder indeed owed its origin to some uncommon and terrible event.
>
> By very slow degrees, and with frequent relapses, that alarmed my friend, I recovered. I remember the first time I became capable of observing outward objects. (46)

When Victor returns to consciousness, he fears that he has exposed his "monster" to Henry. When Henry wants to broach "one subject" regarding the nervous fever, Victor fears the worst: "I trembled. One subject! What could it be? Could he allude to an object on whom I dared not even think?" (47). When the subject turns out to be Henry's suggestion that Victor write to his father, Victor is temporarily relieved. Nevertheless, the reader must note the juxtaposition between terrors: exposing the monster becomes civilized into exposing (and extorting) Victor's duties to honor his father.

Just as abused children often displace their fear from the per-petrator to the tool or weapon used, so too Victor, when in the presence of his laboratory tools and chemicals, undergoes a near relapse:

> When I was otherwise quite restored to health, the sight of a chemical instrument would renew all the agony of my nervous symptoms. Henry saw this, and had removed all my apparatus from my view. He had also changed my apartment; for he had perceived that I had acquired a dislike for the room which had previously been my laboratory. (50)

By removing objects that recall memories, Victor "solves" his psychic pain.[40] Victor then moves into the next stage of trauma survival: he rewrites his history. When he defines himself as someone who "a few years ago, loving and beloved by all, had no sorrow or care" (52), he "forgets" much of what we know about Victor, most noticeably his grief over his mother's death.

This denial allows him to absorb the message of his father's letter: "William is dead!" (53). When Victor returns home, his denial gives way to a glimpse of his own amnesia and responsi-bility for William's death. He sees his Creature; he thinks that the Creature may be responsible for the murder, and "no sooner did that idea cross my imagination, than I became con-vinced of its truth" (57). How does speculating about a possi-bility transform instantly into conviction? This is the way with so-called buried memories. Remembering trauma is less about cognitive thinking than about letting go of defense mecha-nisms, such as the selective amnesia used frequently by abuse survivors. This selective amnesia lets the survivor cognitively remember the event (as in Mary Shelley's making note of God-win's June 13, 1820, letter in her journal) but also requires that she quickly deny her feelings. The "good" daughter does not "read the text," because she believes—desperately—that her privileged status (constructed from the perpetrator's self-appointed good intentions) precludes abuse.

The gender displacement necessary to move from "good daughter" to "bad Victor" offers another window to view Mary Shelley telling truths when we are to think she is telling lies (writing fiction). What we don't know about Victor may also be what Mary Shelley conceals about herself. Victor knows, but he doesn't want to believe. The "logic" of knowing that your body stops at your skin is for the psychologically dense only. For Victor (and, I suspect, for Mary Shelley), the logic that declares experience a verifiable and conscious fact of identity is not a "natural" fact of life.

The complications of experience and memory are traceable from Freud into contemporary critical theory. According to Freud in *Early Psychoanalytic Publications* (1893–1899), "The essential elements of an experience are represented in memory by the inessential elements of the same experience."[41] If inessential elements conceal important memories, this anticipates contemporary critical theory's reliance on the constructed subject. According to Freud, memories do not emerge, they are formed: "It may be indeed questioned whether we have any memories at all *from* our childhood: memories *relating to* our childhood may be all that we possess.[42]

Two years later, Freud redefined this "screen memory," rejecting his earlier idea that such memories "screen off" traumatic recollections. In *The Psychopathology of Everyday Life* (1901), he instead defined screen memories as "indifferent memories [that] owe their preservation not to their own content, but to an associative relation between their content and another which is repressed."[43] Using Freud, we see that *Frankenstein*, a novel about a troubled man's murderous amnesia and dissociative disorder, functions in part as a screen memory for Mary Shelley's anger and confusion resulting from father—daughter covert incest, later written more explicitly in *Mathilda*. We might be tempted to say that in 1817, during the writing of *Frankenstein*, Mary Shelley "knew" (as reflected unconsciously in *Frankenstein*) about a severe incest aftereffect (in Freud's definition, a "content") but could not connect it to any source (in Freud, the "repressed content"). Perhaps this is why psychoanalytic criticism has had such a field day with this novel: Victor's aftereffects spill through the text and inform the plot, but his trauma remains vehemently repressed. Victor would rather die than remember.

Screen memories, like Freudian slips, work along the lines of displacement; but "with the forgetting of names, we *know* that the substitute names are false: with screen memories we are surprised that we possess them at all."[44] We understand the world, our bodies, and our pasts according to the categories our culture makes available to us. In 1901, Freud was troubled by the concept of "infantile amnesia." According to Freud, we are cognitively able to remember our first year of life; and since early childhood experiences "exercise a determining influence for the whole of [a person's] later life,"[45] it is important to challenge the widespread acceptance of infantile amnesia. Freud here ably connects individual repression with cultural determinations of the possible and impossible: "The 'childhood memories' of individuals come in general to acquire the significance of 'screen memories' and in doing so offer a remarkable analogy with the childhood memories a nation preserves in its store of legends and myths."[46] However, when Freud confronted incest and its material aftereffects in hysteria in 1930, he took shelter behind the "fact" of childhood amnesia.

What Freud offers my reading of *Frankenstein* is this: he helps explain the nonliteral abreaction made possible when a woman writer splices unnamed rage into her fiction. In Mary Shelley's early novels, aftereffects of trauma shape and move the character development and plot. Giving aftereffects names and roles offers one of the "conditions for remembering" that Freud articulated in 1901.

When Victor learns of William's death, he knows that he is responsible but cannot remember his role. So the monster did it. The devil made me do it. Boys must be boys. He can't expose his monster, because to do so would cause the myth of his happy family to crumble. Better to let them die one by one than close the collective family coffin with discourse of the kind that exposes the emperor's nakedness. Better even to let Justine die innocently than be the bearer of such news. If we allegorize Justine's murder trial, we see that she is convicted on circumstantial evidence in the same way that sexually abusive fathers (cultural as well as familial) are released. While Justine is convicted of the crime she didn't commit because of her confusion ("on being charged with the fact, the poor girl confirmed the suspicion in a great measure by her extreme confusion of manner" [59]), Clarence Thomas was deemed innocent of sexual harassment charges because no one (except the victim) saw him do it. His confusion and anger, his declaration that he was being victimized by a "high-tech lynching," constituted the proof of his innocence. He was innocent because he couldn't be guilty; Justine is guilty because she cannot be innocent. Logic has little to do with power configurations.

Once Justine dies for his crime, Victor goes into his own hell. He knows he is guilty but can't remember the act: "I had committed deeds of mischief beyond description horrible, and more, much more, (I persuaded myself) was yet behind" (67). Both the parenthetical reference to persuasion and the use of the word *behind* anticipate Freud: persuasions and screens, intentionality and amnesia. Victor is out of physical control, and his solution is that of the confirmed neurotic—to dig deeper inside: "All sound of joy or complacency was torture to me; solitude was my only consolation—deep, dark, deathlike solitude" (67). Victor's symptom here is transparent: the trauma survivor who thrives on trauma fears that happiness and self-satisfaction will spontaneously combust into abuse again. This prophecy works: while Victor abuses himself, his "monster" remains dormant; but as soon as Victor dares to feel joy, his monster comes back to life.

The sexuality of this moment needs to be identified. On vacation in Chamonix, Victor secretly stops chanting to himself: "I, not in deed, but in effect, was the true murderer" (69). Gazing at a sketch of ice, Victor feels himself extend: "My heart, which was before sorrowful, now swelled with something like joy." And when Victor swells, his monster appears: "As I said this, I suddenly beheld the figure of a man, at some distance, advancing towards me with superhuman speed.... It was the wretch whom I had created" (73). Victor feels sexually aroused and is plagued by inchoate memories. He collapses, and the Creature takes over the body. This pattern, although no place in the text as transparent as it is here, accounts for Victor's later association of memories with torture. After his Creature confronts him (that is, after Victor knows that he loses consciousness and "acts out"), Victor exclaims: "Oh! stars, and clouds, and winds, ye are all about to mock me: if ye really pity me, crush sensation and memory" (110). Memories are crushing to Victor, because his amnesia is not a blank slate but rather a waking night terror: "Can you wonder, that sometimes a kind of insanity possessed me, or that I saw continually about me a multitude of filthy animals inflicting on me incessant torture, that often extorted screams and bitter groans" (110).

Victor embodies aftereffects of sexual trauma, of the kind necessary for severe dissociating. First, Victor describes himself with self-loathing: "I, a miserable wretch, haunted by a curse that shut up every avenue to enjoyment" (114). Compare this view to the Creature's self-description: "I, the miserable and the abandoned, am an abortion, to be spurned at, and kicked, and trampled on" (163). (Also, compare this to Mathilda's painful isolation after her father abandons her: "My father had for ever deserted me, leaving me only memories which set an eternal barrier between me and my fellow creatures" [229]. The fact that Victor is an abuser does not necessarily prove that he was abused.[47] Like other abusers, he regards the objectification of human beings and their destruction—most obvious in his construction and then dismemberment of the Creature's bride—as a job, an unfortunate obligation, something he was called on to do. After Victor acknowledges that "company was irksome to me" because "an insurmountable barrier was placed between me and my fellow man,"[48] he explains, "I now began to collect the materials necessary for my new creation, and this was to me like the torture of single drops of water continually falling on the head" (117).

Victor identifies how his construction of a female Creature further infuses him with pain by extending the metaphor to include both past memories and present occupations. Victor knows that his "enjoyment was embittered both by the memory of the past, and the anticipation of the future" (118) but is nevertheless marshalled into the next level of trauma aftereffect: "For an instant I dared to shake off my chains, and look around me with a free and lofty spirit; but the iron had eaten into my flesh, and I sank again, trembling and hopeless, into my miserable self" (119). Victor's fall into the role of abuser should not be attributed to a conscious intent or desire that he become an abuser. He cannot go backward because he cannot tolerate the pain, and he cannot go forward because these same memories have shackled him. The acting out of past pain in present contexts becomes Victor's compulsive pattern.

The repetition compulsion becomes complete when Victor mutilates a female corpse:

> It was indeed a filthy process in which I was engaged. During my first experiment, a kind of enthusiastic frenzy had blinded me to the horror of my employment; my mind was intently fixed on the sequel of my labour, and my eyes were shut to the horror of my proceedings. But now I went to it in cold blood, and my heart often sickened at the work of my hands. (121)

Now playing out the vague script of his haunting memories in cold blood, Victor shows that construction and deconstruction are complicated versions of each other. Three years before he worked to keep his memories at bay when he constructed the Creature; now, again "trembling with passion, [I] tore to pieces the thing on which I was engaged" (123).

After Victor ravages the corpse, he and his Creature switch power positions. This again symbolizes dissociation, where the past becomes more present than the present. Victor experiences this crisis in a night terror, a dream that won't permit the sufferer to wake into full consciousness: "When I awoke ... the words of the fiend rung in my ears like a death-knell, they appeared like a dream, yet distinct and oppressive as a reality" (125). Victor's understanding that there is no one reality but rather many also suggests that, like Mathilda, he feels reality in fragments.

The compulsion to repeat feeds off itself, because the events the repetition compulsion unearths are abusive and painful. When more trauma is laid on the original cluster of traumas, the incentive to repeat becomes greater. The stakes keep getting higher, as does the desire to finally "get it right" and magically break the chain of command. When the repetition compulsion involves violence, rarely does the perpetrator recognize this. When Victor lugs the dismembered corpse to the boat, from which he scatters her into the sea, he comments,

"The remains of the half-finished Creature, whom I had destroyed, lay scattered on the floor, and I almost felt as if I had mangled the living flesh of a human being" (126). He doesn't see what's under his nose, in the same fashion that Mary Shelley critics have absorbed her "excessive and romantic love" for Godwin as something—anything, in fact—other than a clue suggesting covert incest. Victor's reading of the not-corpse at his feet serves similarly as a denial of crime. (I didn't do it if I didn't mean to do it; I didn't do it if I didn't know what I did.) Victor's way of seeing is repeated by well-intentioned literary critics who are fearful of or disinterested in politicizing incest.

But as he prepares to bury the corpse at sea, Victor recognizes his role in the repetition compulsion ("I had ... regarded my promise with a gloomy despair, as a thing that with whatever consequences, must be fulfilled"), and he starts to feel like a criminal: "I felt as if I was about the commission of a dreadful crime, and avoided with shuddering anxiety any encounter with my fellow creatures" (126). His anxiety functions to collapse word with deed, another way of declaring that Victor embodies guilt and pain: "I was ... a dreadful crime." And as if to emphasize this point, once on shore he is indeed treated like a criminal. He is hauled off to the magistrate, Henry Clerval's dead body is discovered, and the townspeople suspect Victor. Before Victor continues his story, he pauses, reminding the reader (Robert Walton) that deeply buried memories bring with them the pain that accompanied the experience: "I must pause here; for it requires all my fortitude to recall the memory" (129).[49] And as I suggested in the previous chapter, for trauma survivors memory has less to do with cognition than with tolerance of pain.

After Henry's murder, Victor has another amnesiac breakdown, thereby preventing further memories from emerging (a process that again allows the monster inside to act out). He describes his reentry into consciousness: "In two months, [I] found myself as awakening from a dream, in a prison, stretched on a wretched bed, surrounded by gaolers, turnkeys, bolts, and all the miserable apparatus of a dungeon." Victor vacillates from amnesia to self-loathing and desired suicide, locating the pain inside himself: "Of what materials was I made, that I could thus resist so many shocks, which, like the turning of the wheel, continually renewed the torture?" (131). Even though Victor is acquitted of murder because Mr. Kirwin is convinced that no man of his class situation could commit such a heinous crime, Victor's dissociation is ironically captured by a witness who declares loudly, "He may be innocent of the murder, but he has certainly a bad conscience" (135). After the trial, Victor, haunted by memories, "took a double dose" of laudanum. As he falls into a drugged sleep he says, "I repassed [replaced?] in my memory my whole life." He wakes to another night terror: "Towards morning I was possessed by a kind of night-mare; I felt the fiend's grasp in my neck, and could not free myself from it; groans and cries rung in my ears" (136).

Overwhelmed by the confusion of his innocence/guilt, Victor "desires" to get caught. He says to his father, Alphonse, "I am the cause of this—I murdered [Justine]. William, Justine and Henry—they all died by my hands." Alphonse commands his son not to confess; accusing Victor of being mad, he says, "I entreat you never to make such an assertion again" (137). But Victor continues: "I am not mad … the sun and the heavens, who have viewed my operations, can bear witness of my truth. I am the assassin of those most innocent victims; they died by my machinations" (137). Alphonse, wishing to "obliterate the memory of the scenes that had taken place," changes the subject. Victor's enforcement of silence becomes routine: "As time passed away, I became more calm: misery had her dwelling in my heart, but I no longer talked" (137).

Victor cannot sustain this silence. After Elizabeth pushes Victor to make a marriage commitment, he tries a more displaced disclosure with her: "I have one secret, Elizabeth, a dreadful one; when revealed to you, it will chill your frame with horror, and then, far from being surprised at my misery, you will only wonder that I survive" (140). Displaced disclosures provide the multiple with short-term peace, but when the pain of repression—denial—disclosure starts the cycle again, the anguish becomes more severe. When the cycle begins again for Victor, he becomes catatonic:

> The tranquility which I now enjoyed did not endure. Memory brought madness with it; and when I thought on what had passed, a real insanity possessed me; sometimes I was furious, and burnt with rage, sometimes low and despondent. I neither spoke nor looked, but sat motionless, bewildered by the multitude of miseries that overcame me. (140)

Victor emerges from his catatonia to make wedding plans; and Victor's monster, true to his word, kills the bride on their wedding night. Victor responds to the murder of Elizabeth as he did to that of Henry—with another amnesiac fit: "A film covered my eyes and my skin was parched with the heat of fever. In this state I lay on a bed, hardly conscious of what had happened; my eyes wandered round the room, as if to seek something that I had lost" (145). Victor wakes again from madness with the desire to confess. He seeks out a criminal judge in his town and tells all: "The story is too connected to be mistaken for a dream, and I have no motive for falsehood," Victor pleads (147). But again, Victor's story is not believed. The judge's disbelief, like his father's, at first enrages Victor; and as before, this anger gives him short-term relief: it allows him to focus on something other than the monster inside himself.

This time Victor does not replay the cycle. Instead, he cracks, promising to follow his Creature wherever he may lead. It is the

monster inside Victor, not his external creation, that has oblit-
erated his family. In a manner typical of severe dissociative disorders, the Creature (Victor's alter) develops talents and skills
that "Victor" doesn't have. The Creature has a separate identity,
reads a different canon, aspires to different life goals, and
assumes the responsibility for the murders.

As Ian Hacking, Frank Putnam, Judith Herman, and others
have noted, it is not unusual for alters to know each other, to
"talk," and, during suicidal phases, to plot the murder of the
core personality. And a murder plot is what is being played out
in the final scene of the novel, when the Creature supplicates
Walton for forgiveness. In his monologue to Walton the Creature identifies the conflation, the spilling over of desire into
autonomy that characterizes the alters. The Creature says, "I
pitied Frankenstein; my pity amounted to horror: I abhorred
myself.... I knew that I was preparing for myself a deadly torture; but I was the slave, not the master of an impulse, which I
detested, yet I could not disobey.... The completion of my
demonical design became an insatiable passion" (162). The
Creature's words echo Victor's. Nobody is in control, and the
expectation that someone's intentions and actions will match
up so that logic can be restored to this scene presents us with a
phenomenological impossibility.

I do not want to focus on the Creature as an isolated agent,
because agency is social, not private or individual. We can
become agents of social change only in collectivity with a
named political movement, not simply by trying hard as earnest
individuals. Nevertheless, I suggest here some ways in which the
Creature's appearance of agency seduces the reader into invest-
ing in the Creature's individuality and therefore occludes for us
the reading I have offered.

The Creature's primary function as an alter is to feel the pain
that numbs Victor and to "act out" this pain. Significantly, the

Creature learns to read, a skill that mocks Victor's amnesia at primary moments in the text. The Creature states, "I cannot describe the delight I felt when I learned the ideas appropriated to each of these sounds, and was able to pronounce them. I distinguished several other words, without being able as yet to understand or apply them" (83). Learning to read serves as the initiation of self-development. Whereas, in the beginning, the personalities born of dissociation are blank slates, as they develop they become readers, who are disconnected from their source (in this case, from the host of Victor). What does it mean when the "monster within" learns to read? It suggests that Victor is far worse off than he imagines, because now he has internal resistance to (self-) integration. It explains why integration, as represented in the famous chase scene offered in the conclusion of Mary Shelley's novel, is suicide.

Significantly, this resistance to integration echoes most readers' relationship to the Creature. After all, the Creature is by far the most likable character in the novel. Because of his penchant for self-improvement, he is also the most fully developed character in the novel. This places the reader on the side of the unconscious Victor, resisting integration of the selves because it means merging the Creature back. The Creature does Victor's bidding in the same way that Mathilda embodies her nameless father's sexual desire. The Creature, more confrontational than Mathilda—a quality we forgive in an eight-foot-tall man—squares off with Victor: "Do your duty towards me" (73). But Victor's duty toward himself would diminish the consciousness of the Creature, which is, of course, not the Creature's (or the reader's) desire. Even though the Creature is Victor's projection, because he is the least repressed and the most unscreened of the aftereffects, we invest him with human qualities and thus invest in his self-growth.

Feminist Speculations

We do not know how to hear Victor's story because reading aftereffects as texts is not part of our present intellectual bag of tricks. Indeed, Mary Shelley is bound up with Victor in complicated ways. It is significant that *Frankenstein* precedes *Mathilda* in composition, and that the trauma and aftereffects that ravage Victor are both more extreme and less translatable into narrative than the experiences that Mathilda relates.

Frankenstein does not thematize incest; it acts out the pain of memory containment, a phenomenon familiar to trauma theory. It portrays a character who dissociates his feelings, his memory, and his actions. While we are not told how he got that way, we can speculate. According to Herman, Putnam, and others, dissociative disorders result from "forgotten" childhood sexual, physical, and emotional abuse.

I move now to the project of reading aftereffects as texts in twentieth-century literature and culture.

CHAPTER FOUR

True Crimes of Motherhood
Mother-Daughter Incest and Dissociative Disorders

PATIENT: Mother, I am frightened.
CHARCOT: Note the emotional outburst. If we let things go unabated we will soon return to the epileptoid behavior.... (The patient cries again: "Oh! Mother.")
CHARCOT: Again, note these screams. You could say it is a lot of noise over nothing.

—C. Goetz, *Charcot the Clinician*

Feminism has historically relied on the mother—daughter bond as a noncontested category for women's connection and social activism.[1] And yet mother—daughter abuse is a very important issue, highlighted in contemporary true crime novels. There are two formula plots for this genre. In the first, a white upper-middle-class woman murders her daughters. Her neighbors and tennis pals are shocked; her husband didn't see it coming. (These narratives flourish in white middle class women's magazines such as *Redbook* and *Woman's Day*.) The second model, typified by Flora Rheta Schreiber's *Sybil*, centers the mother—daughter relationship in incest, not murder. Important elements of plot and politics distinguish this model: the featured presence of abusive mothers; lesbianism in the bodies of women already sanctioned as heterosexual; the production of a multiple-personality daughter, whose unproblematized discourse of confession, disclosure, and confrontation fails to reconstruct the individual (that is, humanism cannot restore the multiple to a single consciousness); and the replacement of the incestuous mother with the mother-therapist. I argue that it is this therapist-mother role which inscribes the misogyny that sustains mother—daughter abuse, first by setting up the crazy mother who "makes" a crazy daughter and then by pitting the crazy mother against the mother-therapist, who emerges at the narrative's close as the good and more deserving mother.

Discussions about incest and its aftereffects almost always configure a father (or father figure) perpetrator and a daughter (or surrogate) victim or survivor. While it is absolutely true that men commit sexual abuse more often than women do, women can also function as perpetrators of incest. By privileging the father—daughter incest paradigm, we successfully inscribe the "sentimental romance" of heterosexuality[2] and cannot account for one of the signal aftereffects of incest: multiple personality disorder (MPD). MPD, recognized by the American Psychiatric Association as an aftereffect of incest only since 1980,[3] frustrates the father—daughter incest paradigm because mother—daughter abuse appears to cause dissociative disorders at a high rate (at least as represented in women's true crime novels). Because mothers are bestowed with the cultural privilege of child welfare, and because children embrace even abusive mothers as allies in early childhood, mother—daughter abuse appears to create severe dissociative disorders. While abusive mothers recast as mother-therapists appear to "cure" MPD, their cure recapitulates a belief in the healing power of motherhood. The "evil mother" dichotomized with the "good mother" honors this desperately felt but unfounded belief.

Indeed, this myth does no good for the therapist, the patient, or the "evil" mother.

In this chapter I use Flora Rheta Schreiber's *Sybil* and Joan Frances Casey's *The Flock: The Autobiography of a Multiple Personality* to show how mother—daughter abuse, the open secret of women's literature, troubles the nostalgic relationship between women that feminism often desperately assumes. I focus this chapter not only on the individual mothers and daughters brought to light by these novels but also on the roles of motherhood and daughterhood. Both novels show that abusive mothers assume power through the social role of motherhood. It is important to recognize that this same social role facilitates the practice of the feminist therapists, who function as surrogate mothers with the power to heal. Daughters who suffer from severe dissociative disorders find wholeness only when they shift loyalty from the evil mother to the good one, a shift often accomplished with bribes and solicitations from the mother-therapist.[4] These mother-therapists are indeed better mothers than the sadistic mothers that precede them, but their cure comes with a price: entrapment, always, in some mother's narrative. When the role of motherhood and its usefulness in feminist therapy are naturalized and idealized, the dissociating daughter is merely reinscribed in another mother's narrative—one that again is not her own. Even with sanity, good daughterhood is a dead-end street.

In *Sybil* the story of Sybil Isabel Dorsett—who was sexually, physically, and verbally abused by her mother, Hattie Dorsett, from infancy—and her relationship with the real[5] Dr. Cornelia B. Wilbur (who still serves as a leading spokesperson about MPD) is narrated by Sybil herself, who, amnesiac and unaware of her sixteen other personalities, knows and feels shame because she "loses time." Vicky, Sybil's memory trace,[6] who emerges when she is twelve but knows the history of the body from the age of two, works with Dr. Wilbur as a co-analysand. "The Peggys"—Peggy Lou and Peggy Ann—interrupt Sybil's life and therapy to express rage and anger, directed at Hattie Dorset. The other twelve personalities appear and confront Dr. Wilbur throughout Sybil's eight years of therapy, and some even try at various times to "murder" Sybil.

In therapy with Dr. Wilbur, Sybil consistently replays tropes that point to child abuse: secrecy, isolation, entrapment. While the aftereffects are ever-present—the most evident of which is her severe MPD—the events themselves (ritualized incest, medical abuse, verbal abuse) are "lost" in the pre—mirror stage talk and not transferable into a comprehensible narrative for the conscious, adult Sybil. While the Peggys know that Hattie molested Sybil, Sybil does not. And while Vicky knows the tale of Sybil's sad plight, she believes she is an entirely separate person from Sybil. Interestingly, even though Hattie's abuse was sadistic, ritualized, and consistent, Sybil does not remember it. She recalls only that Hattie was "at once overprotective and unsympathetic."[7] When one of Sybil's alters "returns" her body to her, leaving Sybil to explain her amnesia to her boss, the police, or a member of the medical community, she repeats in rote, "I am an only child and my parents are very good to me" (*S*, 42).

Hattie perpetrated incest by tying Sybil in a bondage ritual with dishtowels, penetrating her with kitchen utensils, and abusing her with unnecessary enemas. She then enforced silence and repression by "erasing" the event, by veiling it with her role as mother. Hattie reportedly said, "Now don't you dare tell anybody anything about this. If you do, I won't have to punish you. God's wrath will do it for me!" (*S*, 209). (Importantly, the narrator, Flora Schreiber, writes from the psychiatrist's perspective. Thus, Sybil's story is really Cornelia Wilbur's story, just as Freud's case studies of his famous hysterics are his, not theirs.) The Peggys "talk" this trauma because they don't think Hattie Dorsett is their mother; in fact, the fifteen other personalities that take over Sybil's body claim to have no mother at all (*S*, 306). Thus, the alters capably read Hattie as perpetrator only because they refuse to read her as mother. For Sybil, the role and title of "mother" veils all abuse:

> Sybil invested the perpetrator of the tortures with immunity from blame. The buttonhook was at fault, or the enema tip, or the other instruments of torture. The perpetrator, however, by virtue of being her mother, whom one had not only to obey but also to love and honor, was not to blame. (*S*, 222).

This mother—daughter abuse is psychologically dangerous, because the mother's stereotyped social role ameliorates her abusive behavior.[8]

In addition to the social role that protected Hattie's abuse from discovery was Hattie's self-projected image—as an advocate of children's rights, of all things: "Hattie Dorsett enunciated solemn strictures about exemplary child care. Never hit a child, Hattie Dorsett preached, when it is possible to avoid it, and under no circumstances hit a child on the face or head" (*S*, 223). This projected image successfully prohibits Sybil from taking seriously her therapy with Dr. Wilbur until after Hattie's death. Hattie sabotages Sybil's first relationship with Dr. Wilbur by intentionally not giving Sybil a phone message that the doctor had left, to cancel an appointment. With Sybil feeling stood up and abandoned, as Hattie had hoped, her mother caps the moment with another injunction for mother love: "Dr. Wilbur didn't really care for you.... She tells you one thing now. But when she gets you where she wants you, she'll tell you altogether different things. And remember young lady, she'll turn on you if you tell her you don't love your own mother" (*S*, 46). The only reason Sybil has the strength and desire to return to Dr. Wilbur after Hattie's death is that Sybil buffers her mother's warning with Hattie's fundamentalist Christianity and its proscriptions on psychiatric help. (Hattie warned Sybil that Dr. Wilbur would "make [her] crazy ... and then ... put [her] in an institution because that's the way doctors make money" [*S*, 46].)

Sybil, like all abused children, was told never to tell. For this reason, she is "scared about words" (*S*, 298), but also for this reason, she perfected a skill that afforded her nonverbal communication. For Sybil, the only terrain untouched by her mother's abuse and prohibition is drawing. When trapped, Sybil colors her way out of and into amnesia. For example, when the evangelical pastor of her family's Omaha church, hoping to involve her in church activities, asks Sybil to help him scare Satan away by painting his sermons, Sybil agrees. Because the words of the evangelical preacher scare her (it is Vicky who tells Dr. Wilbur that, both in church and in their appointments, Sybil is "scared about words"), Sybil illustrates the sermons from a "scaffold nine feet above [the preacher,] at an easel covered with drawing paper and spanning the entire width of the church" (*S*, 299). Often during these sermons, Sybil would illustrate and "split"[9] into one of her alters. This "strategy of discourse"—drawing and splitting—allows Sybil to negotiate between unnamed events and their potential meanings.[10] We see here that MPD actually helps Sybil to cope. But MPD, in its plethora of visual figures and many-voiced talk, is ultimately antinarrative, that is, it constitutes an endless return to the site of the mother's domination, but by allowing the mother's social role as savior to overwrite her abusive behavior, it fails to name the mother as perpetrator. For Sybil, all that is left are feelings and words disconnected from agents or actors.

Psychoanalysis figures victims of MPD as almost always physically, sexually, and psychologically abused before the age of two, that is, before the Lacanian mirror stage, the moment when the child becomes enraptured with its separateness from its mother. While the mirror stage functions as "the origin of the origin,"[11] for the multiple daughter, this origin is nebulous. Thus Anna O.'s famous talking cure cannot aid the victim of MPD, because the multiple daughter cannot retrace trauma done in the presymbolic with discourse.[12] So even though "the drug of choice for multiples seems to be talk—the kind of talk that permits each of the separate traumas to be identified and relived,"[13] the talk produced by a multiple is abject,[14] and therefore the trauma cannot be easily abreacted. Thus, MPD discourse—(presymbolic) talk, not (narrative) naming—is talk whose signifier does not reflect its signified.[15]

Theories of dissociative disorders as described by Judith Herman, Frank Putnam, Ellen Bass, Laura Davis, and others understand MPD as a condition produced by early childhood sexual and physical abuse that splits the core personality into alters, or multiples, who function as distinct, complex personalities and who may or may not be aware of one another.[16] These personalities are both adaptive and defensive, using the only means available to the disempowered: manipulation of the psyche. Judith Herman writes that "traumatic events violate the autonomy of the person at the level of basic bodily integrity. The body is invaded, injured, defiled."[17] It is for this reason that "the traumatic event ... destroys the belief that one can *be oneself* in relation to others."[18] MPD is dissociation to the extreme; triggered by shame and self-loathing, it represents the release of the rage that victims or survivors embody. Those children who were tortured at a very young, preverbal age and who have nowhere else to turn, turn inward. Dr. Wilbur adds psychological abuse ("demeaning, denigrating, or ridiculing infants and children")[19] to the list of MPD-producing traumas. And Margaret Smith features MPD in her book *Ritual Abuse,* stating that the entrapment of ritual abuse almost always results in MPD.[20]

Because of the escape he failed to offer, Willard Dorsett, Sybil's father, served as an accomplice to Hattie's crime. Importantly, though, he also participated in a bedtime ritual that can be defined as incest. Until the age of nine, Sybil slept in a crib in her parent's bedroom and witnessed the "primal scene." In a list of abusive practices headed by the descriptor "How Can I Know If I Was a Victim of Childhood Sexual Abuse," Bass and Davis include "Made to watch sexual acts or look at sexual parts"[21] as an example. Schreiber writes, "Three or four nights a week, year in and year out, parental intercourse took place within her hearing and vision. And not infrequently, the erect penis was easily visible in the half-light" (*S*, 185). It is important to note that neither the narrator nor the psychiatrist nor the patient blames Willard Dorsett for this display. Instead, Vicky tells Dr. Wilbur that "Hattie Dorsett actually wanted her daughter to look," and the doctor concurs (*S*, 186).

Indeed, Willard is not ever made to take responsibility for his behavior and I am left wondering if this omission is not some extension of male privilege, in this case the privilege not to assume responsibility for parenting. This is made especially clear in the confrontation that Dr. Wilbur has with Willard Dorsett. Dr. Wilbur commands Willard to meet her in her office (in spite of his poor health, advanced age, and difficulty traveling), under the pretense of needing more "hard evidence" to legitimate and authorize the experiences of child abuse revealed by Sybil's alters. In the chapter titled "Confrontation and Verification," Dr. Wilbur stages a showdown that successfully emasculates Willard Dorsett, making clear to the reader who really wields the power of the phallus. After Dr. Wilbur feeds Willard memories from the past, his large stature seems to shrink, and the reader is told:

It was an important moment. Like a mollusk, Willard Dorsett had always stayed within his shell, insulated in the private sea of his own concerns. He had been resolute in pursuing a path of conformity, refusing to look in any other direction. Now the mollusk, out of the sea, was steaming in hot water, its shell cracking. (*S*, 271)

And just in case the drama of Dr. Wilbur's castration of Willard Dorsett is not readily apparent, the narrator tells us, "It was a pivotal moment, the kind that the classic Greek dramatists describe as a *peripety*—the moment in which the action of a drama assumes a quick catastrophic new turn, a reversal" (*S*, 273). It is important that Willard is held accountable only for facilitating Hattie's abuse through his absence. Finally, when Dr. Wilbur repeatedly asks Willard why he allowed Hattie to raise Sybil, even when "this schizophrenic mother came very close to killing her child," Willard is reduced to repeating himself like a traumatized child: "It's a mother's place to raise a child," he chants (*S*, 274).

Enforced voyeurism shows up again in Sybil's life when Sybil watches her mother sexually abuse the small children Hattie baby-sat for on Sundays and witnesses Hattie masturbating the adolescent but "lower-crust" lesbians at the beach (*S*, 204–5). And Sybil's medical records indicate more recognizable forms of child abuse: "The dislocated shoulder, the fractured larynx, the burned hand, the bead in the nose, [nearly suffocating in] the wheat crib, the black eyes, the swollen lips" (*S*, 221). Through this "training," Sybil has developed other aftereffects associated with incest: eating disorders (*S*, 42); time and memory lapses (*S*, 47, 57) that eventually convert into MPD (*S*, 96, 98–99, 207); the acting out of a particular scene (as when alter Peggy Lou breaks glass in an effort to escape Hattie's kitchen [*S*, 66] or "the blonde" hurls herself against walls and glass doors in an attempt to escape traumatic blows to the body [*S*, 432]); the deep shame regarding her body and her inability to stay present

(*S,* 70, 151); the inability to feel anger because, even after her death, Hattie won't allow it (*S,* 72, 75); the unexplained neurological disorders, (*S,* 165); the transference of fear from the perpetrator to the objects of abuse (*S,* 222); and the fear of intimacy and people (*S,* 341). Also evident are Sybil's repressed rage at the teachers who never ask, the grandparents who live above the kitchen and never hear, the family physician who knows but never tells, the father who pretends never to notice, and the religion that declares—to quote the title of Alice Miller's book—"Thou shalt not be aware" of parental abuse.

With the whole culture behind her, the abusive mother is entirely unreadable; she becomes visible only when we read her through her daughter's aftereffects, such as MPD.

In *The Flock: The Autobiography of a Multiple Personality,* Joan Casey, the personality recuperated by therapist Lynn Wilson, experiences a childhood similar to Sybil's. Wilson, a social worker with a university clinic, expresses anxiety over her lack of medical credentials and consults Cornelia Wilbur, relying on Dr. Wilbur to guide her through the process of Joan's therapy and integration. The narrative of *The Flock* is held together by this intertextual therapy-driven matriarchy: Cornelia Wilbur "mothers" Lynn Wilson, who "mothers" Joan Casey; Joan reads *Sybil* with an obsession, feels Sybil is an older sister, and encourages Joan to model Dr. Wilbur's therapy/parenting approach. (Dr. Wilbur denies that she ever used a "parenting" approach and insists that the narrator, Flora Schreiber, embellished this role for the purpose of creating a good story.) Joan has twenty-four personalities who differ in age, gender, and sexual orientation. The personalities of Jo (withdrawn, academic, unfeminine), Renee (fun, sexual, personable), Missy (a needy six-year-old), Iris (a lesbian), Joan Frances (suicidal over unrequited mother worship), Rusty (an illiterate, misogynist boy), and Josie (a two-year-old who hurls herself into walls and through glass and, by so doing, constantly relives and performs her mother's physical abuse) function as primary storytellers in Joan Casey's life. Secrets abound in *The Flock*. Just as Sybil "quickly … reassured herself that what she didn't dare tell had not been told" because "she realized she would never be able to tell" (*S*, 43), so, too, Jo tells Lynn, "It's like I'm carrying around this huge secret that I'm never supposed to tell. But since I don't remember just what I'm supposed to keep secret, [I'm afraid] I'll tell it by mistake."[22]

In *The Flock*, Joan is sexually abused by her father. Long before Missy tells Lynn that Joan was raped by her father, and before Josie replays the scene in Lynn's office (and breaks two of Lynn's ribs in the process), Joan's mother, Nancy, pooh-poohs her daughter's weakness, telling her, "Look at me. You don't see me running to a therapist with every little crisis. My stepfather abused me—you've seen the scars on my back from the beatings—and I came through it without a therapist" (*F*, 24). Indeed, Joan Frances replays her mother's words in her therapist's office: "Joan Frances admitted no blankness, no multiplicity, but provided only vague statements about the ideal childhood her mother claimed she had" (*F*, 56). And while Jo has no early childhood memories of her mother and none of Missy's memories of rape, she does remember "happy" early childhood times with her father—playing driver of his car— until his erection intrudes: "Daddy's hardness under her buttocks and the hard steering wheel in her hands were equally part of the experience" (*F*, 77).

In spite of the father—daughter incest, however, Lynn (and eventually, Joan) believes that Joan's mother's physical brutality, followed by emotional coldness toward Joan, before Joan reached the age of two caused the daughter's MPD. The alter Josie remembers this brutality and "desires" the repetition compulsion of blacking out, by beating her head and body on the wall or floor: "One day when [Mother] screamed in rage at her two-year-old daughter, Josie found herself propelled against a wall. Josie, created in that instinctual certainty that she was about to die, remembered her terror and then a wonderful blackness that brought peace" (*F*, 79). So even though the father assumes the role of incest perpetrator in *The Flock*, it is the preverbal mother-abuse that fuels Joan's dissociation.

Joan embodies the abuse of the incestuous parent and the concomitant neglect and betrayal of the other parent. Unlike Sybil, who has no access to her alters when they talk with Dr. Wilbur, Joan hears her alters' therapy sessions with Lynn but does not have access to their behaviors when they take over the body. And so Joan watches Josie relive a rape scene and then turns to Lynn and her husband, Gordon (who becomes a co-therapist of "the flock," the term Joan uses to describe herself), saying, "Josie was raped by her father" (*F*, 157). Rusty, who hates women and is sure he will grow a penis in time to escape the body, emerges when Ray, Joan's father, initiates father—daughter camping trips (*F*, 172). Rusty can't read because his history of abuse includes the "woods game," a chase-and-entrapment abuse in which Ray writes his lust for Joan in the sand with his urine, then forces his daughter, who transmogrifies into the illiterate Rusty, to read it (*F*, 173). The frustration Rusty feels over his inability to perform the task of reading overshadows his fear of abuse. It is important that Rusty is "raped" by words he cannot read, as is evident in his repetition compulsion during therapy with Gordon (whom he calls "Dad"): "The words ... they're everywhere, Dad. The words, Dad. They're gonna cut me. They're gonna kill me" (*F*, 260). Screaming castration anxiety, Rusty turns into Josie, and Gordon watches as Joan relives the feeling of being "cut" open with Ray's penis, the instrument of the words in the sand.

Joan manifests aftereffects that don't make sense to her because the MPD-producing trauma predates the mirror stage, the organizing moment of narrative. But even though Nancy does not perpetrate incest against her daughter, as Hattie does against Sybil, it is Nancy's abuse that "splits" Joan, because Joan feels she cannot afford escape—either physical or emotional—from her mother.

The narrators and the therapists in both *Sybil* and *The Flock* collude against the crazy biological mothers; in the course of therapy, they become surrogate mothers. This is a dangerous move, since all mothers function as potentially abusive when mother love and mother—child abuse define mothering *on any terms* as something that daughters literally, painfully, need. Furthermore, because abuse from the mother often extends "normal" mother—daughter intrusions (such as excessive medication) mother love is simultaneously lethal and necessary. Thus, this alliance of narrator and therapist against the abusive mother in the "battle for the daughter" misreads the role of the therapist in recovery. Narrative positioning aligns the narrator (and audience) with the female therapists who assume the role of the good mother, castigate the abusive mothers as bad mothers, and retain the role of motherhood as unproblematic. This collusion breaks with a fundamental distance necessary, according to Judith Herman, for the empowerment of women in therapy. According to Herman, a feminist therapist should promise to bear witness, work in solidarity with the survivor, empower the survivor by making her responsible for her decisions and for her truth-telling.[23] But once the feminist therapist asks for emotional support from the survivor in the form of devotion and mother love, a dangerous boundary has been transgressed, a line that, as I will show, Lynn Wilson has clearly crossed.

This transgression takes place because of the transference and countertransference that occur in therapy (processes whereby unconscious wishes and needs are swapped between client and therapist), and because, isolated, Lynn as therapist-mother starts to undergo a secondary victimization, taking on Joan's pain, isolation, and secrecy. The problem begins because Lynn feels isolated in her place of work. She makes it clear that her supervisor does not believe in MPD and that she is hence unable to include him in the diagnostic process. Lynn writes, "The lack of support I feel among my colleagues makes me unwilling to talk with them about this case.... I have been taking my own uncertainty and excitement home" (*F*, 29). Lynn here manifests a particularly dangerous countertransference: she imagines herself indispensable, the all-loving mother who alone knows what Joan needs and who stands with her multiple patient against the world. This countertransference makes Lynn take on the role of rescuer when Joan needs to learn how to help herself. Judith Herman refers to just such a therapist—patient relationship when she describes a therapist who

> come[s] to feel that she is the only one who really understands the patient, and she may become arrogant and adversarial with skeptical colleagues. As she feels increasingly isolated and helpless, the temptations of either grandiose action or flight become irresistible. Sooner or later she will indeed make serious errors. It cannot be reiterated too often: *no one can face trauma alone.* If a therapist finds herself isolated in her professional practice, she should discontinue working with traumatized patients until she has secured an adequate support system.[24]

Perhaps because *The Flock* is narrated through the journals that Lynn Wilson and Joan Casey kept throughout their six years of work together, no "error" of the kind Herman points to is disclosed. But the narrative ends abruptly, with Lynn and Gordon's death in a boating accident. With no (narrative) time to "process" this abandonment, *The Flock* concludes with Joan, energized and alienated in her unresolved grief over her loss of the entire symbolic parental unit. We know, of course, that a crash and possible relapse will probably follow, but *The Flock* ends before such a crash occurs. Our last glimpse of Joan captures her with her husband, her son, and her tenure-track job, none of which inspires great confidence on my part.

The mother-therapist role becomes solidified when the abusive mothers, jealous of the therapists, participate in the therapist—patient relationship with their own transference. When Sybil's and Joan's mothers try to sabotage their daughters' relationships with their therapists, Dr. Wilbur and Lynn Wilson transmogrify into overly protective and threatened mothers themselves. This also functions as a kind of transference, where the crazy mothers' desire to own their daughters is projected onto the therapists themselves, who unwittingly become the characters they oppose. It is here that the therapists threaten to become "phallic mothers,"[25] as the fantasy of the phallic mother is to be everything for the child. While Dr. Wilbur shows more restraint, Lynn Wilson becomes energized and excited by her role as a surrogate mother for Joan, as is evident when she speculates in her journal:

> Gordon's and my success so far is beyond my wildest dreams. We are not only providing what the various personalities need at various times; we are also modeling good parenting and a healthy marriage for all of them. Jo and Missy both watch me carefully to see how I'll respond to their enjoyment of Gordon. Unlike her mother, I'm not envious of the relationship they have. In some respects, the mother role is not a new transition, just one newly recognized. I've known for two years of cuddling Missy and the other very young personalities that I was providing healthy maternal love. Although Renee would never accept hearing this, I mother her as well, using what I learned when my own daughters were teenagers. Like any wise mother of a teenager, I allow Renee to depend on my counsel without ever drawing attention to the fact of her dependency. Mothering Jo is a joy, if for no

other reason than her beginning to realize that, even within her own limited personality, she is a lovely young woman whom I am proud to call my daughter. (*F,* 166).

By becoming a mother again, Lynn can avoid her own empty-nest syndrome.[26] Lynn steps into the role of motherhood without recognizing that this same social role aided and abetted Joan's trauma. Playing out the good daughter role she knows so well, Joan accepts these new parents, referring to Lynn and Gordon as her "therapist-parents" (*F,* 207). Lynn thinks of the postintegration Joan with the same "marvel [she] felt in seeing [her] first grandchild" (*F,* 288). And while Cornelia Wilbur is differently maternal (she smokes during therapy sessions and promises the Peggys a sleeve from her full length mink coat when they integrate with Sybil), in her "exorcism" of Hattie Dorsett she also positions herself as the protective mother replacement:

> "I'm helping you to grow up," the doctor would [say]. "You're getting better, and you're going to be able to use all your talents." The incantation, the exorcising of Hattie Dorsett would proceed: "Your mother taught you not to believe in yourself. I'm going to help you do so." (*S,* 358)

And here we see the ultimate danger for the feminist therapist who colludes with the patriarchal idealization of motherhood: pitting women against each other in a duel that allows the good mother to assume the very same role that constituted the evil mother and fed her sadism. Indeed, it is the *role* of motherhood that conceals and therefore conditions this abuse.

By not confronting the category of motherhood and by identifying only the individuals who occupy social spaces as the agents of transgression, both texts assume as neutral and natural that Hattie and Nancy were simply evil anomalies of motherhood. When Joan attempts a confrontation with her mother, through Joan's selected omission we see how she still feels trapped by her mother's expectation that she will not "remember" her mother's abuse. After telling Nancy that Ray molested and raped her and then "steeling [herself] for [Nancy's] angry denial," Joan is amazed when her mother says, "It makes sense" and "I didn't know" and "Your father always had sexual problems" (*F*, 293–94).

It is important that Joan doesn't ask Nancy to take responsibility for *her* abusive behavior. Both Dr. Wilbur and Joan advance misdirected confrontations that serve to protect the mother roles that the therapists have now assumed. Remember that when Dr. Wilbur confronts Willard, Sybil isn't even in the room to hear and see herself vindicated. In Joan's case, she doesn't confront Nancy with the issue she has spent most of her therapy dollars addressing: the physical and verbal abuse Nancy hurled at her daughter, beginning at birth, when Joan was not the boy her mother wanted, and continuing throughout Joan's adulthood until Lynn "saves" her.

These misdirected confrontations echo the problems raised by replacing the evil mothers with the good mother-therapists. Confronting the role of motherhood threatens to destroy the power of the mother—daughter relationship that Joan and Sybil have with their therapists. Thus, Joan and Sybil both become their therapists "more-than-daughters,"[27] their narratives tying together incestuously. Mothers may die, but daughters may never be autonomous, self-generating women. Significantly, these feminist therapists do not question the role of motherhood, because to do so would threaten their place vis-à-vis their new daughters. Indeed, the signal aftereffect of mother—daughter incest after MPD is the very symbiotic dynamic that sets up the potential abuse: the utter impossibility of maintaining boundaries between mother and daughter. Bass and Davis quote one survivor of mother—daughter incest on this point:

For a while I didn't know where my mother left off and I began. I thought she had a psychic hold on me. I was convinced she knew every thought I had. It was like she was in my body, and she was evil. I felt I was possessed, that I was going to be taken over. I've had a real fear that if I look at all that stuff that I don't like about myself, it will be my mother inside of me.[28]

Women's true crime novels that feature MPD daughters also feature a war of the mothers. The Gothic element of this war is made manifest when daughters never connect the abuser with the social role that sustains, tolerates, and camouflages that abuse.

Because heterosexism foundationalizes the theories that describe cultural practices,[29] mother—daughter abuse remains unnarrativizable. Father-daughter incest is almost always portrayed as an act of sexual seduction and therefore is "normalized" as an obvious extension of heterosexual practice. But abusive mothers are doubly veiled: first, by the power they wield—most often denied in heteropatriarchy—and second, by a culture blinded by the stereotype of mother love. While *Sybil* and *The Flock* describe this unnarrativizable power, they do not expose the abusive mother per se; they reveil her as evil in comparison to the nurturing feminist psychotherapist, who emerges at the novel's end as the good mother. What get lost in this war of the mothers are the voices of the multiple daughters, who always speak from some mother's abyss. In both the genre of women's true crime and the discourse of the contemporary feminist recovery movement, evil mothers assume the position of an *individual's* problem, not a social one. Because dissociation offers an important and heretofore unexamined entrance into subject construction,[30] psychoanalytic feminist theory would do well to position daughters outside the mother's script and to read the potential abusive power inherent in the universal role of motherhood, instead of concealing this power in the romanticized social stereotype that refuses to name the open secret of mother—daughter bond(age).

CHAPTER FIVE

Desiring Daughters, Seductive Sisters
Incested Agency

Truth is nothing other than that which knowledge can apprehend as knowledge only by setting its ignorance to work.

—Jacques Lacan, *Écrits*

As I have suggested throughout *The Politics of Survivorship*, feminist theory needs a working relationship with psychoanalysis in order to forge a politics of liberation, not merely equality. Antipsychoanalytic branches of feminist theory empty the ideological from the psychological, running in fear and terror from the unconscious, thus "confirming the claims by psychoanalytic critics that the unconscious threatens the stability of the supposedly conscious, rational self."[1] I argue that we need a radical politics of the unconscious to understand from a feminist perspective the vexing issue of sexual desire that can emerge in incest. This chapter addresses the most taboo issue within survivor politics and theory: how to account for the desiring daughter and the seductive sister.

Desire

Desire within psychoanalysis does not translate as "want," "need," or "demand." As Jean Laplanche and Jean-Bertrand Pontalis have noted, Lacan understands desire as that which bridges need (a wish for satisfaction by or through a consciously understood object) and demand (the articulation of a conscious need to a hearing audience or subject). While need depends on satisfaction, and demand necessitates a comprehending subject, desire relies on alienation from both the object of desire and its/her recognition.[2]

According to Juliet Mitchell's introduction to *Feminine Sexuality: Jacques Lacan and the École freudienne*, we formulate our object of desire only when we can depend on its denial:

> Lacan states that desire itself, and with it, sexual desire, can only exist by virtue of its alienation. Freud describes how the baby can be observed to hallucinate the milk that has been withdrawn from it and the infant to play throwing-away games to overcome the trauma of its mother's necessary departures. Lacan uses these instances to show that the object that is longed for only comes into existence *as an object* when it is lost to the baby or infant.[3]

Thus, the object of desire is not satisfaction:

> The baby's need can be met, its demand responded to, but its desire only exists because of the initial failure of satisfaction. Desire persists as an effect of a primordial absence and it therefore indicates that, in this area, there is something fundamentally impossible about satisfaction itself. It is this process that, to Lacan, lies behind Freud's statement that 'We must reckon with the possibility that something in the nature of the sexual instinct itself is unfavourable to the realisation of complete satisfaction.'[4]

Desire is an unconscious state of waiting and withholding, not a conscious wish for satiation, fulfillment, completion, or closure. To fulfill a desire is to render it either pleasure or horror. The controversial issue of a child's unconscious sexual desire for her parents, which Freud outlined in the *Three Essays on the Theory of Sexuality* (1905), need not be confused with wants or demands.

Desire constitutes the subject and thus should not be acted on, acted out, or made material; it just need be. Jacqueline Rose, in her introduction to Lacan's *Feminine Sexuality*, says this: "Desire functions much as the zero unit in the numerical chain—its place is both constitutive *and* empty."[5] Indeed, because conscious desire almost invariably involves repression of unconscious desire, to have one's unconscious desire met is an act of trauma and crisis. Desire is performed in fantasy, not flesh:

> Fantasy ... is not the object of desire, but its setting. In fantasy the subject does not pursue the object or its sign: he appears caught up himself in the sequence of images. He forms not representation of the desired object, but is himself represented as participating in the scene.[6]

Desire within fantasy is the full and uncompromising love of the invented self. It is a celebration of the subject's vast potential. Indeed, some psychologists believe that symbolic play, the nexus of symbolism, fantasy, and scene and character creation, marks children on the slippery continuum of "normal."[7] What happens, then, when a parent transgresses in a child's sexual fantasy? A seductive daughter may desire her father, but she does not "want it." And here is the feminist punch: because the unconscious cannot say no, incest, *especially* when desired by the child, cannot be confused with consent. The desiring daughter is not the consenting daughter. Children have the right to sexual fantasies—and to nonsexual boundaries with the imagined objects of desire.

Desire is perverted by those feminists who fail to understand it psychoanalytically. A more egregious extension of the perversion of desire can be found in the 1980 creation of the category "positive incest": positive, apparently, because "the rate of incidence is so high as to make prohibition absurd."[8] In 1980, John Money of Johns Hopkins University declared, "A childhood sexual experience, such as being the partner of a relative or of an older person, need not necessarily affect the child adversely."[9] The coauthor of the original Kinsey Report stated, "It is time to admit that incest need not be a perversion or a symptom of mental illness," because "incest between ... children and adults ... can sometimes be beneficial." Dr. Larry Constantine, assistant clinical professor in psychiatry at Tufts, announced, "Children have the right to express themselves sexually, even with members of their own family," while another researcher posed, "Who knows whether one result [of nonincestuous relationships] may not be the present rash of feverish adolescent sexual activity with its undeniable results?"[10] And while one advocate of positive incest hangs teenage promiscuity on the incest taboo, another sees incest as an appropriate, albeit compensatory, "love": "How many adolescent girls have not said, 'It's the only time I feel someone really loves me'?"[11] Finally, the "pro-incest lobby" (as they call themselves) condemns only incest that takes place in the "lower" classes: "Incest ... is more likely to be negative in the lower classes, where the alleged offender simply has not the requisite training in the refinements of rape."[12] Their adamant classism makes me wonder if positive incest isn't more appropriately called "familial entitlement."

Nevertheless, preserving the daughter's fantasy of desire in no way conditions the parents' decision to abuse.

Seductive Sisters

Feminist postmodernisms refigure the discourse of family dynamics, and one of the narratives that feminist postmodernisms have been most interested in challenging is that of

Freudian psychoanalysis, especially its construct of the nuclear/patriarchal family. Sibling relationships within feminist postmodernity often function as an anti-oedipal narrative. By recasting the nuclear family to expose it as a social construction, rather than a natural unit, feminist postmodernity reveals that siblings not only can transgress the Law of the Father, they can rewrite it. Katherine Dunn's *Geek Love* (1988) offers the most startling example of siblings who revise through embodiment the definition of "family". *Geek Love* does not offer a feminist haven to postmodern literature; rather, it undresses the pro-incest lobby belief in the healthy interrogative function of sibling incest. The nakedness revealed in *Geek Love* is as hard on the eyes as the Binewski family portrayed in this novel.

Geek Love is a novel about the nuclear family constructed, in a very literal sense, by Aloysius (Al) Binewski and Lillian (Lily) Hinchcliff Binewski for the propagation of their occupation: performance in a traveling carnival show called Binewski's Carnival Fabulon. Narrated by Olympia Binewski (Oly), the only surviving "geek," we learn that the Binewski's used Lily's drug addictions to "breed ... [their] own freak show."[13] If the child born from a reproductive experiment is gruesome, Al and Lily keep him or her for the Fabulon and instill in the child a deep respect for its individuality and uniqueness. If a child is born a "norm," they leave him or her in a shopping mall for other "norms" to take in. Their unsuccessful experiments float in formaldehyde in jars; most are fetuses, except one: the lizard girl, whom eldest son Arturo (Arty) murders because he feared she would make more money than him.

Arturo the Aqua Boy, whose ego drives the plot forward, has flippers for hands and feet that "sprouted directly from his torso without intervening hands and legs" (*GL*, 8). As a child, he performs nude in a tank of water; as an adolescent, he reads poetry and philosophy to huge audiences, who marvel at his simultaneous hideousness and beauty; as a young adult, he tells fortunes and eventually makes "callings." Oly, the narrator of *Geek Love* and Arty's sister-wife, reports that "without any of the family taking much notice, Arty became a church.... It wasn't that Arty *got* a church, or created a religion, or even found one. In some peculiar way Arty had always been a church just as an egg is a chicken and an acorn an oak" (*GL*, 114). Arty's callings turn into an institution called Arturism; his thousands of followers in Arturism become members (called "The Admitted") when they pledge their worldly savings and, eventually, their arms and legs. Arturism demands purity, which depends on each follower's intentional and consensual dismemberment.

Arty's sisters closest to him in age, Electra (Elly) and Iphigenia (Iphy), are Siamese twins "with perfect upper bodies joined at the waist and sharing one set of hips and legs" (*GL*, 8). Always "beautiful, slim, huge-eyed," the twins are musical prodigies whose piano duets for four hands "revolutionized the twelve-tone scale" (8). When their piano performances start to outsell Arty's callings, Arty sets out to destroy them. He "gives" the twins in marriage to Vern Bogner, alias "The Bag Man," one of the Admitted who five years earlier had tried to assassinate the Binewski family in a shopping-mall parking lot. On the bogus wedding night, in a Frankensteinian gesture, Lily emerges from her drug fog, realizing that the Bag Man was their attempted assassin. She rushes into the twins' trailer with a loaded gun and shoots the Bag Man as he rapes her daughters. He comes as he dies. The Bag Man impregnates the twins, an event that puts an end to their career. The twins try to abort the child, but Doc P denies them this, saying, "I have a contract with your Arturo, and young Arturo does not wish it. He is looking forward to being an uncle. It's not for me to deny Arturo this pleasure. And it's not for you to defy him" (*GL*, 259). It is Elly and Iphy's attempted escape to an abortion clinic that lands Elly with a botched lobotomy from Doc P's surgical knife (267-68). Mumpo, the twins' boy-child, weighs twenty-six pounds at birth and, once delivered, starts "eating the twins" alive (309).

Oly is a bald albino hunchback whose skills as an elocution-ist prove no threat to Arty's ego, and who, like the youngest child—a blond, blue-eyed boy named Fortunato and nick-named "Chick," who looks like a "norm" but is telekinetic—fears, obeys, and worships Arty. Arty "employed" them both—Oly as his personal maid and masseuse, and Chick as his Arturism surgeon (at first with Doc P and eventually, after Arty punishes Doc P by having her dismembered, unassisted). Chick contains each patient's pain in his own body with his telekinetic gift so that anesthesia is unnecessary. Just as Arty gives the twins to the Bag Man, he gives Chick to Doc P. But he keeps Oly, who births his daughter, solely for himself. Truly a self-made man, Arty becomes the Law of the Father by possessing—both symboli-cally and literally—all of his siblings.

Arty thus usurps from Al the Law of the Father. This Law is a powerful ruse; like the phallus, it functions in name only. As Jane Gallop makes clear in *The Daughter's Seduction*, "It is only the law—and not the body—which constitutes [the father] as patriarch."[14] Arty embodies the Law, stealing it (not inheriting it) from Al. It is important to note that the castration complex is supposed to prevent the son from stealing the Father's Law. But already dismembered, Arty perceives himself as castrated. (Chick tells Oly that "[Arty's] afraid his juice isn't good. He's afraid he can't plant babies" [*GL*, 306]). At first, Arty wields his law by killing Leona the Lizard Girl, by attempting to murder Chick, and by threatening Oly with institutionalization (*GL*, 75-76). And finally, Arty "kills" the patriarch who precedes him: Al "dies" through the only means available to kill the father—through language. Arty tells Oly that he schemes against the family, that he blew Al and Chick's cover in a gambling casino,

a trick that almost ended in literal murder and family separation. Oly responds within the Law of the Father: "Taking money
was against the family; scaring Papa was against the family" (*GL,*
102). Arty just closes his eyes in response, and Oly knows that an
era has come to an end. She says, "I felt robbed. My champion
was revealed as a scam and I was embarrassed at all the years I'd
let myself feel that Papa was any protection at all" (102). The
phallus becomes penis, shrivels, and dies. Al dies without ever
feeling a thing, and Arty assumes the Law, a power that he
wields over his sisters to accomplish what Luce Irigaray refers to
in *Speculum of the Other Woman* when she states, "The seduction
fantasy is really about seducing the daughter to not read her
own text, [and] instead to obey the Law of the Father."[15]

Arty cinches his place as dispenser of the Law by replacing Al
in his only remaining job—as the Fabulon's quack doctor—
with Doc P (short for Phyllis), a paranoid schizophrenic who, in
college, performed stomach surgery on herself because she felt
her body was becoming invaded. Doc P has no credentials and
no history (*GL,* 123-24). The presence of Doc P proves Arty's
law because through his Law, Doc P becomes credentialed,
authorized, and powerful. Most important, through Arty's pos-
session of the Law, Doc P aids Arty in replacing Al. And Al
knows it: "[Al] wasn't working for himself anymore. He was
working for Arty. Everything revolved around Arty, from our
routes and sites to the syrup flavors in the soda fountains" (145).

While it is Al's symbolic passing that permits Arty's ascension
into the Law, it is Alma Witherspoon who authorizes Arty's law
by turning Arty into a man. Significantly, she does this by naming him, not by fucking him. At one of Arty's sermons, she says
what no one has said before: "I want to be like *you*" (*GL,* 178).
Arturism is born in these words, and Alma Witherspoon is the
first member of the Admitted, the first patient of Doc P and
Chick. Oly narrates: "That's the way it began. It was Alma "Pen

Pal" Witherspoon who actually founded what came to be known as 'Arturism' or the 'Arturan Cult.' ... She originated the Concept "Artier than Thou." ... Soon there were enough of the 'Admitted' to give Alma a full-time staff" (*GL*, 184). Alma's words "I want to be like you" institutionalize Arty's church and law. Because of Alma, the Aqua Boy becomes "Aqua Man" (183).

The Law overturns public knowledge and common beliefs, as evidenced by Norval Sanderson, the reporter who is supposed to expose Arty for the fake healer that he is but instead becomes part of the cult (*GL*, 191), and by Vern Bogner, the attempted assassin turned loyal follower. It is important to recognize that Arty preaches the values and ethics of Arturism but doesn't believe what he says:

> [Alma Witherspoon] set up Arturism like a traveling fat farm for nuns. Though she herself had lucked onto Arty while flat broke, all who came after paid what she called a "dowry." Arty said, in private, that the scumbags were required to fork over everything they had in the world, and, if it wasn't enough, they could go home and get their ears pierced or their peckers circumcised and see what that did for them. (*GL*, 185)

The Law translates into the power to *not* believe. While the daughter is made outcast for reading, for naming the proverbial elephant in the living room, the Law protects the patriarch from sacrificing his subjectivity to the ruse.

Norval Sanderson exemplifies the Law's power to overturn "evidence" by embodying and appropriating this evidence for its own purpose. In a newspaper story Norval writes, "Arturism was founded ... on the greed and spite of a transcendental maggot named Arturo Binewski, who used his own genetic defects on the weakness of the unemployed and illiterate to create an insanely self-destructive following that fed his maniacal ego" (*GL*, 189). After Arty laughs at this publicity and uses it in his sermons, Norval chops off a few fingers, claims he had a Ku

Klux Klan veterinarian cut off his balls for Arty (*GL*, 199), and takes charge of the Transcendental Maggot Booth: "The notion was simple and surprisingly popular. Sanderson collected amputated parts from Dr. Phyllis and cut them into small chunks, one chunk in each half-pint jar. His maggot farm was reliable and easy.... Whatever his intentions, Sanderson was with us to stay" (*GL*, 200). This transformation is not to be misunderstood as a change of heart; Norval changes by ideological interpellation.

Incest is the linchpin of the Law, and Arty appropriates this rite of passage too. As Claude Lévi-Strauss states, "The prohibition of incest is less a rule prohibiting marriage with the mother, sister, or daughter, than a rule obliging the mother, sister, or daughter to be given to others. It is the supreme rule of the gift."[16] After Elly tells Arty, "You don't run us" (*GL*, 243), he proves that he does control her—by "giving" the twins away. Oly says to Arty, "The Bag Man says you gave him the twins," and Arty responds, "Just to fuck" (*GL*, 245). Arty then reveals his patriarchal obligation to "traffic" women,[17] when he says to Oly, "You bleeding yet? You need a boyfriend? I don't want you running me through this same grinder, you know" (*GL*, 246). The "grinder" is Arty's projected desire to be the Law; Arty invented this grinder for himself, for he is a self-made, postmodern patriarch. Arty says this of himself: "I'm just an industrial accident! But I made it into something—me! I have to work and think to do it. And don't forget, I was the first keeper. I'm the oldest, the son.... This whole show is mine, the whole family [is mine]" (*GL*, 103).

Oly's response to Arty's attention reveals her interpellation into Arty's law: "I could feel the hot pleasure pumping into my face and couldn't keep myself from grinning back at him" (*GL*, 246). And just as Alma Witherspoon names Arty a man, so Oly names him her patriarch, her keeper, her husband-in-desire: "I'm your girl, Arty," Oly declares, "even with the warts on your ass" (*GL*, 246). With these words, Oly steps into the incest taboo, which, in cultural, psychoanalytic, and political permutations, shows that the patriarch need not seduce the daughter. Instead, he imputes his desire onto her: good daughters obey their fathers/brothers; good daughters anticipate and fulfill their father's/brother's needs; good daughters seduce their fathers/brothers so that the latter don't have to be the agents of transgression.

But Oly's role in the incest taboo complicates feminist articulations of family violence and sexual abuse. Oly contracts with Chick to steal Arty's sperm and inseminate her with it (*GL*, 297). Whether this act represents Arty incesting Oly (because the experience of sixteen years of obeying this tyrannical brother forces her to anticipate—even inaccurately—his needs) or Oly incesting Arty (because she knows what she asks for and gets it without Arty's knowledge or consent) is hard to know. Oly's agency and desire are displaced, and once they are reinscribed, it is hard to know who is molesting whom. Even if I read Oly's behavior as an aftereffect of sixteen years of verbal abuse, and therefore as an extension of Arty's power and desire, Oly's proactive form of resistance disempowers *him* and inscribes *him* as incest victim/survivor, as he is forced to know, as incest survivors do, that his body is permeable, vulnerable, and transgressive without his consent.

Arty's role in sibling incest is steeped in values ascribed to antipsychoanalytic thought, and Oly's intervention/transgression exemplifies a psychoanalytic critique. Arty perceives himself to be autonomous and transcendent. He is certain of his boundaries, and he feels authoritative and unified. He perceives the Fabulon as a totality, a self-contained system; he values his physical deformity as a universalized attribute; his life is centered and linear; he has both closure and hierarchy in his personal vision; his identity relies on homogeneity, uniqueness, and origin. And when Oly steals Arty's sperm, she interrogates each of these characteristics and forces Arty to do the same. But if she is the psychoanalytic critique to Arty's stodgy materialism, she too is changed through the process:

> My focus on Arty was an ailment, noncommunicable, and, even to me all these years later, incomprehensible. Now I despise myself. But even so I remember, in hot floods, the way he slept, still as death, with his face washed flat, stony as a carved tomb and exquisite. His weakness and his ravening bitter needs were terrible, and beautiful, and irresistible as an earthquake. He scalded and smothered anyone he needed, but his needing and the hurt that it caused me were the most life I ever had. (*GL*, 315)

Arty molests his other siblings in emotional and symbolic ways. And it is Chick's internalized guilt for not being good enough (a classic aftereffect of abuse) that causes the literal explosion, the fire, and the end of the Fabulon. Elly murders Mumpo, and Chick feels responsible because it is his job to contain pain. But under Arty's rule, the pain is too diffuse to hold. Chick's last word, "Arty," becomes a testimonial to what happens next:

> The flames spouted outward from [Chick]—pale as light—bursting outward from his belly. He did not scream or move but he spread, and my world exploded with him, and I, watching ... [my] roses—Arty and Al and Chick and the twins—gone dustward as the coals rid themselves of that terrible heat. (*GL*, 318, 319)

Chick blames Arty for the first time in his life, and he "blows." Death by fire leaves no room for the recuperation of monological history. But because of the ashes and bodies, fire also won't allow for the erasure of the past. Instead, the postmodern present emerges at the end of the Fabulon, an end that finds history useful for the dialogue it creates with the present. (A dialogue that is often prohibited in incest families, since keeping secrets is sacred.)

The shocking array of disfigurements—both in body and culture—expose how Arty's rise to power is not an "innocent" fact of nature, and therefore that there is nothing innocent about the frame of reference we call "nature." Arty does not assume the Law through the reality principle. (Under Freudian psychoanalysis the boy-child becomes oedipalized properly when the reality principle allows him to *become* the Law). Rather, Arty ravages his nuclear family for the Law. He usurps his father's role and then "rapes" his siblings in a variety of guises. When we understand the brother's power over his sisters as natural (including the power to "protect" his sisters from other men), we have fallen prey to the complex ideologies of patriarchy, which represent male power as natural because it is institutionalized. Arty uses—and is used by—the incest taboo in a way that returns patriarchal power to culture; and by privileging culture over nature, *Geek Love* lifts the veil from the romanticization of sibling incest. The end of the Fabulon portrays one "answer" to sibling incest: the scapegoat blows and the house comes tumbling down.

Desiring Daughters

In *Thereafter Johnnie* we see a protagonist gripped not by demand, as is Oly, but by desire. *Thereafter Johnnie*, like *Geek Love*, features a child born of incest. But while the agent of incest narrates *Geek Love*, it is the product of incest who narrates *Thereafter Johnnie*. Johnnie, the daughter of incest—the daughter of a daughter who sexually desired her father—is mute until the age of fourteen. When she is seventeen, her mother commits suicide and her mother's lesbian lover, Diotima, leaves Johnnie to care for herself. Johnnie traces her history and connects her birth by incest to slavery. Her life is testimony to the text's overdetermined message: the fulfillment of desire *is* slavery.

Thereafter Johnnie is the most highly eroticized incest narrative I have read to date. An autobiographical novel written by an

African-American, lesbian, feminist English professor, Carolivia Herron, *Thereafter Johnnie*'s feminist message relies on psycho-analytic readings of desire. Johnnie traces her own history in order to live and to speak. In the process, she gives to readers what Patricia, her mother, never had: a narrative that explains the motivations behind Patricia's insatiable sexual demand for her father. We learn that John Christopher Snowdon, an affluent African-American heart surgeon, loves his wife, Camille, and lords over his three daughters, Eva, Cynthia Jane (called "Janie"), and Patricia (called "patPat," her "father's heart beat").

During Hurricane Carol (Herron's real first name is Carol; she combined it with her middle name, Olivia, to arrive at Car-olivia),[18] John Christopher rapes Patricia with his finger. She experiences her first orgasm with pain and fury and stiffens into an *X*, catatonic, her hand frozen to a window. Her mother, Camille, finds her two-year-old catatonic and literally frozen in the pain of escape. She wants to take Patricia to the emergency room, but John Christopher won't have it. (It is important that his name is initialed "JC"; as father, husband, and doctor, John Christopher is the Jesus Christ of the family's world.) Patricia emerges from this coma filled with insatiable sexual passion for her family. In learning the family history, Johnnie collects Camille's, Eva's, and Janie's perspectives on Patricia's lifelong effort to seduce her father sexually.

John Christopher and Patricia never interpret their lives; they merely perform them. Patricia is trapped in the repetition compulsion of sexual desire. Each time her father sates her desire, desire turns to horror and reemerges in a form stronger and more manic than before. It is the other family members who provide or act as interpretations. Camille, the jilted wife, learns that her husband raped her daughter, and to Johnnie she later says, "And it has been my fate to live long enough to know this and not die."[19] Eva was violently—and symbolically—stranger-raped, the same night that John Christopher raped Patricia. Eva serves as patPat's memory trace and, in having survived the experience of a public rape, offers through her own experience a displaced version of patPat's private abuse. Janie demonizes Patricia for her moral depravity. She becomes a nun and voluntarily manifests Johnnie's primary involuntary aftereffect: Janie takes a vow of silence and never speaks again.

When John Christopher learns that the seventeen-year-old patPat is pregnant with his child, he comes to her room with the medical equipment necessary to perform an abortion. She chases him out with a butcher knife. He then banishes her from their home, sets her up in an apartment in Georgetown (explaining that if she appeared too close to his medical practice, she would be bad for his business), and sends her money for food and clothing. She lives as a kept woman. Patricia's lesbian lover, Diotima, tries to convince her to move out from under her father's control, and although they do move into a house together, Diotima can never save or change patPat.

Johnnie, the daughter of patPat and John Christopher, is mute for fourteen years. When she learns she has a father, she speaks. Seventeen years after Johnnie's birth—a perfect symmetry with patPat's age when Johnnie was conceived—on John Christopher's birthday, patPat walks into the Potomac River and drowns. Diotima leaves, and Johnnie is left to trace her history.

Whereas Oly, an elocutionist, makes her profession by the strength of her voice, Johnnie is made mute by witnessing her "grandfatherfather" have sex with her mother: "He is the father who takes my voice. He has his will with my mother, and I, Johnnie, am compelled to see it, to know it.... I am the mute infant propped on pillows on the other bed" (*TJ*, 14). Johnnie does not lose her voice; her grandfatherfather takes it from her:

"Gently the merciless father who takes my voice pulls together the lips of my mother's sex, his daughter, I see it clearly I will not forget what I clearly see" (*TJ*, 15). It is important to note that even though incest is eroticized in *Thereafter Johnnie*, Johnnie, who "inherited" aftereffects of incest, describes John Christopher as "merciless" and as the agent of transgression.

John Christopher uses sex as a punishment for separation. "Salvation," for John Christopher, comes to those who don't allow children to separate from parents. He muses to himself:

> You discovered that you feared something about them and you wanted power over them, you felt the terrifying warning of that power in the fire that stirred upon you thigh. You were in hell.... You could not escape because you desired them, you wanted to be with them, you wanted them to include you. You could not bear to see them dancing there without you apart from you, they were not thinking of you, John Christopher, you had no part in them although you are their father, it wrenched you to see them free of you and you had an uncanny fear for your life. They were daimonic. Separate. You could not bear it. (*TJ*, 50-51)

John Christopher longs for salvation, which he feels he can attain only by advancing "power over" his daughters. This power made itself known in sexual desire ("the fire that stirred upon your thigh"). His desire was to be included in their circle, but their circle was sealed ("you could not escape because you desired them, you wanted to be with them, you wanted them to include you"). Desire turned into anger when he realized that "they were not thinking of you, John Christopher." His role as father-husband-doctor (a holy Trinity of sorts) was shattered when he realized that he "had no part in them although ... their father." The fact of this separation felt life-threatening: "You had an uncanny fear for your life." It cannot be his fault, for he is all-powerful, so "they were daimonic. Separate."

John Christopher interrupts the girls' circle, which has turned into a poetry reading. He lectures them on the rational limits of poetry, then forces them to watch him perform open-heart surgery on a stray female dog so that he can prove to them the frailties of the body. Again he muses:

> See the dog running alive. And come down again tomorrow when I will cut her heart out before your eyes.... Stray bitch. She is in my hands now. I will cut out her heart and strip it—I have to strip the heart and the pericardium in order to keep her body from rejecting her own heart. She won't even recognize her own heart when I am finished.... Come and see. Watch.... I am the truth. (*TJ*, 57-58)

It is a war of the wills. John Christopher declares the body stronger than the mind. He says, "A drowning person who is trying to commit suicide struggles to inhale no matter what she believes about life" (*TJ*, 57). And yet patPat commits suicide by drowning precisely because of her strength of mind over body. While John Christopher can command the dog to accept the heart he stole from her, he cannot teach his daughter the same lesson. He may win over the dog, but he loses the daughter.

Sister Cynthia Jane, before taking a vow of silence, interprets this scene differently for Johnnie, who has come to the convent after her mother's death looking for her history. Sister Cynthia Jane explains that John Christopher

> feared somehow that all three of us were lesbians.... He thought we would be cured by coming down to the hospital and watching him perform open heart surgery on a dog. He tried to show himself as king and god.... Patricia was very much affected.... And when she held the dog's heart in her hands she called it the multifoliate rose. Dad didn't take Patricia's interest in him seriously, it seemed to me, until after the surgery on the dog. (*TJ*, 190)

Cynthia Jane makes errors of interpretation similar to those of John Christopher: her father had good reason to suspect at least one of the girls was lesbian, for indeed, patPat *is*. In addition, we know from the narratives of Eva and Camille that Patricia was a severely depressed child and adolescent. Cynthia Jane's narrative, like John Christopher's rationalization, is littered with denial.

In a chapter titled "The First Time," Herron presents us with the seduction of rape:

> She has never expected this. She has not imagined that something could happen. She struggles to push him away, kicks and twists from under him wrestling his arms from around her body, she turns him away from her and she means it. He knows that she intends truly to push him away and he doesn't fight for her but lies surprised on his back with her holding his shoulders away from her. And she almost rejects him entirely right then except she oddly changes her mind as a strangeness begins its slow circles within her and she opens herself up to him. (*TJ*, 118-19)

Once John Christopher enters her, Patricia's desire turns to horror because "he is no longer her god, nor her king, nor her lover, nor her father, but he is an erected penis urging itself into a female hole" (*D*, 120). Once she is fully in the presence of her horror, of desire sated into crime, she is transported psychologically to a different place, a different rape—the first one: "Shaking and trembling and no one to hold her as she shakes and trembles in her first orgasm, not this time but the first time, the first time, hidden, forgotten, violated by a touch of her father's fingers upon her two-year-old clitoris" (*D*, 120).

Finally, aftereffects from the first molestation shadow the "real" present time: "Whispering the words she had no words for in the beginning, during the first time, as he sleeps fifteen years later her body stiffens into a catatonic X of horror, violation violently enforced pleasure and pain" (*TJ*, 121). Again, rape. Again, isolation. No one to bear witness. No one to know, not even her conscious mind. Desire thus becomes demonic.

In Camille's letter to Johnnie, Patricia's mother documents from her own perspective the same events:

> I still don't understand how Patricia became the way she was. I knew something was wrong when she was about two years old There was a hurricane in Washington, Hurricane Carol, and it actually knocked the steeple off one of the churches downtown. In the middle of the storm I found her petrified and soaked at the window.... She had been watching the storm blowing the treetops. (*TJ*, 179-80)

This scene points to the expansiveness of patriarchal privilege. Even though Camille knows that John Christopher has raped Patricia and therefore is clearly capable of rape, it is easier for her to think that Patricia was first raped by a hurricane, not by her father-husband.

> Her right hand was frozen to the glass of the window that was raised up above her head. It was so strange—it seemed as if she had been struck by lightning just as she had reached up to pull down the window. She was catatonic.... She was soaked through to the skin. I couldn't bend her arms and legs at all and when I picked her up she went into an X shape and wouldn't come out of it. (*TJ*, 180)

Patricia is raped at two, at the age when children first learn that it is safe to set boundaries between themselves and their parents, that one can say no without impunity. Instead, patPat learns that her body is not her own and reaches for a window, an opening to the outside. (Carolivia said that she herself often found safety outside, for the male relative who raped her as a child never abused her outside when she hid under a lilac bush.)[20] Camille thinks Patricia is trying to shut the window, to close out invasion; instead, Patricia becomes frozen to it. Indeed, the repetition compulsion of her sexual desire for John Christopher becomes a frozen need, patPat with her hand frozen to the symbol of boundary, separation, shelter, vision, and home: "It was after that when she started to show those strange feelings for John Christopher. And yet how could a storm have done that? It's as if she had been raped by a hurricane" (*TJ*, 180). Why could John Christopher confess to the rape of patPat only when she was a seventeen-year-old, and not when she was a two-year-old?

Camille's letter continues: "He raped her. I discovered he had raped her. That first time. He finally told me.... She fell asleep. He raped her. It was not coercion from Patricia but rape from her father. And it has been my fate to live long enough to know this and not die" (*TJ*, 181-82). But Camille "knew" that even before rape something had always been wrong with Patricia:

> She told me many, many times that she hated the earth, she hated life and wanted no part of it. She told me she wanted to die. It is an awful thing to hear words like that from my own child. When I asked her why she felt that about life she would start talking about herself as if she were a myth, a myth of a falling city, or nation, or world, or god. (*TJ*, 183)

We might understand Patricia's inability to locate the horror in her own body as an aftereffect in itself. This also highlights one way that survivorship is political: as father-husband-doctor-patriarch, John Christopher does indeed get to "win" his will over his daughter. In addition, he gets to win his will over culture, and thus Patricia's desire-turned-horror is not local but global, not (only) personal but deeply political. Camille has only one question for Johnnie: "And Johnnie, are you reliving all these horrors?" (*TJ*, 183).

The erotics of incest are located in Patricia's desire to control her father. Patricia says seducing her father is a way to take the power back: "I like him angry. I enjoy the heat that leaps from him when he yells at me, when he breaks against me, screaming and pleading for his life. He has my life too. He has had my life. And I'll have him" (*TJ*, 207). Sated desire traps patPat and John Christopher in a battle of wills and hate and love; John Christopher "wins" because of the social power accorded to him.

All of John Christopher's daughters (all four: Cynthia Jane, Eva, Patricia, and Johnnie) are affected by incest, and all four feel it personally. When Patricia returns from San Juan, she visits Eva, who has been hospitalized after a violent stranger rape. At this meeting Patricia tells Eva that she has "had him." When Eva asks her if this is what she wants, Patricia replies, "What I want? Of course it's what I want, it's a necessity" (*TJ*, 194). Eva responds, "A necessity, Patricia? What did he do to you? What makes it so necessary? Have you thought about what made him do that with you—even though you did want it?" (*TJ*, 194). Pat counters, their eyes meeting for the first time, "Would it have been worse for you if Dad had slept with you instead of me?" Eva responds, "No, Patricia, that wouldn't have been worse, I probably would have enjoyed sleeping with Daddy, but I don't know why" (*TJ*, 194–95).

Eva can love Patricia because she can accept her own sexual desire for her father. At the same time, she locates Patricia's desire (and thus, presumably, her own) in some transgression made by John Christopher, some "almost memory."

In contrast, Cynthia Jane's denied desire leads her to demonize Patricia. Of Patricia, Cynthia Jane says, "I hated her and her lack of self-control and the inverted sickness she accentuated in our miserable lives, our sexually perverse family. I hate her" (*TJ*, 196). In debating who has abused whom, Janie yells at Eva: "Why should Patricia feel justified in destroying the family with her passions? Why doesn't she care enough about us, about you and me, not do it? Look what is happening to us" (*TJ*, 199). Why is it easier for Cynthia Jane to make Patricia responsible for destroying the family? Why is it easier for Eva to make John Christopher responsible? Cynthia Jane continues:

I have no free choices left, none at all. All I can do is try to preserve a fragment of myself, a sanity of fasts and meditations,
which I pit against something else in me.... Oh Eva, do you think
there is no vibrancy in me? Do you think Patricia is our father's
only beautiful daughter? (*TJ*, 199-200)

The pain that Cynthia Jane feels is located in herself, not in
the fabric of the family. John Christopher's incestuous attention
to one daughter leads Cynthia Jane to feel unloved, unrecognized, and unimportant. Her sanity—that is, her psychological
attachment to the myth of her own self-control—is located in
fasts and meditations, not engagement with problems or the
psychic integration of pain. The crowning shame for Cynthia
Jane was when "once he yelled at me, Eva, so I wouldn't go
upstairs anymore when he went up there to see her" (*TJ*, 200).
Banishment by father turns Cynthia Jane against Patricia.

Cynthia Jane wants Patricia's love: "She had no business loving my father. She should have loved you and me" (*TJ*, 201).
Without that love, she is filled with rage, enough rage to make
her choose silence. We know what makes Johnnie mute—witnessing father—daughter incest. But what exactly has Cynthia
Jane seen (or felt or heard) that conditions her to choose
enforced, institutionalized silence and spiritual rigidity?

Acting on desire is the repetition compulsion of slavery. In
the last chapter of *Thereafter Johnnie*, the myth is unveiled:

And from these origins has there come this great curse upon our
house: "the females shall be raped and the males shall be murdered." And the males that are not murdered shall be sold, and
to certain ones of the males that are neither murdered nor sold,
to certain of those few males come late into the house marrying,
and to certain of the males born to the house but who nevertheless survive murder and slavery—to these shall be given the
power of revenge upon the females of their own house who con-
sented with the white males for their destruction, these males

shall be given the female children of their own house, and these shall be raped. And raped again. (*TJ*, 239–40)

Why resolve the erotization of father—daughter incest in the institutionalization of slavery? When violence becomes naturalized—that is, understood as common, ordinary, or even necessary to group cohesion and identity—instead of being abreacted—discharged from the unconscious where it manifests itself as distress, depression, or anxiety, to the conscious mind, where it becomes a recognizable pattern of distress but not a compelling or triggering event—it conditions social patterns of oppression, which constitute all subjects who make up that culture. Since rape under slavery was called "capitalism" and therefore, ostensibly, was not marked as abuse, rape for the society born of slavery—that is to say, our own—is an overdetermined symbol of citizenship and subjectivity.

What exactly is the relationship of the social, the historical, and the psychological? To some, the subject is biologically driven, enslaved by a prefigured set of genes and (therefore) futures; to others, the subject is determined by materialist notions of history and culture. Both extremes render impossible (or unimportant) the role of desire in the ideology of the body and the manifestation of desire in institutions and social practices. The third term that mediates these two extremes is the unconscious. Psychoanalysis's privileging of the unconscious and desire allows for a politically progressive theory of subject construction, by establishing, first, the instability of identity (the "split" or "fragmented" self, produced in the mirror stage),[21] and second, that institutional oppressions are indeed oppressive because of their power to enslave the mind (and body). Finally, it is this third term, the unconscious, that allows us to understand the painful issue of incested agency.

The next chapter explores one mass-mediated response to the institutionalization of incest: Oprah Winfrey's video "Scared Silent."

CHAPTER SIX

Oprah Winfrey's "Scared Silent" and the Spectatorship of Incest

Sexual abuse of children is common (best estimates: at least one girl in three, one boy in ten). It is not overreported but vastly underreported (best estimates: under 10 percent of all cases come to the attention of child-protective agencies or police). False complaints are rare (best estimates: under 5 percent of all complaints). Most victims do not disclose their abuse until long after the fact, if ever. Though many suffer long-lasting psychological harm, the great majority never see a therapist.

—Judith Herman, "The Abuses of Memory"

The False Memory Syndrome Foundation

In 1996 cultural representation of incest survivors takes place in the context of an antifeminist political backlash from the False Memory Syndrome (FMS) Foundation,[1] a backlash targeted against incest survivors and their therapists. The popular press has, of course, extensively debated the issue of false memory, and many writers, such as the authors of *The Courage to Heal*, have detected rampant antifeminism and misogyny in the rhetoric of the foundation. Take, for example, the following passage, which accuses feminists of "totalistic thinking":

Emerging political movements almost always exaggerate their "oppression" and attack the powerful and the rich. That is par for the course. In the FMS phenomenon, victimization has become the ideal, the preferred state. Women ... redefine their personalities and reinterpret their pasts to meet that ideal. Celebrities lead the way. To maintain their new image, "victims" become more and more cult-like in their behavior. They must cut themselves off from their families in order to maintain their image.[2]

To the False Memory Syndrome Foundation, women who come out as incest survivors and who choose to separate from abusive family systems are merely "lost." In the newsletter column "Retractor Notices," we find that "Elizabeth Carlson has prepared yellow ribbons for family and friends to wear until the children lost to false memories return. The funds will be used to support the efforts of the retractors through the National Association Against Fraud in Psychotherapy."[3] The section concludes by giving the price and address to write to for these ribbons.

After twenty-one states changed the statute of limitations regarding incest charges[4] and extended the law around the window of the survivor's memory, instead of relying solely on "evidence" of the incest event itself, an organization called the False Memory Syndrome Foundation, directed by Pamela Freyd, a mother who claims to have been "betrayed" by a thirty-something daughter's accusation of childhood sexual abuse, began to challenge the viability of survivors' memories. While a spokesperson from the FMS Foundation told me that as an apolitical, objective, research group they are "not in the business of condemning individual memories,"[5] this claim would seem to be contradicted by the institutional conse-quences of the FMS Foundation.[6] In spite of the fact that the American Psychological Association has rejected the construction of "false memory" as a syndrome and that Judith Herman, author of *Father-Daughter Incest* and *Trauma and Recovery* and a psychiatrist who specializes in incest, has dismissed the FMS Foundation as "an advocacy group for people whose children have accused them of sexual abuse,"[7] I would argue that the foundation poses a very real threat to feminist therapists and their clients.

This chapter examines the political spectacle and spectatorship of incest survivors in two critical contexts: (1) in the False Memory Syndrome Foundation, a "family values" organization with more than six thousand[8] members (at $125 a pop), which has institutionalized this current public backlash against incest survivors; and (2) in Oprah Winfrey's popular television documentary "Scared Silent: Exposing and Ending Child Abuse," aired simultaneously on three major networks in October 1992. I take up both projects together for two reasons. First, Oprah Winfrey's documentary was conceived as a response to the backlash; indeed, the growing backlash unwittingly made possible the popularity and seduction of the incest narratives in the mass media. Second, despite the fact that "Scared Silent" is progressive in some respects, there are some eerie convergences of the ideological projects of the documentary and the foundation.

According to the FMS Foundation, "False Memory Syndrome describes a situation in which a person acquires a memory that is not true but which seems very vivid and real to the person who has it. The memory comes to dominate the life of the person to the detriment of the person and the people involved in the memory."[9] When a foundation spokesperson returned my phone call, she defined false memories as repressed memories that emerge in therapy and that cannot be corroborated by "evidence."[10] False memory has become a syndrome, she explained, because of overzealous, underqualified therapists who rely on Ellen Bass and Laura Davis's *The Courage to Heal,* especially its point that "if you think you were abused and your life shows the symptoms, then you were."[11]

The promotional packet the FMS Foundation sends to parents who feel themselves "falsely accused" includes: a worksheet defining the "syndrome," the history of the foundation, and its mission; an order form for Eleanor Goldstein and Kevin Farmer's *Confabulations: Creating False Memories, Destroying Families,* which "tells the stories of 20 [FMS Foundation] families in their own words, includes interviews with therapists and provides analysis of the impact of the Recovery movement, New Age and radical Feminism in regard to false memories";[12] a xeroxed page of supposedly damning quotations from *The Courage to Heal,* which the FMS Foundation calls "the Bible of the Incest-Memory Recovery Movement" and "a political statement that preaches anger and revenge"; newspaper articles supporting and describing the FMS Foundation, collected in a packet titled *The False Memory Syndrome Phenomenon;* a bulletin (with opportunities to purchase papers) from this year's FMS Foundation conference; a recent *FMS Foundation Newsletter;* and xeroxed essays written by members of the FMS Foundation Professional Advisory Board.[13]

The FMS Foundation began when "a group of families and professionals" responded to "the growing wave of accusations of incest or sexual abuse brought on by adults who recovered 'memories' of events that families and people involved in the memories claim *just could not have happened.*"[14] The power and politics buttressing this position that parents are the final arbiters and truth-tellers about sexual abuse are undercut by the assertion that "the Foundation aims to provide accurate information on current research about the nature of human memory." A pamphlet published by the foundation defines the problem in this way:

Increasingly throughout the country, grown children undergoing therapeutic programs have come to believe that they suffer from "repressed memories" of incest and sexual abuse. While some reports of incest and sexual abuse are surely true, these decade-delayed memories are too often the result of False Memory Syndrome caused by a disastrous "therapeutic" program. False Memory Syndrome has a devastating effect on the victim and typically produces a continuing dependence on the very program that creates the syndrome. False Memory Syndrome proceeds to destroy the psychological well-being not only of the primary victim but—through false accusations of the incest and sexual abuse—other members of the primary victim's family.[15]

According to this pamphlet, a primary function of the foundation is to help "the secondary victims (those falsely accused) to establish reliable methods to discriminate between true and false claims of incest and abuse charges, and the psychological and other reasons they are made, including the intentional or unwitting suggestion of therapists and therapeutic programs." Nowhere does the foundation cite methods for or concern about establishing "reliable methods to discriminate between true and false claims" made by accused parents. The foundation currently "provide[s] information on legal rights, and access to legal counsel, to alleviate or remedy damage done by such accusations resulting from False Memory Syndrome," and in the future hopes to "provide financial assistance to families who need help in paying for polygraph tests, counseling, or legal services."[16]

According to the foundation, 92.2 percent of false accusations are made by thirty-something daughters against middle- and upper-middle-class families.[17] In the same newsletter, a recent legal coup is proudly announced:

Texas therapists have been told that: 1) Their psychological and psychiatric records may be subpoenaed; 2) They may have to bear the expenses of an attorney to file protective orders, unless the client is willing to pay; 3) Personal information may be explored in court if it appears in mental health records.

One Texas attorney has suggested that this ruling might potentially lead to a situation in which a therapist's expert testimony in a child custody case might be discounted as biased if records reveal that the therapist was abused as a child.[18]

While accused parents are the victims, thirty-something daughters and feminist therapists are the "perpetrators" of this new false memory syndrome. Feminist therapists are called "flakes" and "fanatics" who have created a "trendy ... sex abuse industry" that "attracts a lot of people making statements about themselves or others that are patently invalid."[19] The foundation hopes to appeal to the "community ethics" of therapists and challenge any therapeutic practice that does not find resolution in family restoration; for believing incest survivors means failing to grant the nuclear family the power to define the truth. It is the breakdown of the nuclear family that prompts Pamela Freyd to ask, "Does a therapist have a professional responsibility for the impact of her or his diagnosis on the relationship of the client with her or his family or for the impact on the lives of others who are not directly her or his clients?"[20] The question, of course, is rhetorical.

The FMS Foundation employs its own version of "victim politics" (its name for feminism) by intentionally changing the subject—from incest survivor to accused family member. An excerpt, collected in *The FMS Phenomenon* from *Confabulations* reveals this point: "Since sexual abuse of a child is the worst crime we know of—to be falsely accused of such a crime is the worst thing that can happen to a person."[21] The logic here is faulty. Under what system can a false accusation be worse than childhood sexual abuse, which leads to post-traumatic stress disorder, a high rate of suicide attempts, and long-term psychological aftereffects?

Indeed, family vindictiveness rather than scientific neutrality birthed the FMS Foundation. Even though foundation director Pamela Freyd claims to believe that sexual abuse can happen,[22] she rejected the disclosure of one survivor: her daughter Jennifer—a thirty-something feminist clinical psychologist.[23] Pamela and Peter Freyd, a stepbrother and stepsister who married,[24] have launched the FMS Foundation in what seems to me to be a smear campaign against their daughter. This institution born of a family feud is fueled by the confusion, anger, and anxiety shared by other accused parents.

Jennifer Freyd's disclosure of sexual abuse became the "proof" that she is an unreliable narrator of her own experience. She writes:

> Is my father more credible than me because I have a history of lying or not having a firm grasp on reality? No, I am a scientist whose empirical work has been replicated in laboratories around this country and Europe.... Am I not believed because I am a woman? A "female in her thirties" as some of the newspaper articles seem to emphasize? Am I therefore a hopeless hysteric by definition? Is it because the issue is father-daughter incest and as my father's property, I should be silent? ... Indeed, why is my parents' denial at all credible? In the end, is it precisely because I *was* abused that I am to be discredited despite my personal and professional success?[25]

Not only does Jennifer Freyd's "personal and professional success" fail to authorize her credibility but Peter Freyd's known hospitalization for alcoholism does not tarnish his authority over his daughter's narrative.[26] And even Jennifer Freyd's ostensibly unwavering heterosexuality has not protected her from her father's "lesbian baiting" via E-mail. Explaining why the FMS Foundation launched a heavy publicity campaign in the community in Oregon where Jennifer Freyd lives and works, Peter Freyd professed, "We have a lot of members not just from Oregon but with children who are in Oregon involved in rather radical feminist (often lesbian) cult-like groups"—who therefore, presumably, are not to be believed.[27] Of course, Peter Freyd would never read the system under which a father owns a daughter's disclosure as cultist. Indeed, nowhere in FMS literature will you find a survivor speaking outside the narrative of the patriarchal law. The only "survivors" who speak are those who have recanted, and who now see feminism and feminist therapy as "perpetrators."

Feminist therapy offers survivors the option to reject the tautological thinking that declares families of origin always already the final arbiters of truth. The FMS backlash emerges out of the desire not to see the image of the survivor or hear her experience—that is, never to cast her in the role of spectator of the transgression. It is important that the nuclear family's economic and social status is not jeopardized through "false accusations." Master narratives, though, *are* threatened, and it is the master narrative that the incest taboo holds in place (because the incest taboo has historically been a taboo against speech and image, not action).[28] "Survivor discourse" is really under attack.

Survivor Representations: The Silenced, Censored, and Discursive

Remembering is a testament to surviving;
only survivors remember.

—*Affirmations for the Inner Child*

The popular media posit representation of incest survivors as the answer to the problem of authenticity or believability. Privileging the visible reflects the American idealism that envisions letting the marginalized speak for themselves as necessary counterdiscourse. Under the aegis of this idealism, "speaking from experience" allows neutral, context-free "truth" to seep through the web of oppression. Psychoanalysis teaches feminism that we cannot "fix" sexist politics merely by letting the survivor speak, as if speech floats freely in culture from unbiased paradigms and politically uncommitted frames of intelligibility. When the survivor speaks within the ideology of patriarchy—as in courts of law or on television talk shows, where the expert psychiatrist is strategically positioned to fetishize the survivor's pain—she does not have the language necessary to describe *even to herself* her experience of sexual violation. Hoping that the text of self-disclosure will rewrite the context of patriarchy is wishful thinking. More egregious, this wishful thinking can even foreclose the social change it seeks, when the survivor's speech is absorbed by the master narrative that discredits survivors for having survived and denies legitimacy—and therefore political efficacy—to survivor discourse.

In "Survivor Discourse: Transgression or Recuperation?" Linda Alcoff and Laura Gray point out that survivor discourse functions neither as a social panacea (one that actually "ends" child abuse) nor as a political washout:

> The very act of speaking out has become used as performance and spectacle. The growth of this phenomenon raises questions: has it simply replayed confessional modes which recuperate dominant patriarchal discourses without subversive effect, or has it been able to create new spaces within these discourses and to begin to develop an autonomous counterdiscourse, one capable of empowering survivors?[29]

Rejecting the two theoretically fashionable solutions (the neo-Marxist and "materialist" rejection of all things personal or experiential and the liberal-feminist embrace of the "pretheoretical" experiential as necessarily subversive), Alcoff and Gray recommend that we become the "theorists of our own experiences":

> To become the theorists of our own experience requires us to
> become aware of how our subjectivity will be constituted by our
> discourses and aware of the danger that even in our own confes-
> sionals within autonomous spaces we can construct ourselves as
> reified victims or as responsible for our own victimization.[30]

This danger must, of course, be greater when confessionals
occur within mass-mediated spaces; for if one of the primary
ways to become the theorist of one's own experience is to control the production of knowledge that frames experience, no
one individual can "control" representation emanating from
institutionalized apparatuses. Nevertheless, being the "theorist
of one's own experience" appears to have been Oprah Winfrey's desire in producing and hosting her television documentary "Scared Silent: Exposing and Ending Child Abuse." Oprah
Winfrey presides over this documentary as an "out" incest survivor and as an ally of other survivors.

"Scared Silent" opens and closes with the voices of two survivors. The first image is of a nine-year-old white girl, Wendy,
with red hair in pigtails, rocking in a rocking chair. Hardly able
to open her mouth wide enough to shape the words, eyes cast
down, she whispers, "He told me if I told anybody, he was going
to kill me." The second image and voice are Oprah's: she
"comes out" as a survivor and then tells the camera, "We hope
the stories of these abusers and their victims can help *all* the
children and adults among us who have for too long now been
scared silent." Her image promises to give voice and permission
to Wendy and the other survivors on the show. Oprah "comes
out" to establish herself in political solidarity with the other survivors. Her more important role in the documentary, though, is
"to bear witness" to the stories of the other survivors. By bearing witness—an important gift to the survivor of crimes committed in isolation and secrecy—and controlling the means of
production, Oprah potentially delivers what Judith Herman

calls the "first principle" of recovery: "the empowerment of the survivor. She must be the author and arbiter of her own recovery. Others may offer advice, support, assistance, affection, and care, but not cure."[31] It seems to work for Wendy, who at the documentary's end optimistically commands that other children "tell somebody. Tell anybody. *Tell until somebody listens.*" Wendy's changed appearance establishes another of Herman's points: that the act of telling the trauma story transforms the traumatic memory from prenarrative disintegration to postnarrative integration.[32] Significantly, though, it is not really the telling that empowers Wendy but the "listening" that permits her another chance at psychological health, and being heard is not in any survivor's power to control.

The progressiveness of the documentary rests in its reinstatement of the reliability of the survivor. Nevertheless, this progressiveness is undercut by the documentary's overt heterosexism. Some survivors tell their stories, and many of them interpret the personal and political meaning of survivorship. But in too many cases the "expert," who is usually a white male psychiatrist or psychologist, is cast in the interpretive role, and even when his interpretation supports the survivor's right to be believed, he still robs her of the opportunity to "invent" her life's meaning. In "Scared Silent," the privilege to make meaning of abuse follows traditional lines of cultural privilege: "Scared Silent" becomes a documentary about healing the perpetrator, and white, heterosexual, male perpetrators are given many more opportunities to remain "in charge" of their recovery than either white female or African-American female or male perpetrators.

Most important of all, I would argue that like the FMS Foundation, "Scared Silent" is more deeply invested in the survival of the family than in the survival of the survivors. The documentary resolves the pain of survivorship by returning (at least, in

the cases of the white heterosexual men) to the same nuclear
family that produced the conditions under which children are
abused. Thus, while "Scared Silent" offers an optimistic example of the individual's agency to effect social change, its political impact is constrained by liberal notions of recovery. A closer
look at each of the six perpetrators represented in "Scared
Silent" suggests a relationship between cultural privilege and
familial forgiveness.

Del, Eva, and Jan are members of a white, upper-middle-class
family. Del, the father-perpetrator, molested his daughter Eva
and stopped only when Eva told her mother—twenty years
later—in an effort to rescue her younger sister from incest. Jan
acted immediately and effectively; Del was removed from the
house and prosecuted. But in the confrontation between Del
and Eva ("Scared Silent" stages their first encounter since Del
went to prison three years before), Del is allowed to remain the
expert of his family's experience—both in spite *and because* of
his role as perpetrator. In the absence of a moderator for this
confrontation, Del takes charge. Eva says she "just wants some
understanding," and instead of listening to Eva's needs—or dis-
charging his own guilt and shame—Del redeploys clichés of
psychotherapy to establish himself as the authority of his victim's prognosis for healing. When Eva expresses rage that Del
"passed on" his own victimhood to her, Del warns her of her
potential to similarly abuse her children, by marrying a man
just like dear old dad.

Finally, Del shuts Eva down (and shuts her up) with his tears
and bratty insistence that the family stay together. When Eva
was a little girl, Del bought her secrecy by threatening the
breakup of the family as the inevitable result of her disclosure.
Twenty years later, Eva seems fully capable of surviving family
estrangement, but Del will not stand for it. The ultimatum with
which he bought her secrecy earlier stands as a naked projec-

tion of his own castration anxiety; for what exactly *is* a heterosexual patriarch without a family to lord over? For the family of
Del and Eva reconnection does not heal Eva but rather, restores
the phallus to Del.

The second perpetrator represented is an African-American
woman named Tasha. We see Tasha in a group therapy program facilitated by a white male expert. We learn that Tasha's
brother brutally raped her, and that the adults in Tasha's life
neglected her. We also learn that she molested, raped, and
physically abused her male cousins, in an effort to, in her
words, "get back against guys." To force Tasha's accountability
for molesting children, the white male expert and her fellow
group members confront her viciously. The episode is filmed
like a scene of political torture: Tasha's is the only face exposed;
she sits crumpled up, like a captive crumpling under a bright
light; angry words are hurled from a mass of people made
anonymous by blackout, while she cries with shame and terror.
She sits next to the white male expert, whose posture and words
provide "reason" and force "accountability" but do not offer
compassion. In the end he declares that "Tasha will never be
cured," but her release is made possible because she connected
her experience as victim to her behavior of victimizing. Unlike
Del, Tasha is released into a void; we do not witness any reconnection with a nuclear family, and her expert makes no such
prognosis inevitable, or even possible.

Jill, a white, upper-middle-class divorced woman, is a victim
and perpetrator of severe childhood physical abuse. Jill "acci-
dentally" murdered her son, Roger, by beating him with a cur-
tain rod, then hurling the rod at him, puncturing his eyeball
and sending the rod plummeting into his brain. Jill says, "I did-
n't think of myself as an abuser," and indeed, only Roger's
death "makes" her role as abuser real to her and to her family.
Jill is alone, and her journey of healing has no future. We even

learn that Jill's niece has just given up her baby for adoption, fearing that she will pass on this legacy of abuse. The video captures Jill with her brother Dave, searching through old family photos—six generations' worth—tracing the abuse *back*, not recovering forward through familial reconnection.

George, a middle-aged, divorced African-American male, was physically abused as a child and went on to abuse two wives and five children, both physically and psychologically. He now lectures on child abuse across the country, focusing on the devastating effects of psychological and verbal abuse. Tracing his own abuse back to his mother and his mother's house, he returns home to confront his internal demons and talk with his mother about her behavior. As George cries in front of his abuser, remembering how it felt to hear her declare him a failure and how it hurt to be beaten, his aged mother laughs nervously and dismisses his invitation to reconnect, explaining that "slapping a child upside the head" was just how things were done. We last see George preparing to give another lecture on child abuse. By lecturing to perpetrators and parents, George connects himself to the community, but the social text offers no familial immunity—or place to call home—for George.

Wendy, the strawberry blonde who opens the video but has a hard time opening her mouth wide enough to form the words she wants to express, is part of a working-class white family. Her father, Brian, molested her and stopped only when his wife, Roseanne, walked in to witness his abuse. Like Del, Brian serves a short jail term and then returns home. On the one hand, Brian seems more accountable than Del for his behavior: he looks Wendy in the eyes and says, "It was all my fault and it never should have happened to you." But Wendy, only twelve, seems unconvinced by her father's avowed guilt. Brian acknowledges that he stopped molesting Wendy only because his wife "caught" him; he also says that his healing—and the health of his family, in his view—is dependent on his reconnection with them. Wendy and Roseanne seem simultaneously hopeful and leery. The final scene captures Roseanne vigilantly watching Brian and Wendy gardening. The singularity of this act—the watchful and rescuing mother's gaze—suggests the terms under which Brian is "cured": when his wife polices his behavior. Thus, as with Del, Brian's recovery takes precedence over his victim's.

The final perpetrator featured is Patrice, a Hispanic woman who physically abused her children. When she broke the leg of her two-year-old daughter, a children's services agency removed her children from her home. After undergoing therapy and finding "a loving husband," Patrice, like the white men, is allowed to reclaim the social role she held before crossing the line of abuse. Rather than male privilege determining the perpetrator's right to a second chance, the prerequisite seems to be heterosexism—the institutional fodder for family values. This is emphasized by the closing message, delivered first by Brian and Del, last by Wendy and Roseanne, all serving to promote the desirability of the reunited family.

Perhaps because heterosexuality and heterosexism condition survivor spectatorship in "Scared Silent," we find no lesbian representation here. As Shana Rowen Blessing suggests in "How to Be a Political Dyke and an Incest Survivor at the Same Time, or, Why Are All the Dykes I Know Reading *The Courage to Heal?*"[33] there is a relationship between incest survivorship and lesbianism, although exactly what this relationship *means* is unclear.[34] The imposition in Winfrey's documentary of traditional notions of family and gender renders impossible the solution to child abuse offered: to be scared silent is, in fact, a logical extension of the Law of the Father. For the families represented in "Scared Silent," incest stops only because mothers walk through closed doors—or daughters break through them—and they all have the courage to act on what they see and remember. Thus, "Scared Silent" fails to "end" child abuse because its liberal embrace of family values sanctions the father's ownership of his victim's healing as well as his own.

Nevertheless, as I have said, Oprah Winfrey's "Scared Silent" offers one important response to the FMS Foundation: by positioning survivors who are believed, Winfrey opens a space for survivor discourse. This does not mean that Oprah Winfrey's position offers a "solution" to the reactionary politics of the False Memory Syndrome Foundation.

Totalizing theories—those that offer solutions—do not effect progressive social change. For this reason, the problem of sexual abuse and its aftereffects cannot be "solved" by one person, one idea, one moment, one word, one wish, one master theory, or one television production. Instead, politicized incest survivorship demands that we return a retheorized notion of "experience" (contesting experience as an organizing category of personal identity and instead emphasizing the meaning made of experiences as one organizing category of political commitment) to a retheorized notion of "social." This "retheorized social" rejects the sociological determinism of neo-Marxist materialism and reclaims the Lacanian concept of the symbolic order of culture, a move that allows us to repudiate the transparency of experience without rejecting the epistemological potential of personal experience. Such a move allows us to see that incest survivorship is not an identity but is often claimed as such because of the cultural and psychological erasure of the crime and its aftereffects. Survivors face disbelief on the level of truth value ("Did it *really* happen") and import ("Even if it did happen, it wasn't that bad"), and this disbelief confirms survivors' worst fears—that the pathology of abuse resides within their bodies, not within their culture.

Thus, survivorship as I define it emerges when the experiences of sexual violation are made meaningful through the politics of psychoanalytic feminism, with its analyses of heterosexism and of the oppressive nature of the family. Indeed, only by showing how the social makes the experiential discursively "real," and how our most private experiences take shape through and give meaning to the social, can incest survivorship mean anything—political—at all.

Afterword

This book addresses why survivorship is political, not (only) why healing from abuse is good for you. However, I do not understand the realms of the psychological and the political as irreconcilably separate. Indeed, I locate psychology and psychoanalysis as central to any theory of liberation and progressive social change. Since the False Memory Syndrome Foundation came into existence in March 1992, the "politics" of survivorship has taken on new meaning, one encapsulated by right-wing rhetoric and family-values ideology. During these years of survivor backlash, popular media have spent more time representing the False Memory Syndrome Foundation's position (that memories cannot be repressed and retrieved with any degree of accuracy) than representing the social forces that make the sexual, physical and psychological abuse of children in the twentieth-century United States an "ordinary" part of life.

Fairness and Accuracy in Reporting (FAIR), the national media-watch group that offers counterdiscourse to mainstream journalism, recently featured an article on the imbalance and on the unarticulated bias used to promote the false memory syndrome in the popular media. FAIR diagnoses this comprehensive endorsement by mainstream media of the FMS Foundation as "media escapism," a practice that has had serious consequences for child welfare in this country. Focusing on the conjecture of false accusations rather than on the proven cases of child sexual abuse, this media escapism has helped construct a culture where "in opinion polls child abuse is not cited as a public concern or a cause of violence."[1]

The FMS Foundation and its theory that repressed memories are untrustworthy as litigious evidence deserve public representations, attention, and scrutiny. I am in no way advocating censorship. All positions—even ones I may find distasteful, incendiary, or silly—need to be debated fully and publicly, and this engagement does not constitute an "attack." The problem, then, is not that false memory is being discussed but rather that it is being taken up uncritically. The national opinion poll reflecting a citizenship that fails to register child abuse as prevalent and socially debilitating grows from the same ignorance that imagines parents' grievances of false accusations as "worse than" or more prevalent than confirmed cases of childhood sexual abuse. In chapter 6, I countered the faulty logic that a false accusation is worse than molestation. Here I address the False Memory Syndrome Foundation's position that false accusations are "rampant."

The FMS Foundation has six thousand members; in 1995, more than five hundred thousand cases of child sexual abuse have been substantiated, while independent surveys from this time frame suggest that as many as *three million cases of child sexual abuse actually occurred.*[2] Remember the FMS Foundation assumes innocence on the part of its members and uses no system to validate their members' self-appointed innocence. Why would six thousand "unsubstantiated cases" of false accusation be interpreted as more "newsworthy" than five hundred thousand cases of substantiated sexual abuse? How can six thousand people be capable of garnering so much more mainstream media attention and support than five hundred thousand others? Because the opportunity to speak publicly and be believed reflects the power and entitlement of the culturally privileged—not the inherent validity of their position.

What undergirds the privilege and entitlement that have turned such a tide against incest survivors, therapists, and the politics of feminism is not a conspiracy against women and the oppressed but rather one more chink in the armor of family values and the right-wing nostalgia that buttresses it.

Take, for example, Frederick Crews's two-part article "The Revenge of the Repressed,"[3] a literary review that valorizes unsubstantiated declaration of innocences from those who claim to be suffering from an adult child's "false" memory. Significantly, Crews is a "closeted" member of the FMS Foundation and an adviser on their Scientific and Professional Advisory Board. I call him closeted because he withholds this political affiliation in his article. This is no small or minor omission. To fail to identify the political commitments and intellectual paradigms we use to make interpretive sense is to mislead intentionally. Indeed, when we fail to situate ourselves in the intellectual or political traditions that shape our thinking, we project a false sense of neutrality. And this false sense of neutrality is relegated to only certain situations: board members of the FMS Foundation rarely, if ever, fail to mention their academic credentials.

Although Crews looks at two books that verify repression (Lenore Terr's *Unchained Memories: True Stories of Traumatic Memories Lost and Found* and Ellen Bass and Laura Davis's *The Courage to Heal*), he summarily rejects their merit. He saves favorable readings for Elizabeth Loftus and Katherine Ketcham's *The Myth of Repressed Memory: False Memories and Allegations of Sexual Abuse*; Lawrence Wright's *Remembering Satan*; Richard Ofshe and Ethan Watters's *Making Monsters: False Memories, Psychotherapy, and Sexual Hysteria*; and Mark Pendergrast's *Victims of Memory: Incest Accusations and Shattered Lives*. Two of the four books are coauthored by members of the FMS Foundation advisory board.[4]

Wright's book and that of Ofshe and Watters address the case against Paul Ingram, an Olympia, Washington, cop, born-again Christian, and chair of his county's Republican committee, who was accused and confessed to the satanic ritual and sexual abuse of his children. Crews finds the Ingram case "inexpressibly sad" and compares it to the well-publicized 1989 case Eileen Lipsker made against her drunkard father, George Franklin, Sr., who was convicted, on the grounds of her recovered memory, for raping and murdering Eileen's childhood best friend, Susan Nason, decades earlier.[5] Crews finds Ingram's fate more pathetic than George Franklin's: "Whereas the Franklin household, when Eileen Lipsker went public with her vision, no longer contained a married couple or any children, in the Ingram case a devout family of seven was shattered for good."[6] While it may be unfortunate to Crews that Franklin was convicted on the grounds of what Crews perceives to be an unsubstantiated "vision," he withholds King Lear—like tragedy for this devout family of seven, which, in Crews's hierarchy of salvageable life forms, is simply higher on the food chain because of the sacrosanctity bestowed to heterosexual, Christian families.

Indeed, the most tragic of the fallen fathers is the one who writes on his own behalf. Crews promises that Mark Pendergrast's book will "wring the classic emotions of pity and terror from any unbiased reader," mostly because Pendergrast's own two daughters "believe that he did something awful" to one of them; and while they did not accuse Pendergrast of sexual abuse, they *did* separate themselves from him. (Those who value individuation might say they grew up.) Pendergrast believes that they suspect he molested one of them, and he believes that they came to that conclusion after reading *The Courage to Heal.* (Without his daughters' accusation, Pendergrast's six-hundred-page self-defense reads as a glaring unconscious admission—of *something.*) He concludes his book with a letter asking his daughters to come home. Crews hopes "that [the estranged daughters] read not just that letter but the whole of *Victims of Memory,* which ... rests partly on the desperate premise that a 603-page dose of history, logic and exhortation may be able to turn well-coached zealots back into the amiable young women Pendergrast once knew."[7] But what separates the "logic" of the father from the "zealotry" of the daughters? Perhaps the political gravity that declares fathers logical and just and their exhortations noble, and daughters who run from this, hysterical? Indeed, one person's dose of "history" may be another's dose of amnesia.

Crews calls the decade-advanced extension of statutes of limitations in recovered memory cases "legislative backwardness," which, he declares, is "obviously ... not coming from reputable psychological research—which, as we have seen, offers no support of repression even in its mildest form."[8] Psychological research offers no support of repression? Sigmund Freud, Frank Putnam, R. P. Kluft, Judith Herman, and all the others are all simply a bunch of quacks? That is a convenient and cheap way of dismissing one's opposition: convenient, because with one fell swoop, the conversation stops; cheap, because it renders monolithic and totalizing a disparate, energized and eclectic field of study.

Crews concludes the review with this prophecy: that justice, someday, will be done, and those found guilty of child abuse based on recovered memories will be set free, for "simple justice demands that prison sentences resting on a combination of delusion and misinformation be overturned." His fear, however, is that "once the bizarre and sinister features of the recovery movement are widely known," when all "sophisticated readers will not hesitate to distance themselves from it," then "bobbing for repressed memories will be perceived simply as a ludicrous, dismissive aberration from a fundamentally sound psychotherapeutic tradition."[9] Instead, Crews declares, psychoanalysis as a whole is to blame. Indeed, the only sane person among the practitioners of psychology or psychoanalysis are positivists and empiricists who invest "hard" facts with indisputable meaning and hold "interpretive" facts with the contempt they usually reserve for those "children within" lost to UFO abductions. Crews cites a fellow FMS Foundation member for fraternal solidarity:

> In a refreshingly sane essay, Paul R. McHugh, director of the Department of Psychiatry and Behavioral Science at the Johns Hopkins Medical Institutions, recently depicted a long-term struggle, within the mental health disciplines, between what he called empiricists and romanticists—between, that is, those who bind themselves to methodological study of facts and those who "rely upon feelings for evidence, on metaphors for reality, on inspiration and myth for guidance."[10]

What Crews most likes about McHugh's position, though, is not the tired binary McHugh wedges between facts and fiction but that this wedge allows Crews to can the entire debate, and with it the political and social consequences of child sexual abuse. Crews writes, "[McHugh's] essay is especially pertinent because it relegates both psychoanalysis and recovered memory therapy to the romanticist camp, where they surely belong. But it also relegates them to history's ashcan."[11] As Frederick Crews has modeled, when entitlement is challenged, some take this invitation to critical engagement with poststructuralist interventions into the "self-evidence" of empiricism as an opportunity to lose their minds.

In the very least, positioning psychoanalysis as the enemy is politically and intellectually unprogressive, because it renders the interiorization of oppression invisible. Instead, what we need is a radical politics of the unconscious, a politics that distinguishes equality from liberation. Liberation mandates overhauling not only social and material structures but also (ostensibly) private desires, personal lives, and individual experiences. A politics of liberation is not the place for the weak of heart, for it demands the full integration of our (again, ostensibly) personal experiences with a political paradigm that makes intelligible those experiences. Indeed, our personal and individual lives are not more important or valuable than the political ideas that make them meaningful and significant.

I close this book in the company of dogs—rescued dogs, survivors all. At my feet lies Jack, a golden retriever rescued in the winter of 1994 from starvation, neglect, abuse. A six-foot chain in a chicken coop was home. Jack jumps in fear when you pick up a broom, move fast, or drop something. We assure Jack that he will never be hit again, and his slow progression toward trust exemplifies one kind of survivorship.

While writing this book, I moved into the headquarters of GRROWLS: Golden Retriever Rescue Operated With Love—Statewide, New York. My lover, Teri, founded GRROWLS four years ago. Our home phone number is also the GRROWLS line.

Desperate phone calls about abused and neglected animals are routine. Writing a book about survivorship in the setting of a rescue headquarters has reminded me of two things. First, political change must be not separatist in scope but rather integrationist. We need to coalition-build, to define survivorship broadly, to cultivate allies. Second, liberatory ideas need immediate action and application. Both the "personal safety" uncritically embraced by those who separate the psychological from the political and the vulgar empiricism that can see truth only in material evidence are unsatisfactory systems of thought. Indeed, they are kisses in the wind.

Appendix

William Godwin to M. W. Shelley, June 13, 1820

The following is the copy of a letter dispatched by me on the day of its date, but which, as appears from yours of May 26, had never been received.

Skinner Str., Apr. 25, 1820

My Dear Mary

I will make no observation on the letter I have just received from you, lest I should offend. I will merely put down a few plain facts.

In your letter, dated Mar. 14, you make "the following offer. Shelley would make bills for £50 per quarter on his income, to be paid regularly by Brooks: the two first of these bills we can get discounted here, &c, &c."

There is a surprising degree of coincidence between this, & the letter I wrote you three days later, viz, Mar. 17. I there observe that "I had been repeatedly informed by you that the sum of £500 could be made up to me from your resources within a year." I therefore request that Shelley will "put this into my hands through assignments on his banker, such assignments & securities as he used to describe that he had given Peacock for his annuity, which could not be diverted or infringed upon;" & I add that with these "I am persuaded I could complete the business." I conclude this part of the subject with saying that "I should be grieved to press you too hard, & therefore, if the two latter installments, instead of being made for July & October next, were made payable, so secured, at 12 or 15 months from the present time, the business would not fail."

In another part of this same letter, I mention, "This interval, till the terms, April & May, is all I have, in which to effect the compromise, to which my lawyers so earnestly advise me. *Everything therefore seems to depend on the return I shall receive to this letter!*" I add, "Do not let me be led along in a fool's paradise. It is better to look my ruin full in the face at once, than to be amused forever with promises, at the same time that nothing is done."

Now I own I thought I could pretty exactly anticipate "the return I should receive to that letter." I entertained that anticipation in full confidence, & rested upon it with cheerful assurance. There was indeed some difference between my proposition of Mar. 17, & yours of Mar. 14: but I had no doubt that at least "Shelley would make bills for £50 per quarter on his income, to be paid regularly at Brooks's," & that I should receive them in "return to my letter."

It is in vain by words to paint my astonishment at finding, in the first place, when your letter was put into my hands, that it was single. Not a shilling accompanies it. Not the vestige of a bill, or any species of security upon which I could found a negociation. Every thing appears as far off as ever.

What a situation should I have been in, if I had taken Shelley's advice, & opened a negociation in the confidence, that, if they had accepted the offer of £500, he would have enabled me to honour the proposal. Thank God, I escaped that quicksand!

Now my only hope is (if indeed it is worth the name of hope), that the adversary may fail in the coming argument before the judges, respecting a flaw in their proceeding. Hayward says they will fail; but I have no great reliance on that. If they do, they will have to commence their proceedings over again, & this will give me time for a negotiation.

You are in the wrong, when you say that I had "hopes that Shelley would have been on his road to England." On the contrary, I never wished it. What I said was, that "I was left to guess whether your long silence (my letter not having reached you till fifty days after the date) meant, that out of resentment I was to be wholly deserted, or that, prompted by sympathy, Shelley was on his road to England. I could find but these alternatives."

With respect to Lackington, I have nothing to say. As he assured me in person that he did not owe you a farthing, I think that, to say the least, he will find means to baffle Horace Smith. I may be in a mistake.

The present term begins April 19, & ends May 15. I suppose my question will come on in the sittings immediately after term. I thought it would have been sooner.

To come to the point. If Shelley will not immediately send me such bills as I propose, or as you offer, my next request is, that he will let me alone, & not disturb the sadness of my shipwreck, by holding out false lights, & deluding me with appearances of relief when no relief is at hand.

>   *Ever most affectionately yours,*
>   *William Godwin*

June 13, 1820

My question is not yet come on. A great deal of delay has lately arisen from the difficulty of settling between the lawyers of the two parties the precise terms of the question to be argued before the judges. It is now settled. This has protracted the issue to the present term of June. The term ends on the 21st: then begin the sittings.

I can conceive nothing more < >kening [awakening? sickening?] to the heart than this correspondence. My < >ers [letters?] seem never to be received. One is stated to have reached you at the expiration of fifty days from its date. Tomorrow will be fifty days from the date of that of which the above is a transcript. I get letters from you indeed; but they say nothing to this momentous point, & the affair does not advance a single step.

This indeed seems to be the great feature of the whole. The trial took place, Oct. 18, 1819. Immediately Shelley wrote to me with his own hand, assuring me that I might depend upon receiving from him £500 in twelve months from that date. On the 14th of March last you write to me with the express offer of £50 per quarter on Shelley's income. But all this is words only. Not a shilling, not a scrap of a bill, in execution of these tenders, has yet been transmitted to me. If the express purpose had been to delude & to torture me, it could not have been performed more effectually.[1]

>   *Alla Signora Shelley*
>   *Ferma in Posta*
>   *Pisa*
>   *Toscana*
>   *Italia*

Notes

Notes to the Introduction

1. I use "law of heteropatriarchy" to combine two competing notions of heteropatriarchy: the sociological definition, which systematizes male domination, and the Lacanian psychoanalytic definition, which figures the "Name of the Law of the Father" as the child's entrance into the symbolic phase and thus (patriarchal) culture.
2. I use quotes to register my contesting this demonization of Freud.
3. Anita Levy, *Other Women: The Writing of Class, Race, and Gender, 1832–1898* (Princeton, N.J.: Princeton University Press, 1991), 94.
4. M. M. Bakhtin, *The Dialogic Imagination: Four Essays*, trans. Caryl Emerson and Michael Holquist (Austin: University of Texas Press, 1981), 38. Also consider Bakhtin's theory of the relationship between novels and "everyday life": "Another phenomenon in the history of the novel— and one of extreme importance—is the novel's special relationship

with extraliterary genres, with the genres of everyday life and with ideological genres. In its earlier stages, the novel and its preparatory genres had relied upon various extraliterary forms of personal and social
reality, and especially those of rhetoric (there is a theory that actually
traces the novel back to rhetoric). And in later stages of its development the novel makes wide and substantial use of letters, diaries, confessions, the forms and methods of rhetoric associated with recently
established courts and so forth. Since it is constructed in a zone of contact with the incomplete events of a particular present, the novel often
crosses the boundary of what we strictly call fictional literature—making use first of a moral confession, then of a philosophical tract, then
of manifestos that are openly political, then degenerating into the raw
spirituality of a confession, a 'cry of the soul' that has not yet found its
formal contours. These phenomena are precisely what characterize the
novel as a developing genre. After all, the boundaries between fiction
and nonfiction, between literature and nonliterature and so forth are
not laid up in heaven. Every specific situation is historical" (33).

5. Hayden White, "The Historical Text as Literary Artifact," in *Tropics of
   Discourse* (Baltimore: Johns Hopkins University Press, 1978), 98.
6. I use the term *queer* as an umbrella word to include all gay, lesbian,
   bisexual, and transgendered subjects and political positions.
7. I rely here on Judith Butler's notion of performance, which she introduces in *Gender Trouble: Feminism and the Subversion of Identity* (New
   York: Routledge, 1990) and extends in *Bodies That Matter: On the Discursive Limits of "Sex"* (New York: Routledge, 1993): "Performity must
   be understood not as a singular or deliberate 'act,' but rather, as the
   reiterative and citational practice by which discourse produces the
   effects that it names" (*Bodies That Matter*, 2).
8. Eve Kosofsky Sedgwick, *The Epistemology of the Closet* (Berkeley: University of California Press, 1990), 3.
9. I do not understand these two constituencies in a binary pair, for by
   posing queer studies on the one hand and incest survivorship on the
   other, we can erase the specific registers of those who are both survivors and queer. Instead, when using queer studies as a cousin paradigm through which to politicize the incest survivor, I hold separate
   these theories only to be historically sensitive and accurate to their
   different paths into the academy and culture.
10. Heterosexism is an institution and homophobia an ideology. "Het-
    erosexism" refers to the ways in which heterosexuality receives insti-

tutional recognition and homosexuality meets with institutional rejection, ostracization, shame, and punishment. "Homophobia" refers to the feelings that are made material through this institutionalization of sexual and emotional practice: hatred for lesbian and gay people or fear of becoming lesbian or gay.

11. Philip Brockman, "A Fine Day," *New York Native*, no. 175 (August 25, 1986): 13 (quoted in Sedgwick, *Epistemology of the Closet*, 71).

12. Sedgwick, *Epistemology of the Closet*, 81.

13. I understand lesbianism within the psychoanalytic notion that sexuality is not an identity. This puts pressure on the essentialism reflected in both the hate politics of the religious right and the separatist politics of some conservative gay activists. Non-identity-based notions of sexuality do not signify sexual confusion or political fear, or even function as a "real" reflection of sexual practice, but instead point to the instability of identities—all identities—and establish gay and lesbian sexual acts as political practice and choice, not the pathologized consequences of apocalyptic biologism.

14. A friend informed me that my position makes "healing" impossible for the homophobic heterosexual and self-hating lesbian incest survivor. I quite agree. As I argue throughout *The Politics of Survivorship*, healing is possible only in a just world. Healing for us all, then, is a promise contingent on our involvement in progressive political work.

15. Male survivorship is just as politically and intellectually important— and urgent—a subject as female survivorship. Because of the sociological frame of heteropatriarchy, women survive incest differently than men, and my focus here is women's survivorship.

16. I thank Geof Margo for first pointing this out to me.

17. See my Afterword for a critique of the antipsychology that disparages notions of "internalized oppression."

Notes to Chapter 1

1. The topic of repressed memories has been highly contested and publicly debated from 1992, the year the False Memory Syndrome Foundation came into existence, until today. I address this scuffle in chapter 6.

2. Ellen Bass and Laura Davis, *The Courage to Heal* (1988; 3d ed., New York: HarperCollins, 1994), 24.

3. See Linda Gordon, *Heroes of Their Own Lives: The Politics and History of Family Violence* (New York: Penguin, 1988).

4. Florence Rush, *The Best Kept Secret: Sexual Abuse of Children* (New York: McGraw-Hill, 1980).

5. Gordon, *Heroes*, 4.

6. Ibid., 204.

7. Ibid., 219.

8. Ibid., 220, 221.

9. Ibid., 207.

10. Ibid., 248.

11. Ibid., 233, 234.

12. Jean Laplanche and Jean-Bertrand Pontalis, *The Language of Psycho-Analysis*, trans. Donald Nicholson-Smith (New York: W. W. Norton & Co., 1973), 293.

13. I rely on therapists who also may be psychologists and on psychiatrists to define terms. While Carol Tavris and others have renounced therapists as unqualified to perform such a task—and untrustworthy when they do—I use the wisdom of therapists who are substantiated by "researchers" because my focus here is not on the empirical validity of psychological terms and consequences but on their current social and political impact on women. Additionally, because therapists—on account of their accessible writing style and reference base—are read more frequently than research scientists, they have a much greater impact on people's lives and are therefore more important politically, in spite of what some may find poor or substandard qualifications.

14. Bass and Davis, *Courage to Heal*, 25.

15. Ibid. After receiving serious pressure from the False Memory Syndrome Foundation—including a lawsuit—Bass and Davis revised this position. In the third edition of *Courage to Heal*, they write: "If you genuinely think you were abused and your life shows the symptoms, there's a strong likelihood that you were" (26).

16. Patrocinio P. Schweickart, "Reading Ourselves: Toward a Feminist Theory of Reading," in *Gender and Reading*, ed. Elizabeth A. Flynn and Patrocinio P. Schweickart (Baltimore: Johns Hopkins University Press, 1986), 39; Schweickart's emphasis.

17. Ibid., 53.

18. Sigmund Freud, quoted in Jeffrey Moussaieff Masson, *The Assault on Truth* (New York: Farrar, Straus & Giroux, 1984), 9 (from Max Schur's *Freud: Living and Dying*).

19. The Greek root, *hysteros*, means "womb"; the disease featured in 1900 B.C. in the earliest medical manual. See Elizabeth Wright, ed., *Femi-*

nism and Psychoanalysis: A Critical Dictionary (New York: Basil Black-well, 1992), 163.

20. Because Freud uses seduction synonymously with incest, and because seduction connotes consent, which Freud adamantly did not attribute to survivors in 1896, I will hereafter refer to this theory as the "sexual abuse theory," except in cases where doing so contradicts Freud's use of the term.

21. Although Masson understands the move from the seduction theory to the oedipal theory as a betrayal, this understanding fails to see how the oedipal theory is, on one level, an extension of (not a departure from) the seduction theory, in that it merely extends into the realm of social acceptance Freud's consistent desire to "fix" the victim, not the perpetrator or the society that makes abuse an ordinary event.

22. Sigmund Freud, "The Aetiology of Hysteria" (1896), in Masson, *Assault on Truth*, 261.

23. Ibid., 262.

24. Ibid., 264.

25. So much so that Freud's reason for revising the sexual abuse theory was that he couldn't get his patients to comply, to disclose. Instead of seeing this as proof of the psychic burden and also understanding the deep shame that accompanies sexual abuse, Freud understood their resistance as proof he was wrong in 1896.

26. Freud, "Aetiology," 265.

27. Ibid.

28. Laplanche and Pontalis, *Language of Psycho-Analysis*, 405.

29. Ibid., 292–93.

30. Freud, "Aetiology," 266.

31. Ibid., 267.

32. Ibid., 271, 272–73.

33. Ibid., 273.

34. Ibid., 274.

35. Ibid., 276–77.

36. Ibid., 277.

37. Ibid., 279.

38. Ibid., 280.

39. Ibid., 285.

40. Ibid., 286.

41. Masson, *Assault on Truth*, xxx.

42. Alice Miller, *Thou Shalt Not Be Aware: Society's Betrayal of the Child*, trans. Hildegarde Hannum and Hunter Hannum (New York: Meridian Books, 1984), 41.

43. Elizabeth Grosz, *Jacques Lacan: A Feminist Introduction* (New York: Routledge, 1990), 51. Her point here is that both of Freud's theories—the seduction theory and the oedipal—are problematic, and that Lacan's revision connects sexuality to "the acquisition of social identity and a speaking position."

44. Masson, *Assault on Truth*, xxxiv.

45. Laplanche and Pontalis, *Language of Psycho-Analysis*, 405.

46. Sigmund Freud, "On the History of the Psycho-Analytic Movement," quoted in Laplanche and Pontalis, *Language of Psycho-Analysis*, 405.

47. Primal fantasies include seduction, castration, and the primal scene. See Laplanche and Pontalis, *Language of Psycho-Analysis*, 331.

48. Laplanche and Pontalis, *Language of Psycho-Analysis*, 331; my emphasis.

49. Peter Gay, ed., *The Freud Reader* (New York: W. W. Norton & Co., 1989), 96–97.

50. Laplanche and Pontalis, *Language of Psycho-Analysis*, 407.

51. In Sigmund Freud, *Three Essays on the Theory of Sexuality*, ed. J. D. Sutherland (1905); trans. James Strachey (New York: Basic Books, 1978), x.

52. Ibid., xii.

53. Ibid.

54. Ellie Ragland-Sullivan, *Jacques Lacan and the Philosophy of Psychoanalysis* (Urbana and Chicago: University of Illinois Press, 1986), 267.

55. Freud, *Three Essays*, 56.

56. Ibid., 57.

57. Ibid., 89.

58. Ibid., 96.

59. Ibid., 93; my emphasis.

60. Ibid., 93.

61. Claude Lévi-Strauss, *The Elementary Structures of Kinship*, trans. James Haile Bell and John Richard von Sturmer (Boston: Beacon Press, 1969), xxvii.

62. See James Kincaid, *Child Loving: The Erotic Child and Victorian Literature*, 2d ed. (New York: Routledge, 1994).

63. Lévi-Strauss, *Kinship*, 17.

64. Ibid., 18.

65. Ibid., 25.

66. The politics involved in understanding a child's ability to unravel an adult's reputation needs to be unpacked here, since it implies an inversion of the "adultism" upon which patriarchy is based; for if children who broke the silence *could* bring public excoriation to adult molesters, this would suggest that our culture respects, listens, and believes children.

67. "Interpellation," a concept advanced by French Marxist theoretician Louis Althusser (1918–1990), refers to the process by which social influence is rendered invisible, thereby allowing the subject to falsely perceive herself/himself as an entirely free agent. See Althusser, *Lenin and Philosophy and Other Essays*, trans. Ben Brewster (New York: Monthly Review Press, 1971).

68. Judith Herman, *Trauma and Recovery: The Aftermath of Violence* (New York: Basic Books, 1992), 9.

69. Bass and Davis, *Courage to Heal*, 14.

70. Ibid., 64.

71. The implication of full agency here is, of course, untenable. As I said in my Introduction, there is no healing the individual in a sick society. However, it is important to read these gestures of agency as a strategy for skill acquisition, not a manifesto.

72. A sense of power greater than yourself can also be painfully reminiscent of the experience of incest in the first place. Again, though, these are strategies, not elements in a manifesto.

73. Bass and Davis, *Courage to Heal*, 64–65.

74. Herman, *Trauma and Recovery*, 37, 38.

75. Ibid., 37.

76. Ibid., 52–53.

77. Ibid., 181.

78. Barbara Welter, "The Cult of True Womanhood (1820-1860)," *American Quarterly* 18 (1966): 151–74.

79. Alice Miller, *For Your Own Good: Hidden Cruelty in Child-Rearing and the Roots of Violence* (1983), trans. Hildegarde Hannum and Hunter Hannum (1983; reprint, New York: Noonday Press, 1990), xii.

80. Ibid., xii.

81. Ibid., 106.

82. See Norman Holland, *Five Readers Reading* (New Haven: Yale University Press, 1975).

83. See David Bleich, *Subjective Criticism* (Baltimore: Johns Hopkins University Press, 1978).

84. Miller, *Thou Shalt Not Be Aware*, 235.
85. Ibid., 315.
86. Ibid., 120–21.
87. Ibid., 123–24.
88. Ibid., 143.
89. Ibid., 146.
90. Ibid., 229, 316.
91. Ibid., 160.
92. Alice Miller, *The Untouched Key: Tracing Childhood Trauma in Creativity and Destructiveness* (1988), trans. Hildegarde Hannum and Hunter Hannum (New York: Doubleday, 1990), 73.

Notes to Chapter 2

1. Let me define "incest." In accordance with the definition used in contemporary recovery theory, incest does not have to involve touch. The most widely accepted definition of incest is "the imposition of sexually inappropriate acts, or acts with sexual overtones, by … one or more persons who derive authority through ongoing emotional bonding with that child" (E. Sue Blume, *Secret Survivors: Uncovering Incest and Its Effects in Women* [New York: Ballantine, 1985], 4. Although touch may be absent, secrecy, ever-present, becomes more and more difficult to endure, especially if the daughter's denial has made her "forget" the experience (1–20). According to Judith Herman, "Most girls dread discovery of the incest secret and do not reveal it to anyone.… They believe that no recourse is available to them and that disclosure of the secret would lead to disaster" (Judith Lewis Herman, *Father-Daughter Incest* [Cambridge, Mass.: Harvard University Press, 1981], 129). Also, frequency of attack is often used to dismiss the relevance and import of sexual abuse. But as Bass and Davis suggest, "Betrayal takes only a minute. A father can slip his fingers into his daughter's underpants in thirty seconds. After that the world is not the same" (Ellen Bass and Laura Davis, *The Courage to Heal: A Guide for Women Survivors of Child Sexual Abuse* [1988; 3d ed., New York: HarperCollins, 1994], 26).
2. Throughout this book I use "trauma theory" to refer to the process of reading aftereffects as texts, as outlined and described in chapter 1.
3. I put *chooses* in quotation marks, because although it is clearly the wrong word, it is the one a patriarchal culture deems appropriate. No

woman chooses to be raped; selecting among compromises should never be confused with an act of free will.

4. Sylvia Norman's essay is collected in Kenneth Neill Cameron, ed., *Shelley and His Circle: 1773–1822*, Documents in the Carl H. Pforzheimer Library (Cambridge, Mass.: Harvard University Press, 1970), 3:397–423.

5. Ibid., 399.

6. Ibid., 420.

7. Ibid., 408.

8. Ibid., 420.

9. Ibid., 421.

10. Harold Bloom, ed., *Mary Shelley: Modern Critical Views* (New York: Chelsea House, 1985), 1.

11. Ibid., 170.

12. Sigmund Freud, *The Essentials of Psycho-Analysis*, trans. James Strachey (London: Hogarth Press, 1986), 419.

13. Elizabeth Nitchie, introduction to Mary Shelley's *Mathilda* (Chapel Hill: University of North Carolina Press, 1959), vii.

14. Ibid., xiii.

15. Ibid., vii.

16. U. C. Knoepflmacher, "Thoughts on the Aggression of Daughters," in U. C. Knoepflmacher and George Levine, eds., *The Endurance of Frankenstein* (Berkeley: University of California Press, 1979), 115.

17. Anne K. Mellor, *Mary Shelley: Her Life, Her Fiction, Her Monsters* (New York: Routledge, 1988), 195.

18. Emily W. Sunstein, *Mary Shelley: Romance and Reality* (Boston: Little, Brown & Co., 1989)34. For Sunstein's reference and quotation, see Thornton Hunt, "Shelley, By One Who Knew Him," *Atlantic Monthly* 11 (February 1863): 184–204.

19. Herman, *Father-Daugther Incest*, 27.

20. Jane Gallop, *The Daughter's Seduction: Feminism and Psychoanalysis* (Ithaca, N.Y.: Cornell University Press, 1981), 77.

21. Nitchie, introduction to *Mathilda*, vii.

22. Sunstein, *Mary Shelley*, 171.

23. Betty T. Bennett, ed., *The Letters of Mary Wollstonecraft Shelley*, 3 vols (Baltimore: Johns Hopkins University Press, 1980, 1983, 1988), 3:100.

24. Peter H. Marshall, *William Godwin* (New Haven, Conn.: Yale University Press, 1984), 331.

25. Quoted in Knoepflmacher, "Thoughts," 113.
26. Percy Bysshe Shelley, *The Letters of Percy Bysshe Shelley*, ed. Frederick L. Jones, 2 vols. (Oxford: Clarendon Press, 1964), 2:109.
27. Ibid.
28. Paula R. Feldman and Diana Scott-Kilvert, eds., *The Journals of Mary Shelley, 1814–1844*, 2 vols. (Oxford: Clarendon Press, 1987), 1:292.
29. Sunstein, *Mary Shelley*, 171.
30. Ibid. Percy abandoned Harriet Shelley, his first wife, to elope with Mary Godwin in 1814.
31. See Mary Wollstonecraft, *Posthumous Works of the Author of a Vindication of the Rights of Woman*, 4 vols. (London, 1798), 4:97–155.
32. Feldman and Scott-Kilvert, eds., *Journals*, 1:293.
33. Ibid., xvii–xviii.
34. William St. Clair, *The Godwins and the Shelleys: A Biography of a Family* (New York: W. W. Norton & Co., 1989), 467.
35. My speculation offers an important contrast to the precision with which Godwin preserved, ordered, and published Wollstonecraft's letters, which suggests that Godwin concealed *Mathilda* and Mary's letters for the purpose of concealing and silencing Mary's understanding of their relationship.
36. Frederick L. Jones, ed., *Maria Gisborne and Edward E. Williams, Shelley's Friends: Their Journals and Letters* (Norman: University of Oklahoma Press, 1951), 27.
37. As Bennett notes in a footnote in *Letters* (1:68n. 2), Maria Gisborne (1770–1836) was a lifelong friend of both the Shelleys and the Godwins, with the exception of a one-year estrangement from Mary Shelley in 1820–21 (due probably to the fact that Gisborne repeated some gossip from Jane Clairmont). She had cared for Mary when she was a baby and was courted by and refused to marry William Godwin in 1800. Perhaps the most notable element of the relationship between the two women is that Maria Gisborne was the person whom Mary Shelley trusted the most in the early years of her marriage to Percy. In her letters, Mary shares with Maria her bitterness regarding her stepmother, her anxiety about her father's opinion of her, and her anger toward Percy.
38. Jones, ed., *Maria Gisborne*, 27.
39. Ibid., 44.
40. Marshall, *William Godwin*, 331.
41. Knoepflmacher, "Thoughts," 115.

42. Mellor, *Mary Shelley*, xvii; Sunstein, *Mary Shelley*, 193–96, 213, 224, 233, 374.
43. Bennett, eds, *Letters*, 1:218.
44. Ibid., 1:224.
45. Jones, ed., *Maria Gisborne*, 76.
46. Bennett, ed., *Letters*, 1:229.
47. Ibid., 1:245; my emphasis.
48. Ibid., 1:247.
49. Ibid., 1:336.
50. Betty T. Bennett and Charles E. Robinson, eds., *The Mary Shelley Reader* (New York: Oxford University Press, 1990), 175–76. All further page references to this work are noted parenthetically in the text.
51. Gallop, *The Daughter's Seduction*, 78.
52. Blume, *Secret Survivors*, 221.
53. Gallop, *The Daughter's Seduction*, 75.
54. Luce Irigaray, "The Blind Spot of an Old Dream of Symmetry," in *Speculum of the Other Woman*, trans. Gillian C. Gill (Ithaca, N.Y.: Cornell University Press, 1985), 38.
55. Bass and Davis, *Courage to Heal*, 77–95.
56. Sunstein, *Mary Shelley*, 191.
57. Bennett, ed., *Letters*, vol. 1.
58. Feldman and Scott-Kilvert, eds., *Journals*.
59. Bennett, ed., *Letters*, 1:108; young William died on June 7.
60. Irigaray, "Blind Spot," 38.
61. M. M. Bakhtin, "The Problem of the Text," in *Speech Genres and Other Late Essays*, trans. Vern W. McGee (Austin: University of Texas Press, 1986), 126.
62. The living hell created when third parties are absent is not lost on Bakhtin: "The understanding of the Fascist torture chamber or hell ... [is] the absolute lack of being heard, as [in] the absolute absence of a third party" ("Problem of the Text," 126). Bakhtin's configuration helps illuminate Mathilda's isolation; after all, it becomes necessary that she write her history, thereby constructing her subjectivity, only when another displaced third party—Woodville—offers himself as a reader.
63. Herman, *Father-Daughter Incest*, 117.
64. Judith Butler suggests desire is never one's own but rather is something one is forced to own when, inevitably, the Law of the Father cre-

ates the situation where self-expression is relegated to a series of displacements: "The very entry into the cultural field deflects that desire
from its original meaning, with the consequence that desire within
culture is, of necessity, a series of displacements" (Judith Butler, *Gender Trouble: Feminism and the Subversion of Identity* [New York: Routledge, 1990], 65).

65. Andrea Dworkin, *Intercourse* (New York: Free Press, 1987), 150.
66. I put both "fictional" and "real" in quotation marks because the separation between the two is both arbitrary and political. Depositing
events into narrative makes them fictions; at the same time, narrating
a previously unnarrativized experience constructs the event as "real."
67. Claude Lévi-Strauss, *The Elementary Structures of Kinship*, trans. James
Harle Bell and John Richard von Sturmer (Boston: Beacon Press,
1969), 481.
68. Luce Irigaray's "Woman on the Market" offers insight into the
father's role: "The society we know, our own culture, is based on the
exchange of women.... The passage into the social order, into the
symbolic order, into order as such, is assured by the fact that men, or
groups of men, circulate women among themselves, according to a
rule known as the incest of taboo." ("Women on the Market," from
This Sex Which Is Not One, trans. Catherine Porter with Caroline Burke
[Ithaca, N.Y.: Cornell University Press, 1985], 170).
69. Gayle Rubin, "The Traffic in Women: Notes on the 'Political Economy' of Sex," in *Toward an Anthropology of Women*, ed. Rayna Reiter
(New York: Monthly Review Press, 1975), 177.
70. Ibid., 174.
71. Blume, *Secret Survivors*, 51.
72. W. Arens, *The Original Sin: Incest and Its Meaning* (New York and
Oxford: Oxford University Press, 1986), viii.
73. Mary Douglas, *Purity and Danger: An Analysis of Pollution and Taboo*
(1966; reprint, New York: ARK Paperback, 1989), 115.
74. Dworkin, *Intercourse*, 166.
75. Privileging the body over the mind only to "prove" that bodily damage was minimal offers one of the most harmful effects of patriarchal
arrogance to our society. It is important to recognize that someone—
either the dominant gaze or the subject in question—always translates the body's pain through categories available to the mind. The
separation of mind and body and the convenient focus on the site of
a woman's body—whose pain becomes legitimate only when cata-

loged and understood by others—reveals how Western logic obscures, circumvents, or simply overturns subjective inscriptions of the body in pain.

76. Jacques Lacan, "The Signification of the Phallus," in *Écrits: A Selection*, trans. Alan Sheridan (New York: W. W. Norton & Co., 1977), 285.

77. Gallop, *The Daughter's Seduction*, 77.

78. Ibid., 96.

79. Ibid., 77.

80. Dissociation is also called "splitting" in recovery literature. Frank W. Putnam, in "Dissociative Disorders in Children: Behavioral Profiles and Problems," defines dissociation as "a complex psychobiological process that results in a failure to integrate information into the normal stream of consciousness. It produces a range of symptoms and behaviors including a). amnesias; b). disturbances in sense of self; c). trance-like states; d). rapid shifts in mood and behavior; e). perplexing shifts in access to knowledge, memory and skills; f.) auditory and visual hallucinations; and g). vivid imaginary companionship in children and adolescents" (*Child Abuse and Neglect* 17 [1993]: 39). In the same article Putnam has "firmly established a connection between childhood trauma and the development of dissociative disorders in adults."

81. Herman, *Father-Daughter Incest*, 22–35.

82. Ibid., 36–49.

83. According to Lynda E. Boose in "The Father's House and the Daughter in It," the relative openness with which our society now addresses incest does not portend a liberal future; rather, "the subject has changed venues and now rests in the hands of a new and more powerful set of cultural fathers." In fact, these new fathers rule with a more ruthless reign than their predecessors: "In 1987, after a six-year study conducted by doctors from Harvard Medical School and Massachusetts General Hospital, headed by Harvard psychiatrist Muriel Sugarman, a new phenomenon termed 'divorce incest' was identified, in which the children typically were not abused *until* the divorce or separation took place. Having followed a group of '19 children age 6 or younger whom the researchers believed had been sexually abused by their biological father during visits after separation or divorce,' the study reported that at the court level, in spite of substantial documentation of incest by social-service agencies, 'allegations were disbelieved in 73.7 percent of the cases,' and not one of the men

accused was prosecuted. In fact, the judicial system seemed so loath to side against the privileges of the father that 'in nearly 60 percent of the cases, the children were forced to have [continued] visits with their fathers'" (Lynda Boose, "The Father's House and the Daugther in It," in *Daughters and Fathers*, ed. Lynda E. Boose and Betty S. Flowers [Baltimore: Johns Hopkins University Press, 1989], 71n. 5).

84. Bass and Davis, *Courage to Heal*, 31.

85. This idealism is ultimately intellectually unsupportable, because there is no such thing as healing the self in a sick society.

86. Arens, *The Original Sin*, vii.

87. Diane Price Herndl, "The Writing Cure: Charlotte Perkins Gilman, Anna O., and 'Hysterical' Writing," *National Women's Studies Association Journal* 1, 1 (1988): 68.

88. Bennett, ed., *Letters*, 1:103.

Notes to Chapter 3

1. Abreaction is "emotional discharge whereby the subject liberates himself [or herself] from the affect attached to the memory of a traumatic event in such a way that this affect is not able to become (or to remain) pathogenic. Abreaction may be provoked in the course of psychotherapy, especially under hypnosis, and produce a cathartic effect. It may also come about spontaneously, either a short or a long interval after the original trauma" (Jean Laplanche and Jean-Bertrand Pontalis, *The Language of Psycho-Analysis*, trans. Donald Nicholson-Smith [New York: W. W. Norton & Co., 1973], 1). Abreaction has recently come under attack from the proponents of the False Memory Syndrome Foundation, for reasons that I address in chapter 6.

2. Marilyn Gaull, *Romanticism: The Human Context* (New York and London: W. W. Norton & Co., 1988), 247.

3. Betty T. Bennett and Charles E. Robinson, eds., *The Mary Shelley Reader* (New York: Oxford University Press, 1990), 170.

4. Emily W. Sunstein, *Mary Shelley: Romance and Reality* (Boston: Little, Brown & Co., 1989), 34.

5. According to Jacques Lacan in "The Signification of the Phallus," the phallus is not an organ: "It is even less the organ, penis or clitoris, that it symbolizes.... For the phallus is a signifier, a signifier whose function, in the intersubjective economy of the analysis, lifts the veil perhaps from the function it performed in the mysteries. For it is a

signifier intended to designate as a whole the effects of the signified, in that the signifier conditions them by its presence as a signifier" (*Écrits: A Selection*, trans. Alan Sheridan [New York: W. W. Norton & Co., 1971], 285).

6. Sunstein, *Mary Shelley*, 89.

7. Ibid., 108.

8. Georges Bataille, *Erotism: Death and Sensuality*, trans. Mary Dalwood (San Francisco: City Lights Books, 1986), 56–67.

9. Sunstein, *Mary Shelley*, 111; my emphasis.

10. William Veeder, *Mary Shelley and Frankenstein: The Fate of Androgyny* (Chicago: University of Chicago Press, 1986), 7. Note that paralysis of the arms is also one of Anna O.'s signal disorders, also motivated by her "passionate fond[ness]" (62) for her father. See Josef Breuer and Sigmund Freud, Case Histories, "Fräulein Anna O.," in *The Freud Reader*, ed. Peter Gay (New York: W. W. Norton & Co., 1989), 61–78.

11. Veeder, *Mary Shelley*, 8.

12. Ibid., 18.

13. Ibid., 125.

14. Ibid., 127.

15. Lynda Zwinger, *Daughters, Fathers, and the Novel: The Sentimental Romance of Heterosexuality* (Madison: University of Wisconsin Press, 1991), 127.

16. Ibid., 4.

17. Harold Bloom, ed., *Mary Shelley: Modern Critical Views* (New York: Chelsea House, 1985), 1.

18. Certainly, the national hysteria generated over the 1991 Clarence Thomas hearings suggests the existence of tremendous conflict and anxiety about precisely what counts as proof when women's bodies are the texts in question. In "Testimony of Silence; A Psychohistorical Perspective on the Thomas-Hill Hearings," *Journal of Psychohistory*, 19, 3 (winter 1992): 257–68, Dan Dervin refers to Anita Hill as "the messenger sacrificed for delivering her message" and explains why this sacrifice takes place: "[Anita Hill] is guilty, however, not of sexual transgression or of violating taboo, but of an equivalent crime in the turbulence of the unconscious: for speaking of it" (263).

19. Kenneth Adams, *Silently Seduced: When Parents Make Their Children Partners: Understanding Covert Incest* (Deerfield Beach, Fla.: Health Communications, Inc., 1991), 9.

20. Ibid.

21. Ibid., 10. An anonymous reader for New York University Press pointed out that same-sex covert incest is also common for girls, especially ones who play empathic daughter-husband to oppressed or abused mother. It is interesting—and highly problematic—that Adams uses only a heterosexual paradigm for this study, because the culturally inscribed mother—daughter bond/bind can also be fruitfully understood as covertly incestuous.

22. Anne K. Mellor, *Mary Shelley: Her Life, Her Fiction, Her Monsters* (New York: Routledge, 1988), chap. 1.

23. Sunstein, *Mary Shelley*, 42.

24. Ibid., 90.

25. Ibid.

26. As I suggested in chapter 1, the seduction theory did not have to be abandoned for Freud to identify erotic desire within children.

27. Sigmund Freud, "An Autobiographical Study," in *The Freud Reader*, 21. Freud's "obligation" here was to protect the patriarchal system that sustained him. As I suggested in chapter 2, the most outspoken critics of this gesture are Alice Miller (in *Thou Shalt Not Be Aware*) and Jeffrey Moussaieff Masson (in *The Assault on Truth*).

28. Veeder, *Mary Shelley*, 134.

29. Zwinger, *Daughters*, 9.

30. Paula R. Feldman and Diana Scott-Kilvert, eds., *The Journals of Mary Shelley, 1814–1844*, 2 vols. (Oxford: Clarendon Press, 1987, 1:324.

31. Ibid., 1:324–25n. 4.

32. I cite here those recent articles on *Frankenstein* that have received the most critical attention. While there is clearly a good deal of overlap in the different schools, I list three groupings for organizational ease.

   The psychoanalytic criticism: Peter Brooks, "Godlike Science/ Unhallowed Arts: Language and Monstrosity in *Frankenstein*," *New Literary History* 9 (1978): 591–605; Sandra Gilbert and Susan Gubar, "Horror's Twin: Mary Shelley's Monstrous Eve," chapter 7 of *The Madwoman in the Attic: The Woman Writer and the Nineteenth-Century Literary Imagination* (New Haven, Conn.: Yale University Press, 1979); Margaret Homans, "Bearing Demons: Frankenstein's Circumvention of the Maternal," in *Bearing the Word: Language and Female Experience in Nineteenth-Century Women's Writing* (Chicago: University of Chicago Press, 1986); Barbara Johnson, "My Monster/Myself," *Diacritics* 12 (1982): 2–10; U. C. Knoepflmacher, "Thoughts on the Aggression of Daughters," in *The Endurance of Frankenstein*, ed U. C. Knoepflmacher and George Levine (Berkeley: University of California Press, 1979), 119; Anne K. Mellor, "Possessing Nature: The Female in *Frankenstein*," in *Romanticism and Feminism*, ed. Anne K. Mellor (Bloomington: Indiana University Press, 1988), 220–32; Ellen Moers, *Literary Women* (Garden City, N.Y.: Doubleday, 1977); Marc Rubinstein, "'My Accursed Origin': The Search for the Mother in *Frankenstein*," *Studies in Romanticism* 15 (1976): 165–94.

The Feminist Criticism: James B. Carson, "Bringing the Author Forward: *Frankenstein* through Mary Shelley's Letters," *Criticism* 30, 4 (1988): 431–53; Kate Ellis, "Monsters in the Garden: Mary Shelley and the Bourgeois Family," in *The Endurance of Frankenstein*, ed. Knoepflmacher and Levine, 123–42; Gilbert and Gubar, "Horror's Twin," chapter 7 of *The Madwoman in the Attic*; Burton Hatlen, "Milton, Mary Shelley, and Patriarchy," *Bucknell Review* 28, 2 (1983): 155–64; Devon Hodges, "*Frankenstein* and the Feminine Subversion of the Novel," *Tulsa Studies in Women's Literature* 2, 2 (1983): 155–64; Mellor, *Mary Shelley*.

The science-fiction criticism: Anca Vlaspolos, "*Frankenstein*'s Hidden Skeleton: The Psychopolitics of Oppression," *Science Fiction Studies* 10, 2 (1983): 125–36.

33. Frank W. Putnam, "Dissociative Disorders in Children: Behavioral Profiles and Problems," *Child Abuse and Neglect* 17 (1993): 40.

34. Ibid., 41.

35. Ian Hacking, "Two Souls in One Body," *Critical Inquiry* 17, 4 (1991): 856.

36. Ibid., 861.

37. Philip M. Coons, "The Differential Diagnoses of Multiple Personality," *Psychiatric Clinics of North America* 7 (March 1984): 53 (quoted in Hacking, "Two Souls," 850).

38. Mary Shelley, *Frankenstein*, in *The Mary Shelley Reader*, ed. Bennett and Robinson, 40. All further page references to this work are noted parenthetically in the text.

39. Barbara Johnson's "My Monster/Myself" also situates *Frankenstein* as a work of autobiography; according to Johnson, Mary Shelley perceived herself as the "monster" within Mary Wollstonecraft: "Mary herself was in fact the unwitting murderous intruder present on her own parents' wedding night: their decision to marry was due to the fact that Mary Wollstonecraft was already carrying the child that was to kill her" (152).

40. This is the objective behind social values prevalent in dysfunctional families that impose silence, which falsely understand talking about a painful experience as a cause and further aggravation of the pain.

41. Sigmund Freud, *Early Psychoanalytic Publications* (1893–1899), vol. 3 of *The Standard Edition of the Complete Psychoanalytical Works of Sigmund Freud*, ed. James Strachey (London: Hogarth Press), 302.

42. Ibid., 322.

43. Sigmund Freud, "Childhood Memories and Screen Memories," in *The Psychopathology of Everyday Life* (1901), vol. 6 of *The Standard Edition*, ed. Strachey, 43.

44. Ibid., 45.

45. Ibid., 46.

46. Ibid., 47–48.

47. Judith Herman explodes the myth that abuse survivors inevitably become abusers when she says, "Survivors of childhood abuse are far more likely to be victimized or to harm themselves than to victimize other people.... Survivors seem most disposed to direct their aggression at themselves" (*Trauma and Recovery: The Aftermath of Violence* [New York: Basic Books, 1992], 113).

48. Again, this can profitably be compared to Mathilda's observation: "I never dared give words to my dark tale, I was impressed more strongly with the withering fear that I was in truth a marked creature, a pariah, only fit for death" (Shelley, *Mathilda*, 239).

49. It is important that Walton plays the same role for Victor that Woodville does for Mathilda, that of the third party whose vision and voice provide the context for crisis and (even veiled) self-disclosure. As Marlene Longenecker has pointed out to me in conversation, it is additionally significant that both names begin with a *W* and thus echo the third party who contextualizes Mary Shelley's own personal crisis, William Godwin.

Notes to Chapter 4

1. See, for example, the work of Nancy Friday and Nancy Chodorow.

2. See Lynda Zwinger's *Daughters, Fathers and the Novel: The Sentimental Romance of Heterosexuality* (Madison: University of Wisconsin, Press, 1991).

3. Frances Howland, M.D., afterword to Joan Frances Casey and Lynn Wilson, *The Flock: The Autobiography of a Multiple Personality* (New York: Fawcett, 1991), 299; American Psychiatric Association, *Diagnostic and*

Statistical Manual of Mental Disorders, 4th ed. (Washington, D.C.: American Psychiatric Press, 1994), 484–88 (hereafter cited as *DSM IV*).

4. For example, Sybil's therapist, Cornelia Wilbur, finds her estranged patient walking the streets at night. (Of course, one wonders why a psychiatrist trails after her patients after office hours!) She wraps her patient in her own mink coat and promises that once Sybil finds wholeness she can have a sleeve of this mink coat (Flora Rheta Schreiber, *Sybil* [New York: Warner Books, 1973], 370).

5. It is important to note that Cornelia Wilbur (the psychiatrist) and Flora Schreiber (the narrator) are two of only a handful of "characters" in true crime novels who use their real names. Typically in the genre of true crime fiction, real names are reserved only for the guilty.

6. The memory trace is the alter who knows the history of all the other alters. She carries the memory, pain, and triumph of the others, and when social demands require that the victim produce memory and history, this alter often cues in.

7. Schreiber, *Sybil*, p. 37. All further page references to this work are noted parenthetically, with *S* and the page number, in the text.

8. As Jane Gallop puts it, "The phallic mother is more dangerous because less obviously phallic. If the phallus 'can only play its role when veiled (Lacan)', then the phallic mother is more phallic precisely by being less obvious" (*The Daughter's Seduction: Feminism and Psycho-analysis* [Ithaca, N.Y.: Cornell University Press, 1981], 118).

9. Ellen Bass and Laura Davis define "splitting" as a common dissociative aftereffect of sexual abuse: "In its milder form, you live exclusively on the mental level, in your thoughts, and aren't fully present. At its most extreme, you literally leave your body" (*The Courage to Heal*, 3d ed. [New York: Harper & Row, 1994], 219).

10. Julia Kristeva shows how this allows "the subject to articulate abrupt passages between the real, the imaginary and the symbolic" ("The True-Real," trans. Sean Hand, in *The Kristeva Reader*, ed. Toril Moi [New York: Basil Blackwell, 1986], 218). Sybil, when splitting, talks in the presymbolic real and inscribes truth in what Kristeva calls "hysterical discourse": "In hysterical discourse, truth, when not weighed down by the symptom, often assumes the obsessive, unsayable and emotionally charged weft of visual representation. Floating in isolation, this vision of an unnamed real rejects all nomination and any possible narrative" (227).

11. Judith Roof, *A Lure of Knowledge: Lesbian Sexuality and Theory* (New York: Columbia University Press, 1991), 93.
12. See Josef Breuer and Sigmund Freud, Case Histories, "Fräulein Anna O." in *The Freud Reader*, ed. Peter Gay (New York: W. W. Norton & Co., 1989), 61–78; and Diane Hunter's brilliant essay "Hysteria, Psychoanalysis, and Feminism: The Case of Anna O.," in *The (M)other Tongue: Essays in Psychoanalytic Interpretation*, ed. Shirley Nelson Garner, Claire Kahane, and Madelon Sprengnether (Ithaca, N.Y.: Cornell University Press, 1985), 89–115.
13. Howland, afterword to Casey and Wilson's *The Flock*, 300.
14. The abject is "neither subject nor object. [It] makes clear the impossible and untenable identity of each.... The abject is an impossible object, still part of the subject: an object the subject tries to expel but which is uneliminable.... These ingested/expelled objects are neither part of the body nor separate from it.... The abject is undecidably both inside and outside (like the skin of milk); dead and alive (like the corpse); autonomous and engulfing (like infection). It signals the precarious grasp the subject has over its identity and bodily boundaries, the ever-present possibility of sliding back into the corporeal abyss out of which it was formed" (Elizabeth Wright, ed., *Feminism and Psychoanalysis: A Critical Dictionary* [New York: Basil Blackwell, 1992], 197–98).
15. *Sign, signifier,* and *signified* are terms borrowed from Ferdinand de Saussure and used in poststructural theories to explain how language functions as an "institution" to shape personal relations and social structures. A sign is the linguistic relationship between the signifier and signified, a signifier is the arbitrary word assigned to a concept, and a signified is the concept itself.
16. Bass and Davis, *Courage to Heal*, 423–24.
17. Judith Herman, *Trauma and Recovery: The Aftermath of Violence* (New York: Basic Books, 1992), 52–53.
18. Ibid., 53.
19. Cornelia Wilbur, M.D., "Multiple Personality and Child Abuse: An Overview," *Psychiatric Clinics of North America* 7, 1 (1984): 4.
20. Margaret Smith, *Ritual Abuse* (New York: HarperCollins, 1993).
21. Bass and Davis, *Courage to Heal*, 25.
22. Casey and Wilson, *The Flock*, 30. Further references to pages in this work are noted parenthetically, with *F* and the page number, in the text.

23. Herman, *Trauma and Recovery*, chap. 7.
24. Ibid.
25. The phallic mother is not the same as the "collusive" or "powerless" mother (Janis Tyler Johnson, *Mothers of Incest Survivors: Another Side of the Story* [Bloomington: Indiana University Press, 1992], 1–6); these terms represent mothers who either act as co-perpetrators or are co-victims of father—daughter incest. The conflation of the phallic mother with the collusive or powerless mother reenacts the larger misreading that psychoanalysis has endured in the name of material-ist feminist critique: substituting the psychic mother (the mother that resides in the unconscious and is bound up with fantasy) for the social (historical) mother. The phallic mother begins as a fantasy for both mother and infant. For the pre—mirror stage infant, she is the fantasy of the "absolutely powerful" but "sexually neutral" mother (Wright, ed., *Feminism and Psychoanalysis*, 314). (While the phallic mother functions as a fantasy for the child, for the phallic mother herself this fantasy crosses into what Kristeva calls the *true-real*, a term I explore later.) The child does not perceive itself as separate or dis-tinct from the mother until the mirror stage, when "the child acquires an image of the mother as a total being, a coherent union of her composite parts, separate from the child" (Wright, ed., *Feminism and Psychoanalysis*, 314). But the phallic mother resists this separation and replaces the child's independence (to function for itself) with her need to "grant the child everything, to be its object of desire, and in turn, to be the subject who desires the child as her object." While the phallic mother intends no harm, "there is something psychically crippling about the unmediated pre-oedipal mother-child relation, where each offers the other a perfect satisfaction of desire.... This relation is stifling, and if unmediated, induces psychosis." In the mother—child relationship defined by the phallic mother (and rep-resented in popular culture through women's true crime novels), "the child may mean everything to [the mother], and she remain[s] everything for the child, leaving no room for growth and indepen-dence." The phallic mother functions as the "basis of the persecutory image of psychosis" (Wright, ed., *Feminism and Psychoanalysis*, 315).
26. In the prologue Lynn writes, "When I first met Joan, on a snowy day in 1981, I was approaching a transition in my life. My daughter Lisa, youngest of five, was finishing her final year at home. For the first time in thirty years, I would have no children with me. For the first

time in our seventeen years of marriage, my second husband, Gordon, and I would be alone together" (*F*, 1).

27. As earlier chapters have posited, in Mary Shelley's early fiction, especially her incest narratives *Mathilda* (1819) and *Frankenstein* (1818), incest assumes the place of "normal" familial extensions, not obviously marked transgressions. This phrase of Mary Shelley's, "more-than-daughter," is a symptomatic repetition revealing, I believe, the particular pain that occurs when abuse is normalized and naturalized by social practice. I use this phrase here because the transgression from therapist to surrogate mother is, ultimately, a transgression of incest.

28. Bass and Davis, *Courage to Heal*, 109.

29. See, for example, a most intriguing side comment by Nancy Chodorow in *The Reproduction of Mothering: Psychoanalysis and the Sociology of Gender* (Berkeley: University of California Press, 1978): "Mother—daughter incest may be the most 'socially-regressive' in the sense of a basic threat to species survival, since a mother and son can at least produce a child. But the threat of mother—daughter incestuous and exclusive involvement has been met by a girl's entry into the Oedipus situation and her change of genital erotic object" (132). Not only does the daughter become responsible for the incest potential of the phallic mother here but, we are told, if she plays her heterosexually determining cards right, then she need not fret about mother invasion at all.

30. See Thomas J. Hurley III and Brenden O'Regan, *Multiple Personality— Mirrors of a New Model of Mind?*, special issue of *Investigations: Institute of Noetic Sciences* 1, 3/4 (1985).

Notes to Chapter 5

1. Judith Mayne, *Cinema and Specatorship* (New York: Routledge, 1993), 38.

2. Lacan distinguishes "desire from concepts with which it is often confused, such as need and demand. Need is directed towards a specific object and is satisfied by it. Demands are formulated and addressed to others; where they are still aimed at an object, this is not essential to them, since the articulated demand is essentially a demand for love. Desire appears in the rift which separates need and demand; it cannot be reduced to demand, in that it seeks to impose itself without taking the language or the unconscious of the other into account,

and insists upon absolute recognition from him" (Jean Laplanche and Jean-Bertrand Pontalis, *The Language of Psycho-Analysis*, trans. Donald Nicholson-Smith [New York: W. W. Norton & Co., 1973], 483).

3. Juliet Mitchell, "Introduction—I," in *Feminine Sexuality: Jacques Lacan and the École freudienne*, ed. Juliet Mitchell and Jacqueline Rose, trans. Jacqueline Rose (London: Macmillan Press, 1982), 5–6.

4. Ibid., 6.

5. Jacqueline Rose, "Introduction—II," in *Feminine Sexuality*, ed. Mitchell and Rose, 32.

6. Jean Laplanche and Jean-Bertrand Pontalis, "Fantasy and the Origins of Sexuality" (1964), in *Formations of Fantasy*, ed. Victor Burgin, James Donald, and Cora Kaplan (London and New York: Methuen, 1986), 26.

7. Teri A. Vigars, "Symbolic Play in Autism: Is There a Developmental Trend?" (paper, Department of Human Development and Family Studies, Cornell University, 1995).

8. Benjamin DeMott, "The Pro-Incest Lobby," *Psychology Today*, March 1980, 12 (quoted in Louise Armstrong, *Rocking the Cradle of Sexual Politics* [New York: Addison-Wesley, 1994], 55).

9. "Attacking the Last Taboo," *Time*, April 14, 1980, 72. (quoted in Armstrong, *Rocking the Cradle*, 55).

10. Ibid.

11. DeMott, "The Pro-Incest Lobby," 12 (quoted in Armstrong, *Rocking the Cradle*, 55).

12. Armstrong, *Rocking the Cradle*, 58.

13. Katherine Dunn, *Geek Love* (New York: Warner Books, 1988), 7. Further page references to this novel are cited parenthetically, with *GL* and the page number, in the text.

14. Jane Gallop, *The Daughter's Seduction: Feminism and Psychoanalysis* (Ithaca, N.Y.: Cornell University Press, 1981), 77.

15. Luce Irigaray, "The Blind Spot of an Old Dream of Symmetry," in *Speculum of the Other Woman*, trans. Gillian C. Gill (Ithaca, N.Y.: Cornell University Press, 1985), 38.

16. Claude Lévi-Strauss, *The Elementary Structures of Kinship*, trans. James Harle Bell and John Richard von Sturmer (Boston: Beacon Press, 1969), 481.

17. Gayle Rubin redefines the gift in "The Traffic in Women: Notes on the 'Political Economy' of Sex," in *Toward an Anthropology of Women*, ed. Rayna Reiter (New York: Monthly Review Press, 1975), 157–210.

18. Donna Britt, "The Author, the Relative and a Question of Incest: Carolivia Herron's Disputed Tale of Childhood Horror," *Washington Post*, June 25, 1991, D1.

19. Carolivia Herron, *Thereafter Johnnie* (New York: Vintage Books, 1991), 182. Further page references to this novel are cited parenthetically, with *TJ* and the page number, in the text.

20. Britt, "The Author, the Relative," D1.

21. See Jacques Lacan, "The Mirror Stage as Formative of the Function of the I as Revealed in Psychoanalytic Experience," in *Écrits*, trans. Alan Sheridan (New York: W. W. Norton & Co., 1977), 1–7.

Notes to Chapter 6

1. The FMS Foundation is located at 3401 Market Street, Suite 130, Philadelphia, PA 19104. It costs between $100 and $125 to become a member for a year. Their phone numbers are 215-387-1917 and 1-800-568-8882. An emerging organization called the Coalition For Accuracy About Abuse offers education and advocacy for survivors and allies and contests the false claims of scientific neutrality proffered by the FMS Foundation. For information about a local chapter of the coalition, contact the Family Violence and Sexual Assault Institute, 1310 Clinic Drive, Tyler, TX 75701 (telephone: 903-595-6600).

2. *FMS Foundation Newsletter*, vol. 2, no. 9 (October 1993): 6.

3. "Retractor Notices," *FMS Foundation Newsletter*, vol. 2, no. 10 (November 1993): 6.

4. Daniel Goleman, "Childhood Trauma: Memory or Invention?" *New York Times*, July 21, 1992, 6, in *The FMS Phenomenon*, 6.

5. Telephone interview, June 2, 1993.

6. Apart from member surveys—structured questionnaires that seek to understand the family history only as reflected by the point of view of the accused parent, the FMS Foundation has conducted no research to date, as far as I can discern.

7. Judith Herman, "The Abuses of Memory," Backtalk editorial, *Mother Jones*, March/April 1993, 3.

8. The False Memory Syndrome Foundation deceptively inflates its membership to include all phone calls received by its office. Thus, they declare in a recent newsletter that they have thirteen thousand members, when, in fact, they include as supporters researchers like me who contest their position. They write, "If any other medical product had more than 13,000 complaints, it would be taken off the mar-

ket. Not only is there no way to take 'therapy' off the market, there is no way for people affected by the therapy to have their complaints considered" (*FMS Foundation Newlsetter*, vol. 3, no. 5 [May 1994]: 1).

9. FMS Foundation stationery, back page.

10. Even "evidence" does not validate the survivor: "Physical evidence does not prove truth, merely that the memory has elements of reality" (Irene Wielawski, "Unlocking the Secrets of Memory," *Los Angeles Times*, October 3, 1991, in *The FMS Phenomenon*, 3).

11. Ellen Bass and Laura Davis, *The Courage to Heal*, 2d ed. (New York: HarperCollins, 1988), 22. As stated earlier, in the third edition, Bass and Davis revise this point. They write: "If you genuinely think you were abused and your life shows the symptoms, there's a strong likelihood that you were" (26).

12. *The FMS Phenomenon*, 41. Half of the proceeds from the purchase of *Confabulations* go back to the foundation.

13. These essays include: Robyn M. Dawes, "Biases of Retrospection," *Issues in Child Abuse Accusations* 1, 3 (1991): 25–27; Harold I. Lief, "Psychiatry's Challenge: Defining an Appropriate Therapeutic Role when Child Abuse Is Suspected," *Psychiatric News*, August 21, 1992; Elizabeth F. Loftus, "The Reality of Repressed Memories" (unpublished manuscript, 1992); Paul R. McHugh, "Psychiatric Misadventures," *American Scholar* 61, 4 (1992): 497–510; Andrew Meacham, "Study Disputes Link between Eating Disorders, Sexual Abuse," *Changes* (April 1993): 22.

14. FMS Foundation stationery, back page; my emphasis.

15. *False Memory Syndrome Foundation* (pamphlet, 1992).

16. Ibid.

17. *FMS Foundation Newsletter*, vol. 2, no. 4 (May 1993): 9.

18. Ibid., 12–13.

19. Bill Taylor, "What if Sexual Abuse Memories Are Wrong?" *Toronto Star*, May 16, 1992, G1+, in *The FMS Phenomenon*, 19.

20. *FMS Foundation Newsletter*, vol. 2, no. 4 (May 1993): 2.

21. Excerpt from *Confabulations*, in *The FMS Phenomenon*, 40.

22. Pamela Freyd: "Do I believe children are sometimes abused by their parents? Absolutely. But to the degree that we are being asked to accept? Absolutely not" (Bill Taylor, "True or False?" *Toronto Star*, May 18, 1992 [quoted in *The FMS Phenomenon*, 21]).

23. Jennifer Freyd, "Personal Perspectives on the Delayed Memory Debate," *Family Violence and Sexual Assault Bulletin* 9, 3 (1993): 26.

24. Ibid., 28.
25. Ibid., 30.
26. Bass and Davis, *Courage to Heal,* 490.
27. Freyd, "Personal Perspectives," 29.
28. As noted by Claude Lévi-Strauss (*The Elementary Structures of Kinship,* trans. James Harle Bell and John Richard von Sturmer [Boston: Beacon Press, 1969]) and extended by Gayle Rubin ("The Traffic in Women: Notes on the 'Political Economy' of Sex," in *Toward an Anthropology of Women,* ed. Rayna Reiter [New York: Monthly Review Press, 1975]), the incest taboo functions to protect the patriarch's duty to exchange his daughter, to "traffic" her in a patriarchal marketplace—and an acceptable gift should be unused.
29. Linda Alcoff and Laura Gray, "Survivor Discourse: Transgression on Recuperation?" *Signs* 18, 2 (1993): 275.
30. Ibid., 284.
31. Judith Herman, *Trauma and Recovery: The Aftermath of Violence* (New York: Basic Books, 1992), 133.
32. Ibid., 175.
33. This essay is from a special edition of *Lesbian Ethics* (4, 3 [spring 1992]: 122–28) that focuses exclusively on lesbian incest survivors.
34. Lesbianism can, of course, serve as a useful contradiction to those sexual abuses contained by normative heterosexuality. But for closeted lesbians, lesbianism can also function as a repetition of the incest narrative via homophobia and heterosexism, by closeting sexuality and thereby revisiting the isolation and secrecy that signifies victimhood.

Notes to the Afterword

1. Mike Males, "'Recovered Memory,' Child Abuse and Media Escapism," *Extra! (The Journal of FAIR)* (September/October 1994): 11.
2. Ibid.
3. Frederick Crews, "The Revenge of the Repressed," parts 1 and 2, *New York Review of Books* (November 1994): 54–60; (December 1994): 49–57.
4. Loftus (co-author of *The Myth of Repressed Memory*) and Ofshe (co-author of *Making Monsters*) are also members of the FMS Foundation and advisers on their Scientific and Professional Advisory Board.
5. In 1995, U.S. District Judge D. Lowell Jensen overturned the 1990 conviction and life sentence of George Franklin, Sr., for the 1969

murder of eight-year-old Susan Nason. As this book goes to press, the retrial of George Franklin will begin (*Syracuse Herald American*, Sunday, January 21, 1996, A13).

6. Crews, "Revenge of the Repressed," part 1, 58.
7. Ibid., part 2, 52.
8. Ibid., part 2, 49.
9. Ibid., part 2, 52.
10. Ibid., part 2, 57–58.
11. Ibid., part 2, 58.

Note to the Appendix

1. Donald Reiman, ed., *Shelley and His Circle*, Documents in the Carl H. Pforzheimer Library, vol. 8 (Cambridge: Harvard University Press, 1986), 1069–72.

Bibliography

Adams, Kenneth M. *Silently Seduced: When Parents Make Their Children Partners: Understanding Covert Incest.* Deerfield Beach, Fla: Health Communications, Inc., 1991.

Alcoff, Linda, and Laura Gray. "Survivor Discourse: Transgression or Recuperation?" *Signs* 18, 2 (1993): 260–90.

Althusser, Louis. *Lenin and Philosophy and Other Essays.* New York: Monthly Review Press, 1971.

American Psychiatric Association. *Diagnostic and Statistical Manual of Mental Disorders.* 4th ed. (*DSM–IV*). Washington, D.C.: American Psychiatric Press, 1994.

Anzaldúa, Gloria, ed. *Making Face, Making Soul—Haciendo caras: Creative and Critical Perspectives by Feminists of Color.* San Francisco: aunt lute books, 1990.

Arens, W. *The Original Sin: Incest and Its Meaning.* New York and Oxford: Oxford University Press, 1986.

Armstrong, Louise. *Rocking the Cradle of Sexual Politics*. New York: Addison-Wesley, 1994.

Bakhtin, M. M. *The Dialogic Imagination: Four Essays*. Translated by Caryl Emerson and Michael Holquist. Austin: University of Texas Press, 1981.

———. "The Problem of the Text in Linguistics, Philology, and the Human Sciences: An Experiment in Philosophical Analysis." Pp. 103–31 in *Speech Genres and Other Late Essays*. Translated by Vern. W. McGee. Austin: University of Texas Press, 1986.

Bass, Ellen, and Laura Davis. *The Courage to Heal: A Guide for Women Survivors of Child Sexual Abuse*. 3d edition. New York: HarperCollins, 1988, 1994.

Bataille, Georges. *Erotism: Death and Sensuality*. Translated by Mary Dalwood. San Francisco: City Lights Books, 1986.

Bennett, Betty T., ed. *The Letters of Mary Wollstonecraft Shelley*. 3 vols. Baltimore: Johns Hopkins University Press, 1980, 1983, 1988.

Bennett, Betty T., and Charles E. Robinson, eds. *The Mary Shelley Reader*. New York: Oxford University Press, 1990.

Bijkerk, Inie, and Kathy Evert. *When You're Ready: A Woman's Healing from Childhood Physical and Sexual Abuse by Her Mother*. Rockville, Md.: Launch Press, 1987.

Bleich, David. *Subjective Criticism*. Baltimore: Johns Hopkins University Press, 1978.

Blessing, Shana Rowen. "How to Be a Political Dyke and an Incest Survivor at the Same Time, or, Why Are All the Dykes I Know Reading *The Courage to Heal?*" *Lesbian Ethics* 4, 3 (spring 1992): 122–28.

Bloom, Harold, ed. *Mary Shelley: Modern Critical Views*. New York: Chelsea House, 1985.

Blume, E. Sue. *Secret Survivors: Uncovering Incest and Its Effects on Women*. New York: Ballantine, 1985.

Boose, Lynda E., and Betty S. Flowers, eds. *Daughters and Fathers*. Baltimore: Johns Hopkins University Press, 1989.

Breuer, Josef, and Sigmund Freud. *Studies in Hysteria* (1895). Translated by James Strachey. New York: Basic Books, 1955.

Britt, Donna. "The Author, the Relative and a Question of Incest: Carolivia Herron's Disputed Tale of Childhood Horror." *Washington Post*, June 25, 1991, D1.

Butler, Judith. *Bodies That Matter: On the Discursive Limits of "Sex."* New York: Routledge, 1993.

———. *Gender Trouble: Feminism and the Subversion of Identity*. New York: Routledge, 1990.

Byerly, Greg, and Rick Rubin. *Incest: The Last Taboo—An Annotated Bibliography.* New York: Garland, 1983.

Calof, David. "Facing the Truth about False Memory." *Family Therapy Network* (September/October 1993): 39–45.

Cameron, Kenneth Neill, ed. *Shelley and His Circle: 1773–1822.* Documents in the Carl H. Pforzheimer Library, vol. 3. Cambridge, Mass.: Harvard University Press, 1970.

Casey, Joan Frances, and Lynn Wilson. *The Flock: The Autobiography of a Multiple Personality.* New York: Fawcett, 1991.

Chodorow, Nancy. *The Reproduction of Mothering: Psychoanalysis and the Sociology of Gender.* Berkeley: University of California Press, 1978.

Clairmont, Claire. *The Journals of Claire Clairmont.* Edited by Marion Kingston Stocking. Cambridge, Mass.: Harvard University Press, 1968.

Crews, Frederick. "The Revenge of the Repressed." Parts 1 and 2. *New York Review of Books,* November 17, 1994, 54–60; December 1, 1994, 49–58.

Cronin, James. "False Memory: The Controversy Surrounding 'False Memory' and Child Abuse." *Z Magazine* (April 1994): 31–37.

Daly, Lawrence, and J. Frank Pacifico. "Opening the Doors to the Past: Decayed Delayed Disclosures of Memories of Years Gone By." *Champion Magazine* (December 1991): 43–47. In *The FMS Phenomenon,* 36–39.

"Dangerous Obsession: The Truth about Repressed Memories." *McCall's,* June 1993, 98ff.

Davis, Laura. *Allies in Healing: When the Person You Love Was Sexually Abused as a Child.* New York: HarperCollins, 1991.

Dawes, Robyn M. "Biases of Retrospection." *Issues in Child Abuse Accusations* 1, 3 (1991): 25–28.

Dervin, Dan. "Testimony of Silence: A Psychohistorical Perspective on the Thomas-Hill Hearings." *Journal of Psychohistory,* 19, 3 (1992): 257–68.

Douglas, Mary. *Purity and Danger: An Analysis of Pollution and Taboo.* 1966. Reprint, New York: ARK Paperbacks, 1989.

Dunn, Katherine. *Geek Love.* New York: Warner Books, 1988.

Dworkin, Andrea. *Intercourse.* New York: Free Press, 1987.

False Memory Syndrome (FMS) Phenomenon. Philadelphia: FMS Foundation, 1992.

Feldman, Paula R., and Diana Scott-Kilvert, eds. *The Journals of Mary Shelley, 1814–1844.* 2 vols. Oxford: Clarendon Press, 1987.

Foucault, Michel. *The Archeology of Knowledge and the Discourse on Language.* Translated by A. M. Sheridan Smith. New York: Pantheon Books, 1972.

———. *The History of Sexuality.* Vol. 1: *An Introduction.* Translated by Robert Hurley. 1987. Reprint, New York: Vintage Press, 1990.

Freud, Sigmund. "The Aetiology of Hysteria" (1896). Pp. 259–90 in Masson, *Assault on Truth.*

———. *The Essentials of Psychoanalysis.* Translated by James Strachey. London: Hogarth Press, 1986.

———. *The Freud Reader.* Edited by Peter Gay. New York: W. W. Norton & Co., 1989.

———. *The Standard Edition of the Complete Psychological Works of Sigmund Freud.* 24 vols. Edited by James Strachey. London: Hogarth Press, 1953–1974.

———. *Three Essays on the Theory of Sexuality* (1905). Translated by James Strachey. Introduction by Steven Marcus. Edited by J. D. Sutherland. New York: Basic Books, 1978.

Freyd, Jennifer. "Personal Perspectives on the Delayed Memory Debate." *Family Violence and Sexual Assault Bulletin* 9, 3 (1993): 28–32.

Friday, Nancy. *My Mother/My Self: The Daughter's Search for Identity.* New York: Delacorte, 1977.

Gallop, Jane. *The Daughter's Seduction: Feminism and Psychoanalysis.* Ithaca, N.Y.: Cornell University Press, 1981.

Gaull, Marilyn. *English Romanticism: The Human Context.* New York and London: W. W. Norton & Co., 1988.

Geraci, Joseph. "Interview: Hollida Wakefield and Ralph Underwager" (Amsterdam, June 1991). *PAIDIKA: The Journal of Pedophilia* 3, 1 (winter 1993).

Gilbert, Sandra M., and Susan Gubar. *The Madwoman in the Attic: The Woman Writer and the Nineteenth-Century Literary Imagination.* New Haven, Conn.: Yale University Press, 1979.

Goetz, C., ed. and trans. *Charcot the Clinician: The Tuesday Lessons. Excerpts from Nine Case Presentations on General Neurology Delivered at the Salpetriere Hospital in 1887–88.* New York: Raven Press, 1987.

Goleman, Daniel. "Childhood Trauma: Memory or Invention?" *New York Times,* July 21, 1992. See also *The FMS Phenomenon,* 6–7.

Gordan, Linda. *Heroes of Their Own Lives: The Politics of Family Violence.* New York: Penguin, 1988.

Grosz, Elizabeth. *Jacques Lacan: A Feminist Introduction.* New York: Routledge, 1990.

Hacking, Ian. "Making Up People." Pp. 68–69 in Edward Stein, ed., *Forms of Desire: Sexual Orientation and the Social Constructionist Controversy.* New York: Routledge, 1992.

———. "Two Souls in One Body." *Critical Inquiry* 17, 4 (1991): 838–67.

Hall, Karen J. "Sisters in Collusion: Safety and Revolt in Shirley Jackson's *We Have Always Lived in the Castle.*" Pp. 110–19 in Jo Anna S. Mink and Janet Doubler Ward, eds., *The Significance of Sibling Relationships in Literature.* Bowling Green, Ohio: Bowling Green State University Popular Press, 1993, 110–19.

Herman, Judith. "The Abuses of Memory." Backtalk editorial. *Mother Jones*, March/April 1993, 3–4.

————. *Father-Daughter Incest.* Cambridge, Mass.: Harvard University Press, 1981.

————. *Trauma and Recovery: The Aftermath of Violence.* New York: Basic Books, 1992.

Herndl, Diane Price. "The Writing Cure: Charlotte Perkins Gilman, Anna O., and 'Hysterical' Writing.'" *National Women's Studies Association Journal* 1, 1 (1988): 52–74.

Herron, Carolivia. *Thereafter Johnnie.* New York: Vintage Books, 1991.

Hirsch, Kim. S. "Legislating Memory." *Ms.*, July/August 1994, 91.

Holland, Norman N. *Five Readers Reading.* New Haven, Conn.: Yale University Press, 1975.

hooks, bell. *Sisters of the Yam: Black Women and Self-Recovery.* Boston: South End Press, 1993.

Howland, Frances, M.D. Afterword to *The Flock.* See Casey and Wilson, *The Flock*, 299–303.

Hunter, Diane. "Hysteria, Psychoanalysis, and Feminism: The Case of Anna O." Pp. 89–115 in Shirley Nelson Garner, Claire Kahane, and Madelon Sprengnether, eds., *The (M)other Tongue: Essays in Psychoanalytic Interpretation.* Ithaca, N.Y.: Cornell University Press, 1985.

Hurley, Thomas J., III, and Brenden O'Regan. "Multiple Personality—Mirrors of a New Model of Mind?" Special issue of *Investigations: Institute of Noetic Sciences* 1, 3/4 (1985).

Irigaray, Luce. "The Blind Spot of an Old Dream of Symmetry." Pp. 13–129 in *Speculum of the Other Woman.* Translated by Gillian C. Gill. Ithaca, N.Y.: Cornell University Press, 1985.

————. "Women on the Market." Pp. 170–91 in *This Sex Which Is Not One.* Translated by Catherine Porter and Caroline Burke. Ithaca, N.Y.: Cornell University Press, 1985.

Johnson, Barbara. "My Monster/Myself." *Diacritics* 12 (1982): 2–10.

Johnson, Janis Tyler. *Mothers of Incest Survivors: Another Side of the Story.* Bloomington: Indiana University Press, 1992.

Jones, Frederick L., ed. *Maria Gisborne and Edward E. Williams, Shelley's Friends: Their Journals and Letters.* Norman: University of Oklahoma Press, 1951.

Kincaid, James. *Child Loving: The Erotic Child and Victorian Literature*, 2d ed. New York: Routledge, 1994.

Kitzinger, Celia, and Rachel Perkins. *Changing Our Minds: Lesbian Feminism and Psychology*. New York: New York University Press, 1993.

Kluft, R. P. *Childhood Antecedents of Multiple Personality*. Washington, D.C.: American Psychiatric Press, 1985.

Knoepflmacher, U. C., and George Levine, eds. *The Endurance of Frankenstein*. Berkeley: University of California Press, 1979.

Kristeva, Julia. "The True–Real." Translated by Sean Hand. In Toril Moi, ed., *The Kristeva Reader*. New York: Basil Blackwell, 1986.

Lacan, Jacques. *Écrits: A Selection*. Translated by Alan Sheridan. New York: W. W. Norton & Co., 1977.

———. *Feminine Sexuality: Jacques Lacan and the "École freudienne."* Edited by Juliet Mitchell and Jacqueline Rose. Translated by Jacqueline Rose. London: Macmillan Press, 1982.

———. *The Four Fundamental Concepts of Psycho-Analysis*. Edited by Jacques-Alain Miller. Translated by Alan Sheridan. New York: W. W. Norton & Co., 1981.

Laplanche, Jean, and Pontalis, Jean-Bertrand. "Fantasy and the Origins of Sexuality" (1964). Pp. 5–34 in Victor Burgin, James Donald, and Cora Kaplan, eds., *Formations of Fantasy*. London and New York: Methuen, 1986.

———. *The Language of Psycho-Analysis*. Translated by Donald Nicholson-Smith. New York: W. W. Norton & Co., 1973.

Lévi-Strauss, Claude. *The Elementary Structures of Kinship*. Translated by James Harle Bell and John Richard von Sturmer. Boston: Beacon Press, 1969.

Levy, Anita. *Other Women: The Writing of Class, Race, and Gender, 1832–1898*. Princeton, N.J.: Princeton University Press, 1991.

Lief, Harold I. "Psychiatry's Challenge: Defining an Appropriate Therapeutic Role when Child Abuse Is Suspected." *Psychiatric News*, August 21, 1992.

Loftus, Elizabeth F. "The Reality of Repressed Memories." Unpublished manuscript, 1992.

Males, Mike. "'Recovered Memory,' Child Abuse and Media Escapism." *Extra! (The Journal of FAIR)* (September/October 1994): 10–11.

Marshall, Peter H. *William Godwin*. New Haven, Conn.: Yale University Press, 1984.

Masciarotte, Gloria-Jean. "C'mon, Girl: Oprah Winfrey and the Discourse of Feminine Talk." *Genders* 11 (1991): 83–110.

Masson, Jeffrey Moussaieff. *The Assault on Truth.* New York: Farrar, Straus & Giroux, 1984.

Mayne, Judith. *Cinema and Spectatorship.* New York: Routledge, 1993.

McHugh, Paul R. "Psychiatric Misadventures." *American Scholar* 61, 4 (1992): 497–510.

Mellor, Anne K. *Mary Shelley: Her Life, Her Fiction, Her Monsters.* New York: Routledge, 1988.

Miller, Alice. *Banished Knowledge: Facing Childhood Injuries* (1988). Translated by Leila Vennewitz. New York: Doubleday, 1990.

———. *The Drama of the Gifted Child* (1979). Translated by Ruth Ward. 1981. Reprint, New York: Basic Books, 1990.

———. *For Your Own Good: Hidden Cruelty in Child-rearing and the Roots of Violence* (1980). Translated by Hildegarde Hannum and Hunter Hannum. 1983. Reprint, New York: Noonday Press, 1990.

———. *Thou Shalt Not Be Aware: Society's Betrayal of the Child.* Translated by Hildegarde Hannum and Hunter Hannum. New York: Meridian Book, 1984.

———. *The Untouched Key: Tracing Childhood Trauma in Creativity and Destructiveness* (1988). Translated by Hildegarde Hannum and Hunter Hannum. New York: Doubleday, 1990.

Nitchie, Elizabeth. *Mary Shelley: Author of Frankenstein.* New Brunswick, N.J.: Rutgers University Press, 1953.

———. "Mary Shelley's *Mathilda*: An Unpublished Story and Its Biographical Significance." *Studies in Philology* 40 (1943): 447–62. Reprinted in Nitchie, *Mary Shelley*, 211–17.

———. Introduction to Mary Shelley's *Mathilda.* Chapel Hill: University of North Carolina Press, 1959, vii–xv.

Putnam, Frank W. "Dissociative Disorders in Children: Behavioral Profiles and Problems." *Child Abuse and Neglect* 17 (1993): 39–45.

———. "The Disturbance of 'Self' in Victims of Child Sexual Abuse." Pp. 113–32 in R. Kluft, ed., *Incest-Related Syndromes of Adult Psychopathology.* Washington, D.C.: American Psychiatric Press, 1990.

Ragland-Sullivan, Ellie. *Jacques Lacan and the Philosophy of Psychoanalysis.* Urbana and Chicago: University of Illinois Press, 1986.

Reiman, Donald, ed. *Shelley and His Circle.* Documents in the Carl H. Pforzheimer Library, vol. 8. Cambridge, Mass.: Harvard University Press, 1986.

Roof, Judith. *A Lure of Knowledge: Lesbian Sexuality and Theory.* New York: Columbia University Press, 1991.

Rubin, Gayle. "The Traffic in Women: Notes on the 'Political Economy' of Sex." Pp. 157–210 in Rayna Reiter, ed., *Toward an Anthropology of Women.* New York: Monthly Review Press, 1975.

Rush, Florence. *The Best Kept Secret: Sexual Abuse of Children.* New York: McGraw-Hill, 1980.

"Rush to Judgment: America Is Now at War against Child Abuse, but Some Recent Cases Suggest We May Be Pushing Too Hard, Too Fast." *Newsweek,* April 19, 1993, 54–60.

St. Clair, William. *The Godwins and the Shelleys: A Biography of a Family.* New York: W. W. Norton & Co., 1989.

Schreiber, Flora Rheta. *Sybil.* New York: Warner Books, 1973.

Schweickart, Patrocinio P. "Reading Ourselves: Toward a Feminist Theory of Reading." Pp. 31–62 in Elizabeth A. Flynn and Patrocinio P. Schweickart, eds., *Gender and Reading.* Baltimore: Johns Hopkins University Press, 1986.

Scott, Joan. "The Evidence of Experience." *Critical Inquiry* 17, 4 (1991): 773–97.

Sedgwick, Eve Kosofsky. *The Epistemology of the Closet.* Berkeley: University of California Press, 1990.

Shelley, Percy Bysshe. *The Letters of Percy Bysshe Shelley.* Edited by Frederick L. Jones. 2 vols. Oxford: Clarendon Press, 1964.

Sifford, Darrell. "Accusations of Sex Abuse, Years Later." *Philadelphia Inquirer,* November 24, 1991. See also *The FMS Phenomenon,* 11–12.

———. "Perilous Journey: The Labyrinth of Past Sexual Abuse." *Philadelphia Inquirer,* February 13, 1992. See also *The FMS Phenomenon,* 10.

———. "When Tales of Sexual Abuse Aren't True." *Philadelphia Inquirer,* January 5, 1992. See also *The FMS Phenomenon,* 13–14.

———. "When Therapists 'Find' Childhood Sexual Abuse." *Philadelphia Inquirer,* March 15, 1992. See also *The FMS Phenomenon,* 9.

Smith, Margaret. *Ritual Abuse.* New York: HarperCollins, 1993.

Sunstein, Emily W. *Mary Shelley: Romance and Reality.* Boston: Little, Brown & Co., 1989.

Tavris, Carol. "Beware the Incest Survivor Machine." *New York Times Book Review,* January 3, 1993: 1ff.

Taylor, Bill. "Therapist Turned Patient's World Upside Down." *Toronto Star,* May 19, 1992. See also *The FMS Phenomenon,* 23–24.

———. "True or False? The Psychiatric Community Knows Incest Is Real, but Worries That when Over-Eager Therapists Uncover Repressed Memories That Are False, Families Can Be Needlessly Torn Apart." *Toronto Star,* May 18, 1992. See also *The FMS Phenomenon,* 21–22.

———. "What If Sexual Abuse Memories Are Wrong?" *Toronto Star*, May 16, 1992. See also *The FMS Phenomenon*, 19–21.

Toefexis, Anastasia. "When Can Memories Be Trusted?" *Time*, October 28, 1991, 86–88. See also *The FMS Phenomenon*, 405.

Twitchell, James B. *Forbidden Partners: The Incest Taboo in Modern Culture*. New York: Columbia University Press, 1987.

Veeder, William. *Mary Shelley and Frankenstein: The Fate of Androgyny*. Chicago: University of Chicago Press, 1986.

Vigars, Teri A. "Symbolic Play in Autism: Is There a Development Trend?" Paper, Cornell University, 1995.

Wartick, Nancy. "A Question of Abuse: More and More Americans Are Suddenly Recalling Traumatic Childhood Events—But How Many of Their Memories Are Real?" *American Health* (May 1993): 62–67.

Watters, Ethan. "Doors of Memory." *Mother Jones*, January/February 1993, 24ff.

Weeks, Jeffrey. *Sexuality and Its Discontents: Meanings, Myths and Modern Sexualities*. New York: Routledge, 1985.

Welter, Barbara. "The Cult of True Womanhood, 1820–1860." *American Quarterly* 18 (1966): 151–74.

White, Hayden. *Tropics of Discourse: Essays in Cultural Criticism*. Baltimore: Johns Hopkins University Press, 1978.

Whitley, Glenna. "Abuse of Trust." *D Magazine* (January 1992): 36–39. See also *The FMS Phenomenon* 15–18.

Wielawski, Irene. "Unlocking the Secrets of Memory." *Los Angeles Times*, October 3, 1991. See also *The FMS Phenomenon*, 103.

Wilbur, Cornelia B., M.D. "Multiple Personality and Child Abuse: An Overview." *Psychiatric Clinics of North America* 7, 1 (1984): 3–7.

Wollstonecraft, Mary. *Posthumous Works of the Author of a Vindication of the Rights of Woman*. 4 vols. London, 1798.

Wylie, Mary Sykes. "The Shadow of a Doubt." *Family Therapy Networker* (September/October 1993): 18ff.

Wright, Elizabeth, ed. *Feminism and Psychoanalysis: A Critical Dictionary*. New York: Basil Blackwell, 1992.

Zwinger, Lynda. *Daughters, Fathers, and the Novel: The Sentimental Romance of Heterosexuality*. Madison: University of Wisconsin Press, 1991.

Index